I0419254

Drawing Amazing
OPTICAL
ILLUSIONS

Easy Lessons for
Drawing 3D Trick Art
Step-by-Step

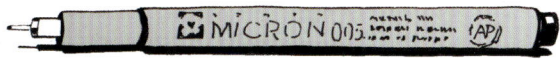

Tom McPherson

Drawing Amazing Optical Illusions
Easy Lessons for Drawing 3D Trick Art Step-by-Step
Tom McPherson

Editor: Kelly Reed
Project manager: Lisa Brazieal
Marketing coordinator: Katie Walker
Copyeditor: Joan Dixon
Cover design: Aren Straiger
Interior design: Andrei Pasternak
Composition: Danielle Foster

ISBN: 979-8-88814-156-4
1st Edition (1st printing, November 2024)
© 2024 Tom McPherson
All images © Tom McPherson unless otherwise noted.

Rocky Nook Inc.
1010 B Street, Suite 350
San Rafael, CA 94901
USA

www.rockynook.com

Distributed in the UK and Europe by Publishers Group UK
Distributed in the U.S. and all other territories by Publishers Group West

Library of Congress Control Number: 2023944104

All rights reserved. No part of the material protected by this copyright notice may be reproduced or utilized in any form, electronic or mechanical, including photocopying, recording, or by any information storage and retrieval system, without written permission of the publisher.
Many of the designations in this book used by manufacturers and sellers to distinguish their products are claimed as trademarks of their respective companies. Where those designations appear in this book, and Rocky Nook was aware of a trademark claim, the designations have been printed in caps or initial caps. All product names and services identified throughout this book are used in editorial fashion only and for the benefit of such companies with no intention of infringement of the trademark. They are not intended to convey endorsement or other affiliation with this book. While reasonable care has been exercised in the preparation of this book, the publisher and author assume no responsibility for errors or omissions, or for damages resulting from the use of the information contained herein or from the use of the discs or programs that may accompany it.

This book is printed on acid-free paper.
Printed in China.

Drawing Amazing

OPTICAL

ILLUSIONS

Easy Lessons for
Drawing 3D Trick Art
Step-by-Step

Tom McPherson

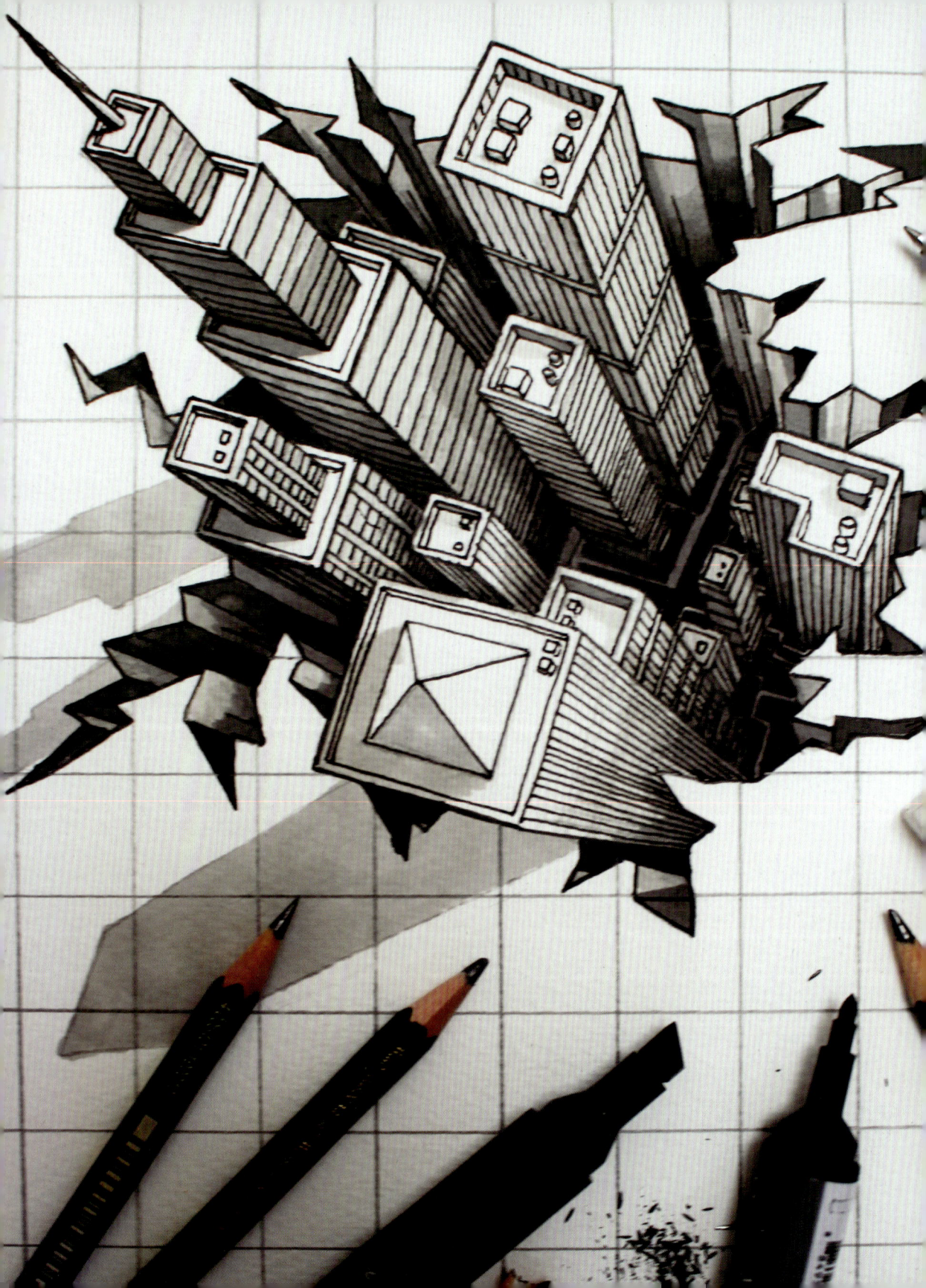

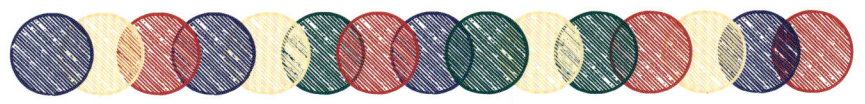

CONTENTS

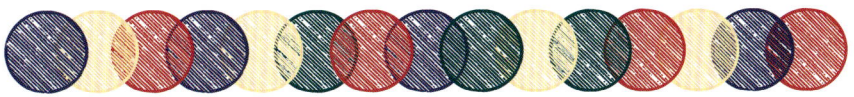

Introduction

Optical illusions are fascinating because they trick our perception of reality. They create images that go against what we expect, often leaving us puzzled and amazed. These illusions exploit how our brains naturally make assumptions about what we see, leading us to perceive things that aren't there. The most convincing optical illusions are so compelling that they remain convincing even when we know they are a trick.

Whether you are a beginner or an experienced artist, this book will guide you through drawing amazing optical illusions with clear, concise instructions and step-by-step illustrations.

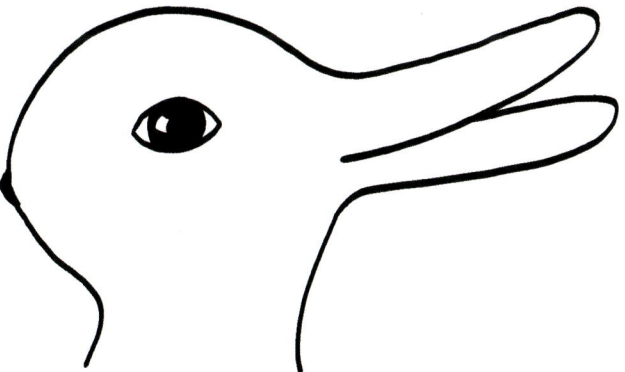

The rabbit-duck illusion is an ambiguous image that can be perceived as either a rabbit facing left or a duck facing right. It demonstrates the brain's ability to interpret visual images in multiple ways.

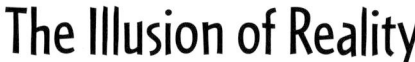

The Illusion of Reality

Whenever we see a flat image showing a realistic-looking three-dimensional object or scene, we are looking at an illusion of reality. Drawings can create the illusion of reality by using various techniques to fool the mind's eye into seeing a seemingly realistic image. We often accept that photographs are accurate depictions of three-dimensional reality even though they are flat. In this sense, all images that aim to create realistic representations of reality use tricks to fool the mind's eye.

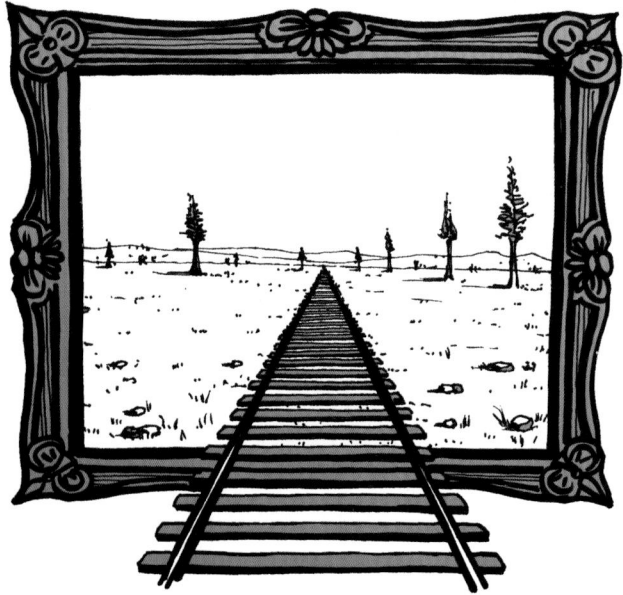

A picture frame serves as a visual boundary, guiding the viewer's focus and shaping their perception of depth within an image. For instance, when a train track extends beyond the confines of the frame, it triggers the viewer's brain to sense the continuation of the tracks, amplifying the sense of depth and realism in the scene's perspective. The frame acts as a window through which we can depict the world, creating a sense of spatial depth and realism.

The Eye-Brain Partnership

Light never enters the brain, leaving it forever in the dark. We see a constructed mental image created by a partnership between the eye and the brain. This process involves the intricate coordination between the eyes' ability to capture visual data and the brain's sophisticated mechanisms for interpreting this data.

Our brains can occasionally be tricked into misinterpreting what we see, giving us false information. Optical illusions use this ability to fool the brain.

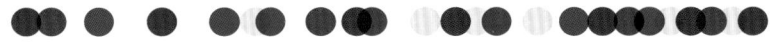

We generally see only what we are looking for. For example, if you start looking for a range of red objects, you will slowly notice all the red objects in your field of view. These red objects will suddenly seem obvious, yet you may not have noticed them before you started to look. Once you are looking for red objects, you might begin to observe many subtle variations of red, from cold blueish-red objects to warmer yellowish-red objects. The more you look, the more subtlety you will notice in what you see.

We seem hard-wired to look for patterns, connections, spatial logic, and beauty. As a visual artist, careful observation is the foundational activity that feeds creativity. Creative optical illusions use the brain's natural bias, particularly its bias towards spatial logic, to trick us into seeing images that are, in fact, not as they seem.

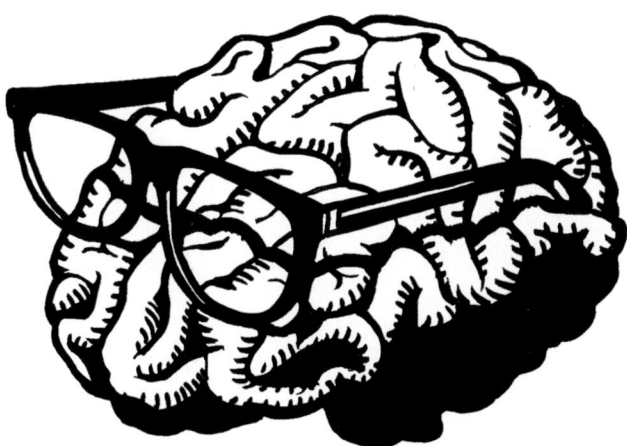

The Brain with Glasses: The image of a human brain with glasses suggests that the brain metaphorically "sees" or comprehends things despite lacking physical vision.

Hand-Eye-Brain Partnership

The hand-eye-brain partnership is a complex coordination between the muscle memory of the hand, the observations of the eye, and the interpretations of the brain. This partnership can create a state of flow that is critical to confident drawing.

When drawing, we observe our subject and analyze its proportions, angles, and spatial relationships.

It is important to train your eye to perceive details accurately. Look at the shapes of the subject and try to see them as flat. Then, notice the shapes behind the positive shapes of the subject; these are the negative shapes.

Each drawing can be thought of as a flat image of interlinked positive and negative shapes. Positive shapes make up the objects, and negative shapes make up the areas of the background between the objects. In a drawing, these positive and negative shapes should fit together like pieces of a jigsaw puzzle. If one of the puzzle pieces does not fit, consider the accuracy of the surrounding puzzle pieces and improve their accuracy until they all fit together.

When drawing, we can use a range of techniques, including size, perspective, shading, and overlapping objects, to simulate the appearance of depth that our eye-brain partnership will recognize. All realistic drawing is a form of illusion.

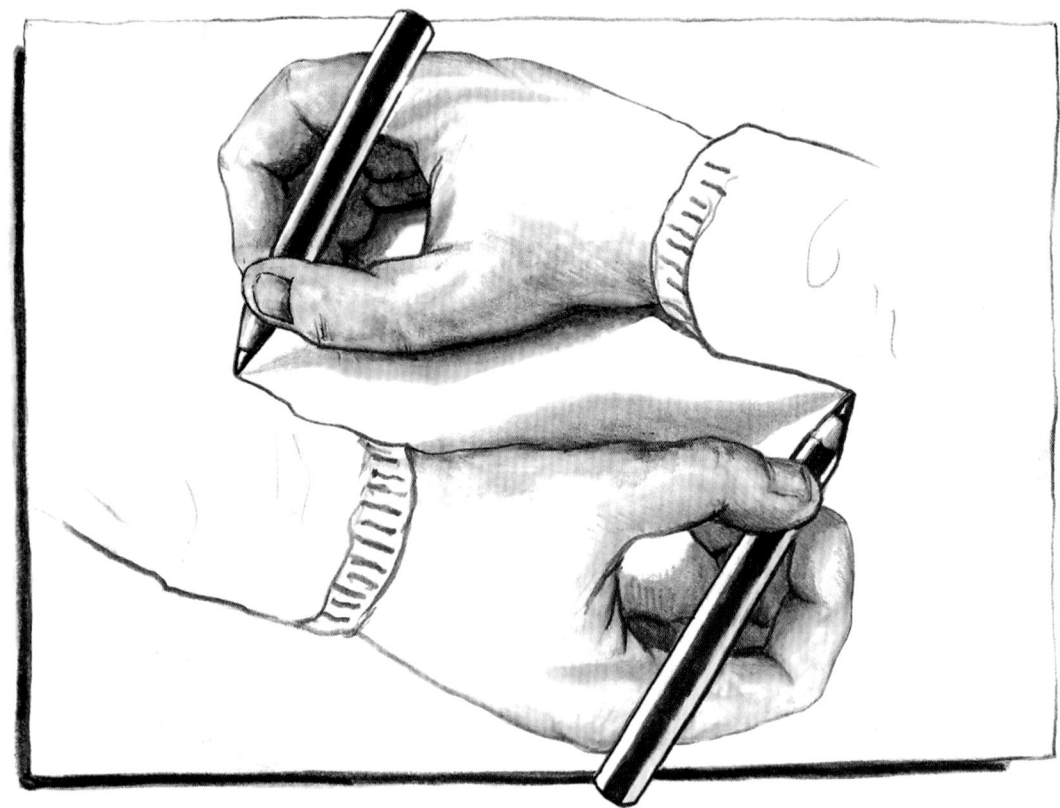

Drawing Hands: This sketch is based on the famous "Drawing Hands" image by M.C. Escher. This work shows two hands drawing each other in a perpetual loop. M.C. Escher was a Dutch artist renowned for his optical illusions, which play with perspective, geometry, and paradoxes, challenging viewers' perceptions.

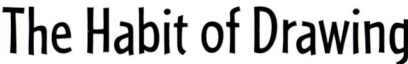

The Habit of Drawing

If you make drawing a habit, you will improve your drawing skills over time. Regular practice enhances muscle memory, meaning that drawing techniques will become second nature, leading to greater hand-eye coordination and precision in your drawings. Trust that over time, your drawing skills will continue to improve.

Six Steps to Make Drawing a Habit

1: Time

Set aside dedicated time for drawing practice each day or week. Even short practice sessions can make a significant impact over time. Consistent practice is critical. Make drawing a part of your routine and prioritize it as a regular activity.

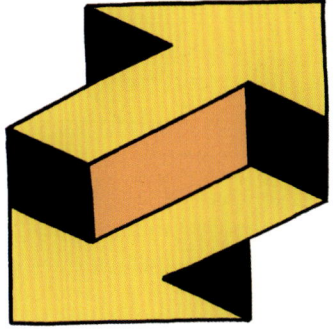

Two-Way Arrow:
The two-way arrow optical illusion is an image of a single shape that depicts a three-dimensional arrow pointing in two directions. The three-dimensional quality of each arrow is shared, so depending on how the viewer interprets the image, the viewer can only see one three-dimensional arrow at a time.

2: Space

Select a quiet and well-lit area where you can focus on your drawing without distractions. Make sure the space has good light and is comfortable. Consider a drawing board upon which to place your drawing paper. Keep your drawing tools organized and simple.

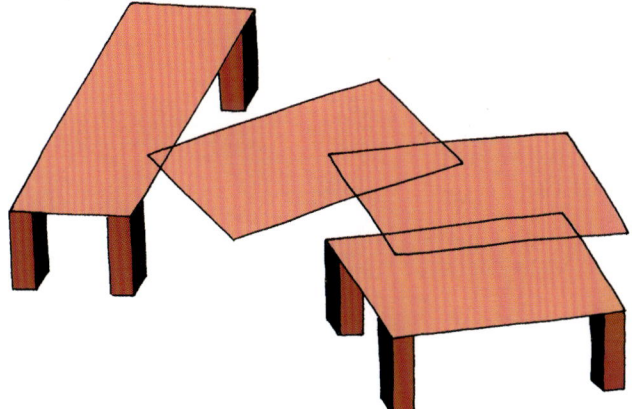

Shepard Table Illusion: The Shepard table illusion is an optical illusion created by Roger Shepard, an American cognitive psychologist. It consists of a set of tabletops whose apparent sizes change despite their actual sizes remaining constant. This distortion occurs due to the surrounding context and perspective cues, challenging the viewer's perception of scale and size.

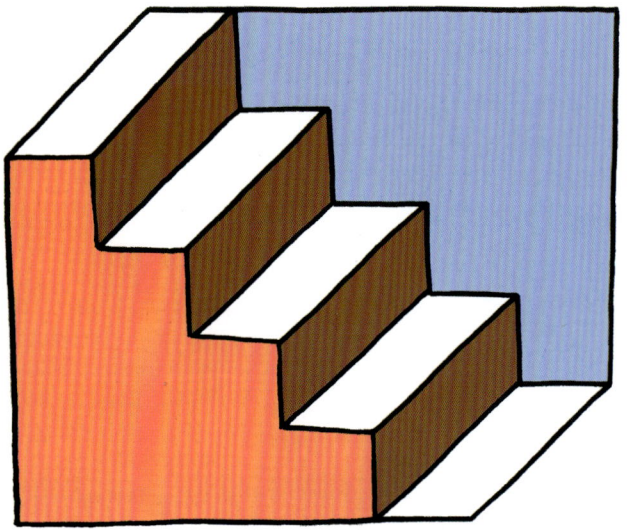

3: The Growth Mindset

Developing a growth mindset is crucial for improving any skill. Challenge yourself to draw things you find a little tricky. Aim for progress rather than perfection, as drawing is a journey of discovery. One of the significant aspects of drawing is that there is always room for improvement and learning, whatever your skill level.

The Schröder Stairs: The Schröder Stairs optical illusion is a famous ambiguous optical illusion that simultaneously depicts a staircase ascending and descending depending on the viewer's visual interpretation of the back wall in the image.

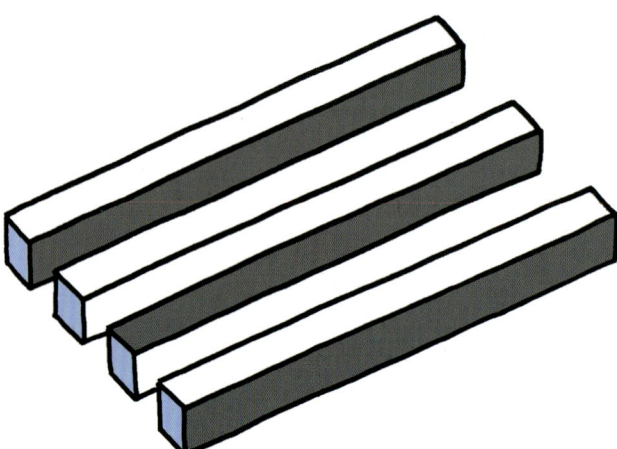

4: Track Your Progress

To track your progress effectively, consider dating or numbering your drawings and storing them in a folder or drawer. This will give you a clear record of your progress over time. Reflecting on your past drawings can provide valuable insights into your growth as an artist.

Four Bars: This image resembles a simple set of bars, but how many are there? Four Bars is an example of an impossible object illusion, an object that appears real when drawn but would be impossible to exist.

5: Experiment and Explore

Give yourself the freedom to explore new techniques, styles, and subjects. Experimenting boosts creativity, which, at its core, is the ability to make new connections and see new possibilities. Explore various subjects and drawing styles and look for new visual connections between lines, shapes, tones, and colors.

6: A Lifelong Journey

Drawing is a rewarding lifelong journey that offers real personal growth and self-discovery opportunities. Drawing encourages keen observation and a deeper appreciation for the beauty and complexity of the visual world.

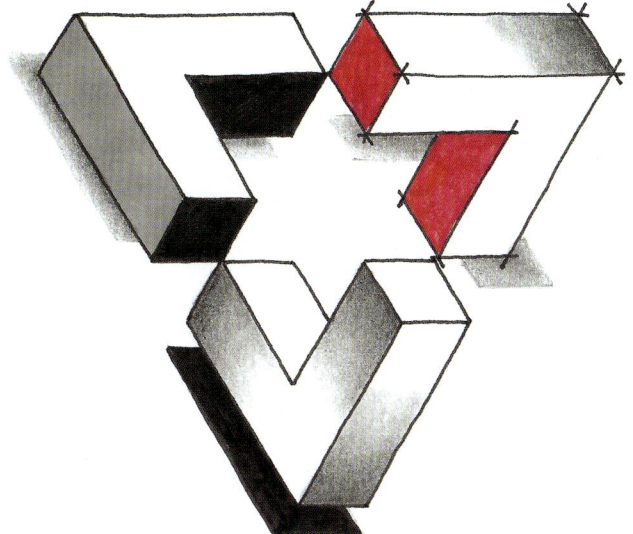

This is my experimental version of the famous Impossible Triangle illusion. Whenever you draw an optical illusion, it is rewarding to consider your own unique alternative versions.

Why I Draw Optical Illusions

Since an early age, I have been deeply interested in observing shapes and the spaces between them. I am fascinated by how the world we see seems to change as we move through it. The process of drawing has helped me appreciate the beauty found in nature and in our everyday surroundings.

It is good to question the visual world. A building might seem very small when viewed from a great distance, but its size seems to change as we walk towards it, as the building takes up more of our field of view. When we enter a building, the interior space becomes our total visual world.

It is interesting to question the reality of how we observe the world around us. The reality we see is perhaps just a persistent illusion, and optical illusions are like cracks in this reality. My fascination with optical illusions grew out of my interest in these ideas. I like to question what I observe.

The study of optical illusions provides an amazing opportunity to create images that explore ideas of perception and question the line between illusion and reality.

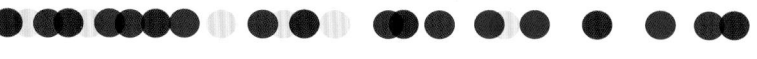

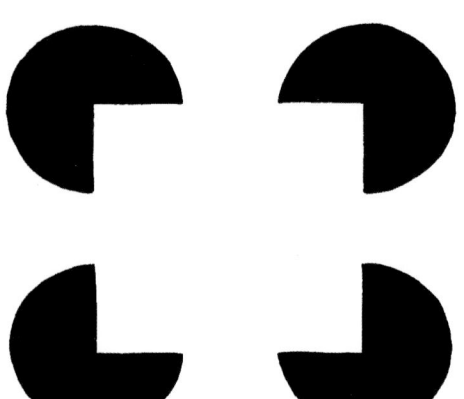

The Kanizsa square illusion creates the perception of a white square in the center of four black shapes, even though no square exists. The viewer's brain fills in missing information to perceive a square based on incomplete visual cues.

In this illusion, a two-dimensional drawing depicts a three-dimensional wireframe cube casting a shadow. This effect is achieved through shading and perspective, tricking the viewer's brain into perceiving depth and solidity where there is none, resulting in a compelling three-dimensional illusion.

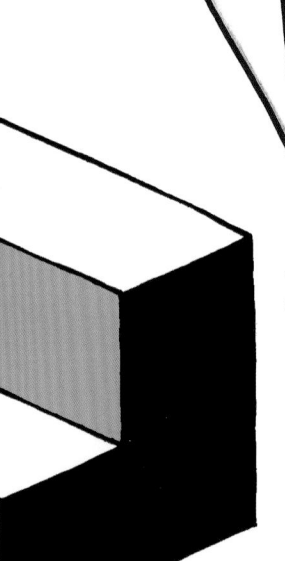

In this illusion, we can observe a three-dimensional cube with a missing area that can also be perceived as a smaller three-dimensional cube.

8

A Short History of Optical Illusions

Humans seem to have an impulse to create images driven by our evolutionary instincts. The ability to manifest objects through drawing marks on a wall has had a deep power and meaning throughout history, often challenging our perceptions and our understanding of the world.

Early Beginnings

Some ancient cave paintings, dating back more than 30,000 years, are thought to have been painted onto specifically shaped cave walls that, when illuminated by a flickering fire in a dark cave, would create the illusion of movement in the animals depicted. If this theory is correct, it indicates an ancient interest in optical illusions.

Ancient art often experimented with new ways to create the illusion of depth on a flat surface. For example, Ancient Egyptian art used a "composite perspective" technique, drawing people from the most descriptive angle. For example, heads and legs were shown in profile, while torsos were depicted from the front.

The ancient Greek philosopher Aristotle's keen quest for knowledge encompassed an interest in vision and optical illusions, including pareidolia—the tendency to perceive meaningful images, like animals and faces, in otherwise meaningless visual patterns like rocks and clouds.

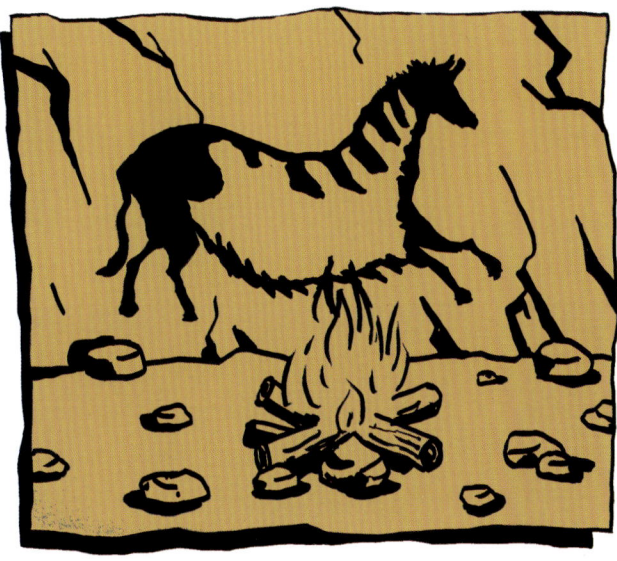

Ancient cave paintings often depicted hunted animals. We do not know for sure why these images were so important to their communities.

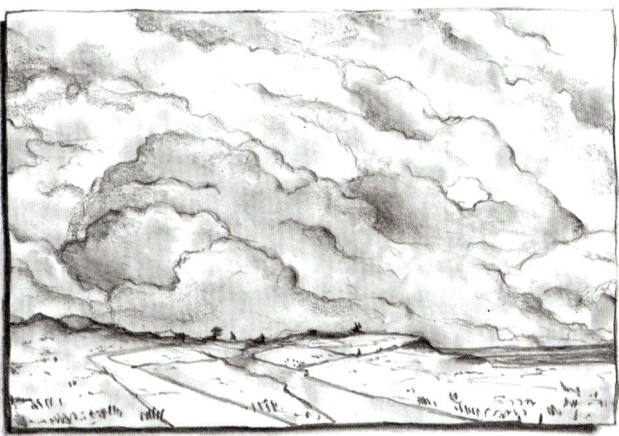

In this pareidolia illustration, we can see a landscape and a cloud that is also a rabbit.

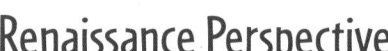

Renaissance Perspective

The Renaissance was a European cultural movement during the 14th to 17th centuries, characterized by renewed interest in art, science, and discovery.

The rules of linear perspective were developed during the Renaissance by artists such as Filippo Brunelleschi and Leon Battista Alberti. Renaissance artists were fascinated by how objects appeared smaller and seemed to converge at a vanishing point in the distance. Through study and observation, the foundations of linear perspective were discovered. Linear perspective is a drawing technique that accurately depicts depth on a two-dimensional surface, using the concept of receding parallel lines converging at an imaginary vanishing point, often on the eye-level horizon line of the viewer.

The discovery of linear perspective transformed how depth could be depicted in artwork, leading to new ways to create the illusion of realism.

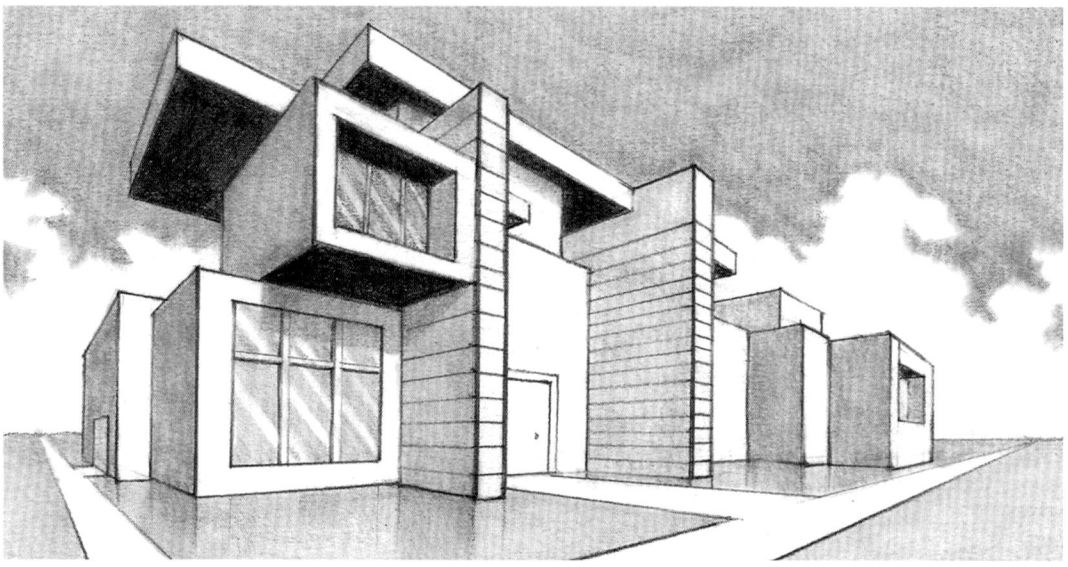

This is an example of two-point perspective, which is a type of linear perspective. When drawing buildings in two-point perspective, the nearest part of the building to the viewer is generally a vertical corner of the building. We can see the straight lines of the sides of the building receding to the left and right vanishing points on the horizon. Vanishing points are imaginary points where two parallel lines seem to meet, for example, at the end of a straight train track. The two vanishing points are on a horizontal line, which represents the eye level of the viewer when they are looking straight ahead. The horizon line in linear perspective is an imaginary line that is dependent on the height of the eye level of the viewer. Linear perspective is a powerful drawing technique to depict the illusion of depth in an image.

Camera Obscura

In the 17th century, artists like Vermeer and Canaletto used various optical devices to aid their creative process. Among these tools was the camera obscura, a darkened box with a small hole through which light enters to project an image onto a surface, often ground glass, providing a reference image for the artist to trace. The camera obscura was a precursor of modern photography. Artists have always used any techniques they can to enhance their image-making.

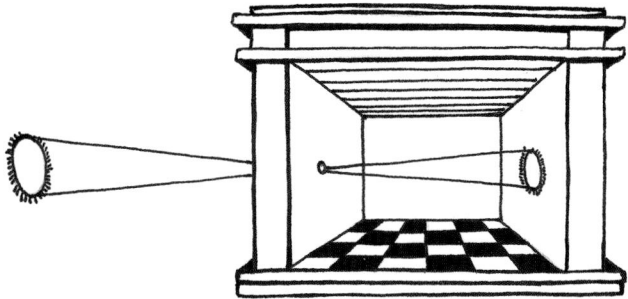

This is an illustration of a room that is also a camera obscura; light enters the darkened room through a hole and illuminates an image of the outside on the facing wall. The image is upside down due to the way light travels in straight lines, crossing at the hole and so inverting the image.

Trompe L'oeil

Trompe-l'œil, French for "deceive the eye," has roots in ancient art but experienced a resurgence during the Renaissance. Artists sought to create realistic illusions that tricked viewers into believing they saw three-dimensional objects on a flat surface.

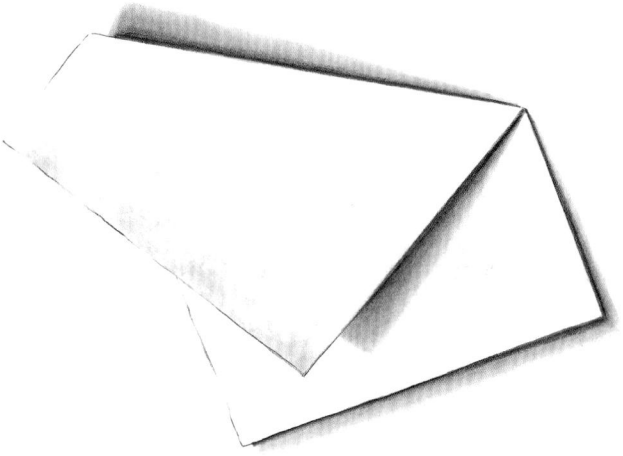

In this illusion, we can observe a simple trompe l'oeil drawing of a folded piece of paper.

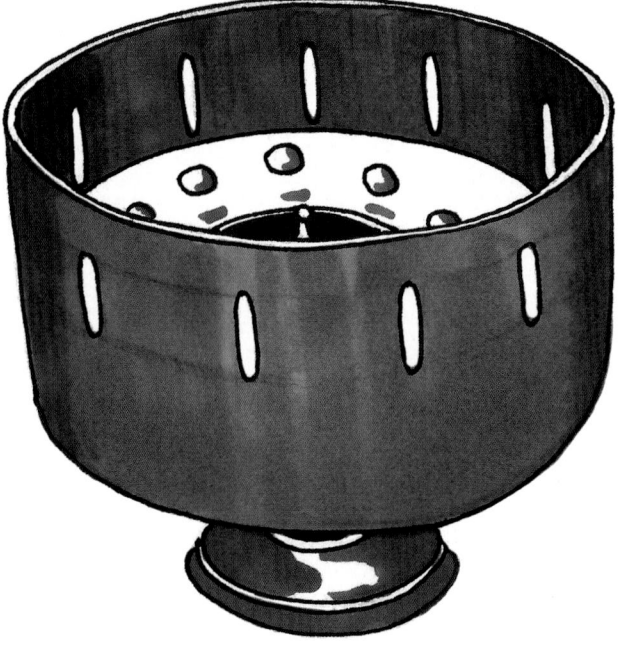

A zoetrope consists of a cylinder that is mounted on a central axis so it can spin freely. Around the cylinder are a series of vertical slits through which the viewer can see a series of illustrations of sequential stages of a moving object, for example, a bouncing ball or a bird flying. The sequential images are organized in such a way as to create a loop. When the cylinder is spun, each image is seen in rapid sequence, creating the illusion of movement due to the persistence of vision.

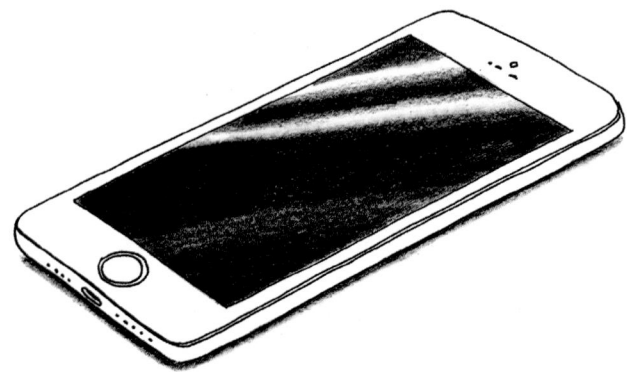

A simple drawing of a mobile phone.

Zoetrope

The zoetrope is a device that can create a moving image. It was invented in 1833 by William George Horner. It produces the illusion of movement by viewing a series of images through narrow slits in a rotating cylinder. When the images are viewed through the slits in the drum, when it is spinning fast, the slightly differing images blur together to create an illusion of motion.

The illusion of motion is based on the principle of the persistence of vision; our brain retains an image briefly after it is seen. The zoetrope changes the images viewed very fast, and our brain blends the images to create a sense of motion.

The principle of persistence of vision laid the foundations for motion pictures, leading to the birth of the modern movie industry.

The Digital Age

Optical illusions can be created in this digital age with increasingly sophisticated artificial intelligence (AI) and digital software. There is a powerful connection between the hand-drawn image and the brain that drew it, but at the same time, we should embrace the newest technology and use it as a tool. At its core, visual art is fascinated by the optical world.

Linear Perspective

Linear Perspective is a drawing technique that creates the illusion of depth on a two-dimensional surface. It is based on the principle that parallel straight lines appear to converge at a single point in the far distance, called the vanishing point. The vanishing point is an imaginary point in space. When looking at a straight path receding into the distance, the parallel lines of the path seem to meet, but this is just an illusion created by how our eye-brain partnership depicts the world. It is impossible to stand on a vanishing point.

Linear perspective also uses an imaginary horizontal line called the horizon line. The horizon line in linear perspective represents the eye level of the viewer of the image. The linear perspective horizon line is an imaginary line, unlike the geographic horizon line that we see between the Earth and the sky. If you were looking straight out the window in a plane, the perspective horizon line would be above the geographic horizon line if the aircraft were flying in the sky.

Anamorphic Perspective

The discovery of anamorphic perspective in the Renaissance introduced distorted images that only revealed their true form from one specific fixed point of view.

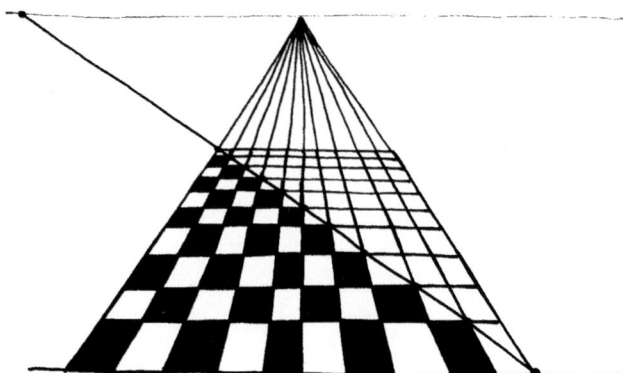

An example of a grid in linear perspective. Each of the tiles is evenly spaced on the horizontal baseline and recedes to the vanishing point on the eye-level horizon line above the baseline. To work out even receding tiles, a diagonal guideline is needed from the right baseline tile to the left point of the furthest horizontal line of the floor tiles. At each point where the guideline crosses the straight lines that recede to the vanishing point, a horizontal line can be made, which accurately represents the length of the receding lines in one-point perspective.

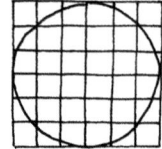

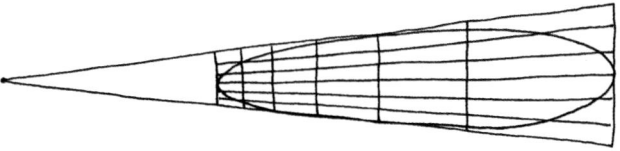

Anamorphic Grid of a Circle: A circle in a 6x6 grid of squares and then the same circle in an anamorphic grid. When viewed from the direction of the dot at the point of the anamorphic grid, the distorted circle will appear undistorted if viewed from a low angle.

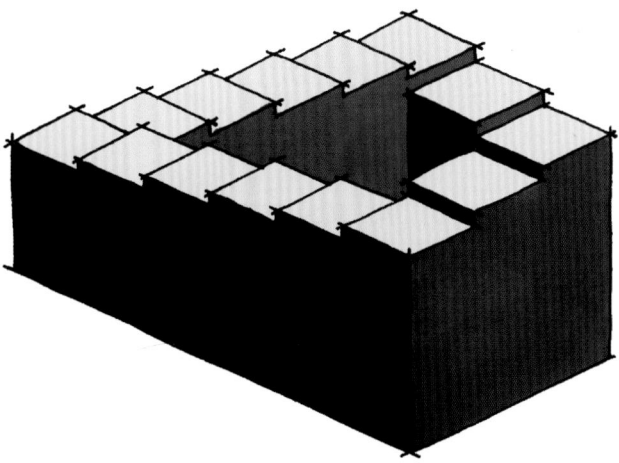

This drawing is based on M.C. Escher's "Endless Stairs," a lithographic print depicting a continuous staircase that appears to either rise or descend endlessly, defying traditional notions of geometry.

Anamorphic 3D optical illusions challenge conventional artistic representation by creating realistic, solid-looking 3D objects that appear powerfully realistic and seem to jump out from the picture's surface when viewed from one fixed point of view.

Impossible Shapes

M.C. Escher (1898–1972) was a Dutch artist fascinated with optical illusions, particularly impossible shapes. Impossible shapes break the logic of geometry, challenging viewers with conflicting visual information.

Impossible shapes are a type of optical illusion that shows an image of a solid-looking three-dimensional object that would be impossible to exist as a three-dimensional shape because the image breaks the laws of physical geometry.

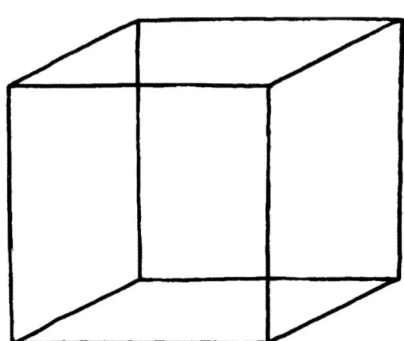

The Necker Cube is a famous example of an ambiguous optical illusion, as it can be perceived in two orientations. When viewing the cube, we can see it as either facing upward or downward, with the front face of the cube being interpreted as either closer or farther away, causing the image to flip between the two possible interpretations. The Necker Cube is named after the Swiss crystallographer Louis Albert Necker, who first described it in 1832.

The Four Main Types of Optical Illusions

The following are the most common types of optical illusion images.

Ambiguous Illusions

Ambiguous illusions are pictures or objects that can instantly switch from one interpretation to another. A famous example is the Necker cube, which can look like a receding cube and then switch to an advancing cube.

Distorting Illusions

Distorting illusions distort the size and position of objects and the spaces around them, creating an image that tricks the viewer into thinking it is something it is not.

A famous example is the Müller-Lyer illusion, which consists of two lines of equal length but with different fins at the ends of the lines. The line with closed fins appears shorter than the line with open fins. Anamorphic perspective is a drawing technique used in many distorting illusions of solid-looking 3D shapes, for example, floating shapes.

Impossible Shapes

Impossible shapes depict an object that looks solid and three-dimensional when drawn but is impossible to exist in reality due to inherent inconsistencies in the object's geometry.

A famous example is the Impossible Trident, also known as the Devil's Fork, which consists of three cylindrical prongs at one end and a rectangular base with just two prongs at the other end.

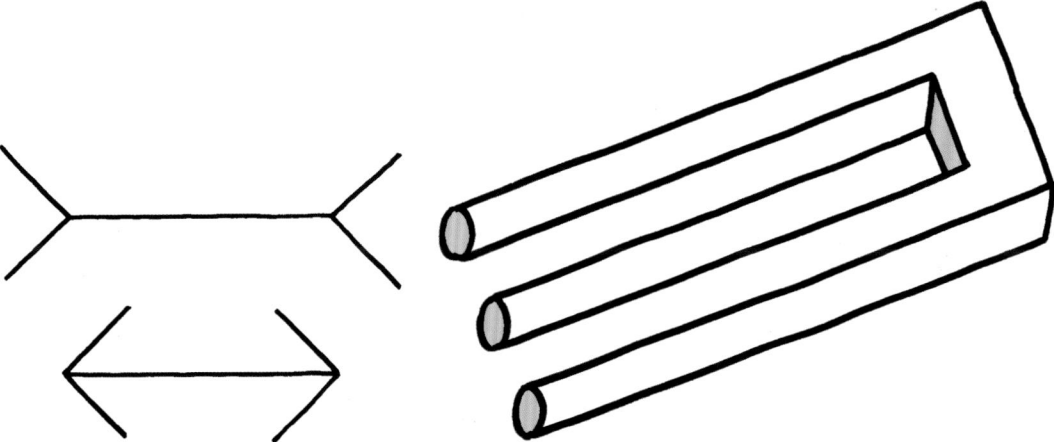

The Müller-Lyer illusion was first described by Franz Carl Müller-Lyer, a German sociologist, in 1889. The illusion is an example of how our perception of size is influenced by visual context.

The Impossible Trident was developed by D.H. Schuster, an American psychologist, from images that were published in the 1960s. The illusion is an example of an impossible shape, a shape that would be impossible to exist as a real shape, but which can be drawn as a realistic looking optical illusion.

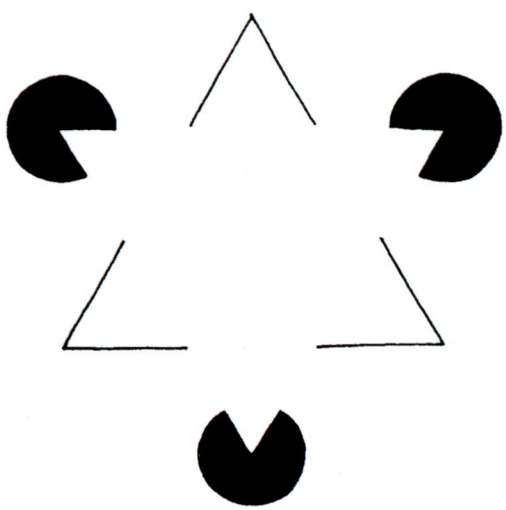

The Kanizsa Triangle is a variation on the Kanizsa Square, creating the sense of a shape that is not within the image.

Fiction Illusions

Fiction illusions use shapes, and empty spaces imply an extra shape that does not exist but seems natural. A famous example is the Kanizsa triangle, which uses three circles, each with a missing segment, that, when placed correctly, creates the impression of a triangle. The illusion tricks our mind into seeing a triangle that does not exist.

Drawing Tools

The drawing tools you use will directly affect the drawings you make. If you improve the quality of your tools, your drawings will instantly improve.

The best way to improve your drawing tools is to select just a few that are good and discover what they can do. Over time, using a few essential drawing tools will become second nature.

Never let the art supplies you have limit your pleasure in drawing. All the images in this book can be adequately made with just a standard writing pencil, an eraser, and some copy paper.

The Importance of Paper

Choosing the right drawing paper is crucial as it directly impacts the final drawing. When drawing optical illusions, it is best to select a smooth, thick white paper so that the illusion looks separate from the paper on which it is drawn. This way, the illusion can seem to pop out of the paper dramatically.

Paper Weight

Paper weight is a crucial factor in determining the durability and quality of the drawing surface. A higher paper weight means a thicker paper. Drawing paper for everyday drawing is best around 70 to 80 lbs, but if you want thicker more durable paper consider a heavy-weight drawing paper of around 90 to 115 lbs.

A good-quality thick paper will also allow you to add extra darkness when using dark pencils or pen work to your drawings. The paper surface will absorb the marks more than light paper, making dark areas look dense and deep. This is particularly important for the drawing techniques in this book, where the result will look best if the paper seems untouched, apart from the image drawn.

Recommended Paper

Bristol board A4 100-120 lbs white paper: Bristol board is a thick, smooth white paper that works well with pencil and pen drawings.

Pencils

Graphite pencils are the most versatile tools for creating stunning optical illusions. Graphite pencils are composed of a graphite core encased in wood. These pencils come in various grades, each indicating the hardness or softness of the lead. The right graphite pencil is crucial for achieving desired effects in optical illusion drawings.

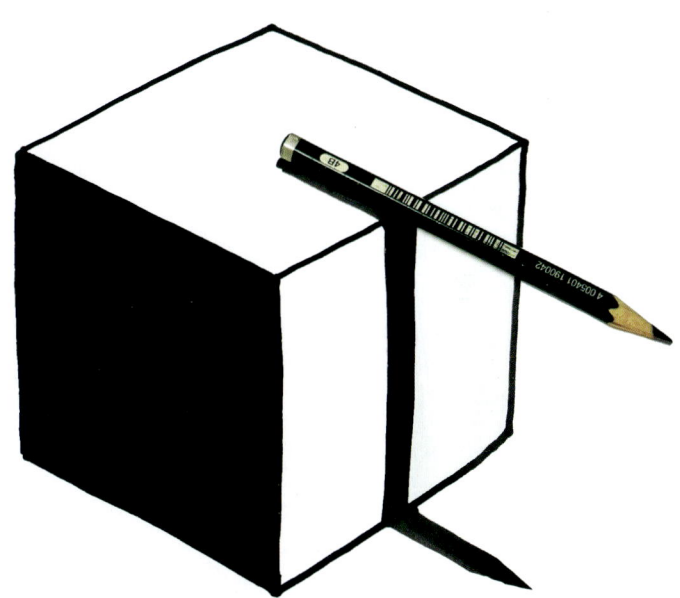

17

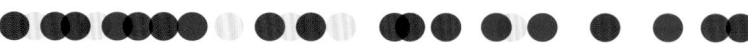

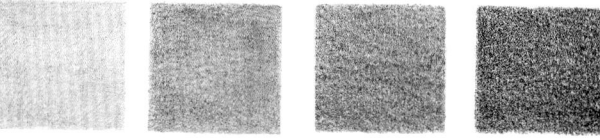

HB   2B   4B   6B

Grades of Pencils

Graphite pencils are graded on a scale ranging from 9H (hard) to 9B (soft). Hard pencils (H) produce lighter lines and are suitable for drawing fine details and intricate patterns in optical illusions. Soft pencils (B) are ideal for creating darker, bolder lines and shading. Having a range of pencils offers versatility in achieving various qualities of lines and various tonal values when shading.

Understanding graphite pencil grades and incorporating the drawing tips in this chapter will allow you to use pencils to their full potential when drawing optical illusions.

Recommended Pencils

Faber-Castell 9000 4B pencil: I prefer to use one pencil grade for most of my drawings. Over time, the range of tonal values and marks it can create has become second nature to me. Each brand of pencil has different qualities, so you should experiment with a few before settling on your favorite.

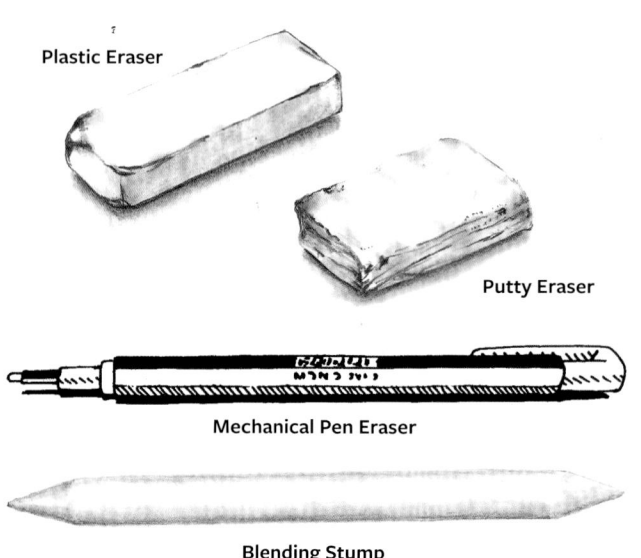

Plastic Eraser

Putty Eraser

Mechanical Pen Eraser

Blending Stump

Erasers

Plastic Erasers: Plastic erasers, often white or colored, are firm erasers that efficiently remove pencil marks with minimal paper abrasion. They are suitable for detailed work and precise erasing, leaving clean surfaces to separate optical illusions from the drawing paper.

Putty Erasers: Putty erasers are soft and malleable and can be kneaded and shaped for specific erasing needs. Their soft composition makes them ideal for lifting graphite marks. They are also ideal for removing unwanted

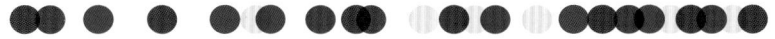

smudges from undrawn areas of a picture, enabling the image to look separate from the paper it is drawn on, which should be the aim of all optical illusion drawings.

Mechanical Pen Erasers: Mechanical pen erasers offer precise erasing for fine details. Their fine retractable eraser tips make them recommended for controlling specific areas of a drawing.

Blending Stumps: These rolled paper sticks can be used for delicate blending of pencil shading, creating flat, even tones and smooth transitions between light and dark areas of your drawing.

Recommended Erasers

Staedtler Mars plastic eraser: This eraser works well with the Bristol board paper I use. It is useful to have an eraser that can clean up any smudges within the drawing and erase soft areas and details of pencil work so that there is no trace of the erased areas. Choose an eraser that works well with the paper and pencils you are using, as your drawings will improve when all three tools work in combination.

Pens

Fine-liner Pens: These pens have a consistent line width, which is useful when drawing optical illusions. They are ideal for drawing over the initial pencil lines and come in various thicknesses, providing flexibility for creating precise details.

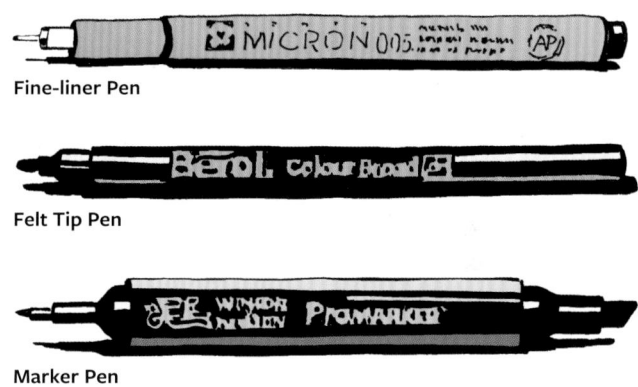

Fine-liner Pen

Felt Tip Pen

Marker Pen

Felt Tip Pens: Great for smooth, continuous lines, felt tip pens are reliable for outlining and coloring in flat areas in optical illusions or for the outlines of a large drawing. They come in various sizes and colors.

Marker Pens: When drawing optical illusions, markers provide smooth and consistent coverage of flat or graded shading of tonal values, allowing you to create a high level of smoothness in tonal values. A set of gray markers with various shades helps achieve various tonal values of grey in optical illusions. These markers, typically light to dark grays, can enhance the illusion's realism. By layering and blending these gray tones, you can create three-dimensional effects, gradients, and intricate details, making marker pens valuable in creating captivating optical illusions.

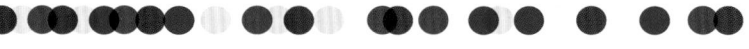

Pen Thicknesses

Pen thickness plays an important role in drawing optical illusions, as it can significantly impact the viewer's perception of depth. Thicker lines will appear closer, while thinner lines can be seen to be farther away.

Most drawings of optical illusions need a consistent line thickness to work well. When the thickness of the line is consistent, the shape of the illusion will be the focus of the image. Try to keep to a consistent thickness of line within each optical illusion.

Fine-tip pen

Medium-tip pen

Bold-tip pen

Fine-tip pens: Fine-tip pens have a very narrow and precise point, making them ideal for intricate details and fine lines in optical illusions.

Medium-tip pens: Medium-tip pens have a slightly broader point compared to fine-tip pens, offering a balance between precision and coverage.

Bold-tip pens: Bold-tip pens have a broad point, allowing bold, thick lines to fill large areas and create strong contrasts within the optical illusion.

Recommended Pens

Pilot VBall 0.7mm or 0.5mm black ink pen: I like the darkness of the black ink and the smooth flow the pen makes when drawing.

Pigma Micron fine liner black pens: These precision pens are available in a range of narrow thicknesses.

Winsor & Newton Promarker: These marker pens are available in a range of gray tonal values, ideal for adding smooth or graded shading.

Overview

Start with just a few drawing tools and get to know them well. Over time, you can add a few extra drawing tools and discover new possibilities for creating impressive optical illusions.

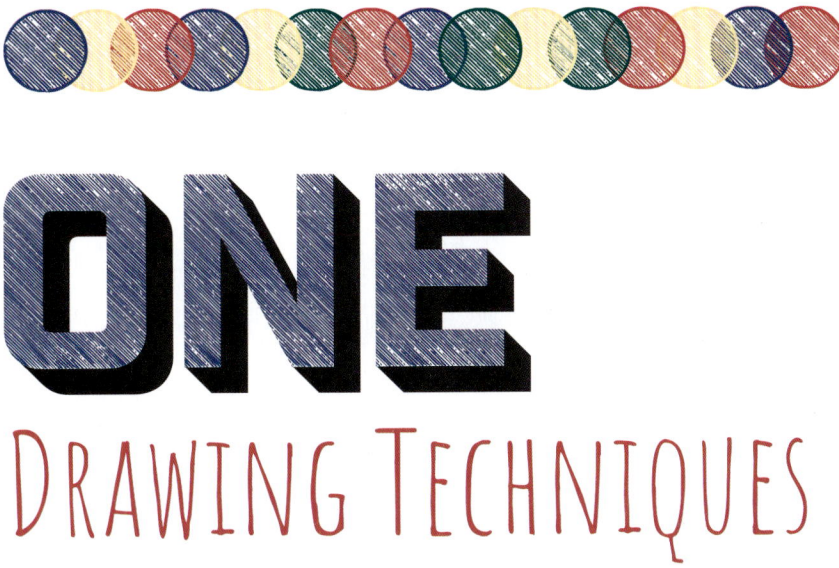

ONE
Drawing Techniques

Optical illusions are most effective when the image is precisely drawn and highly realistic, as this will enhance the power of the illusion. You will see real improvements over time if you strive for creative experimentation and learning rather than perfectionism. You will learn more if you keep and number or date all your drawings. Remember, drawing takes effort and is a process to master over time.

Below are the main drawing techniques you will need.

Line Drawing

A line is a fundamental element used to represent the boundary or edge of an object. Observe the lines used within the optical illusion you are drawing and try to notice how these lines interconnect to make the shapes needed for the optical illusion to work well.

Look at each line's angle and consider how it relates to all the other angles of lines within the image. When drawing optical illusions, you will need to develop the ability to depict the outlines of shapes accurately and evenly.

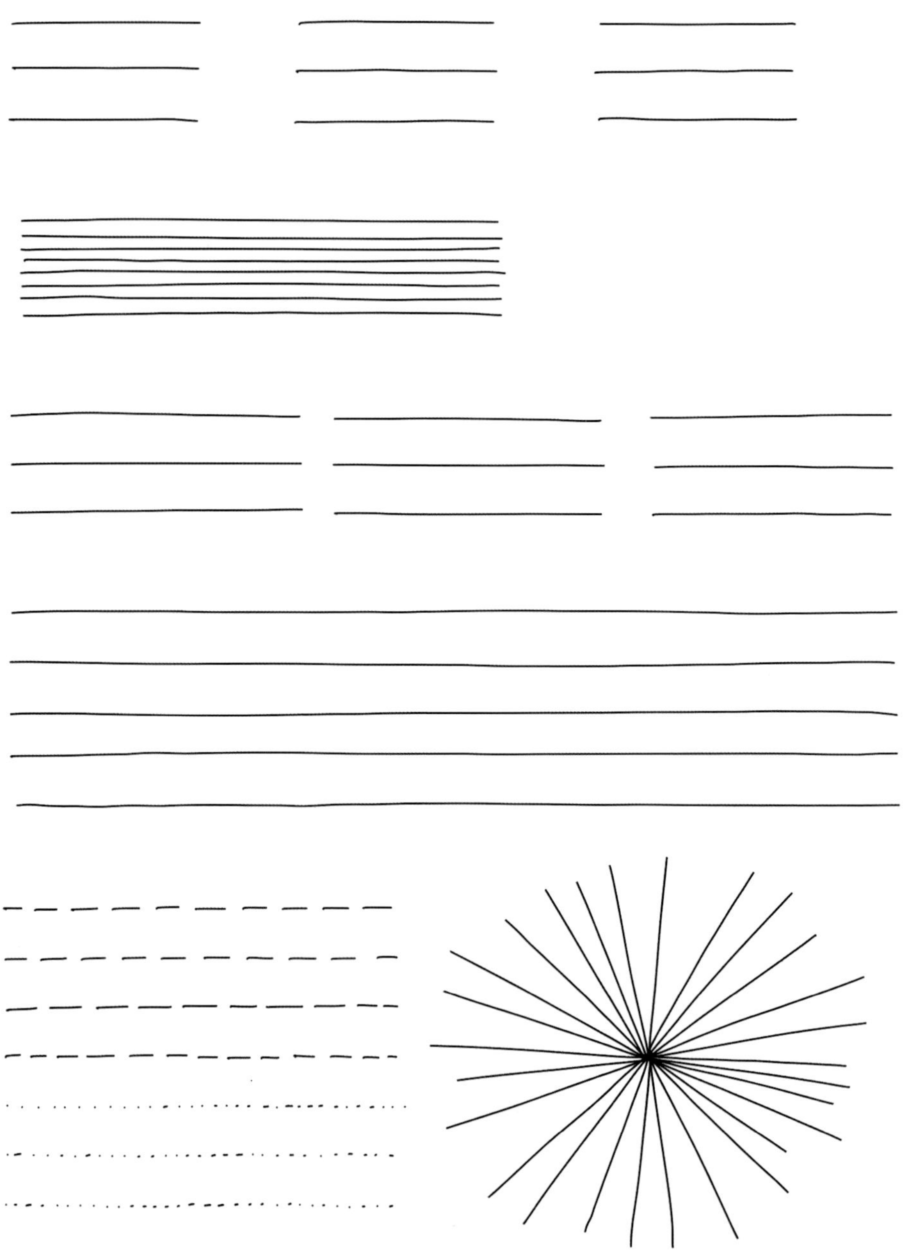

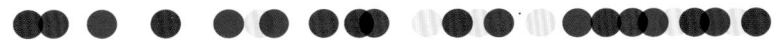

When drawing optical illusions it can be useful to use a ruler to enhance the accuracy of straight lines. If you like to draw straight lines without a guide, so that your drawing has a consistent style of line, it is helpful to practice some simple drawing techniques. Start with drawing straight lines, from dot to dot, and then progress with longer lines. You could also experiment with dotted lines and straight lines radiating from a point.

Shapes and Forms

Shapes are two-dimensional areas defined by boundaries created by lines. These lines can be made in several ways, for example, outlines, color changes, and tonal value changes. They are flat, lacking depth or volume.

In contrast, forms are three-dimensional shapes with depth and a sense of solidity. When drawing, we must use shapes to represent forms.

When starting a drawing, define the basic shapes first; details can be added at the end of the drawing. Try to work out how they work together. In most optical illusions, you might find fewer shapes within the image than you initially imagined. Once you have defined the basic shapes, consider

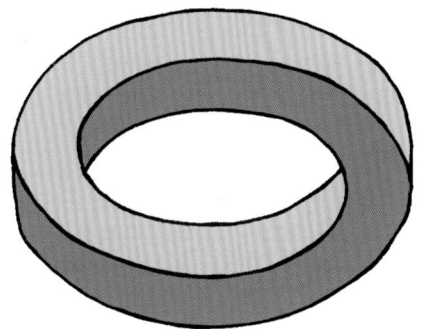

adding levels of detail and precision, ensuring that your drawings engage the viewer with a powerful and intriguing optical illusion.

Shapes can be either geometric or organic. Geometric shapes most often consist of straight lines, curves, and angles. Common geometric shapes include circles, squares, and triangles. Organic shapes are usually found in nature, with irregular, free-flowing outlines. Common organic shapes include clouds or trees. Most optical illusions use geometric forms.

Tonal Values

Tonal values refer to the range of tones in a drawing from light to dark. It is a good idea to notice the range of tonal values in an optical illusion before you start shading, as tonal values in a drawing must work together to create a strong image.

When adding shading, try to use a limited number of tonal values. The right combination of tonal values can significantly increase your drawing's power and sense of form and depth.

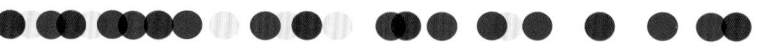

Most three-dimensional geometric forms have no more than three sides visible at any time. We can observe two sides of a form simultaneously and either the top or the bottom if we are looking downwards or upwards.

We can use three tonal values to represent the three visible sides of a form, simplifying and dramatizing the three-dimensional quality of the form we are drawing.

Three Tonal Values for 3D Forms

Light tones: Light tones can depict areas where light directly hits the object.

Mid-tones: Mid-tones can be added to surfaces that are not directly facing the light.

Dark tones: Dark tones can be added to surfaces that face directly away from the light. These areas are the darkest areas of a form.

Graded and Flat Shading

Graded Shading: Graded shading involves smoothly transitioning between different tonal values to create gradual changes in light and shadow, enhancing the realism and solidity of the object.

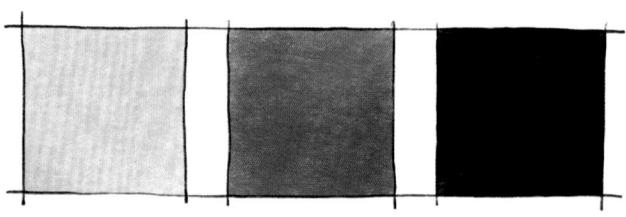

Flat Shading: Flat shading involves applying uniform, even tonal values without variation. It is best to use the side of a pencil point, start with a light tone, and slowly darken the tonal value by adding flat shaded tonal layers on top of each other, resulting in a flatter, smoother tonal value.

Shadows

Shadows are areas in a drawing where light is blocked or absorbed, resulting in darker tones. When carefully placed shadows are added to a drawing, you can increase the sense of light, depth, and space within the various elements.

Define Forms: Use shadows to define the three-dimensional structure of the forms within your drawings, creating the illusion of solidity.

Create Contrast: Use a range of tonal values, including light, mid-tone, and dark, to create contrast within your optical illusion. This contrast helps objects stand out from their surroundings and adds visual interest to the artwork.

Add Depth: By varying the intensity and placement of shadows, you can create the illusion of objects receding into space or overlapping with one another. This adds visual complexity to your optical illusions and enhances your artwork's realism, depth, and visual impact.

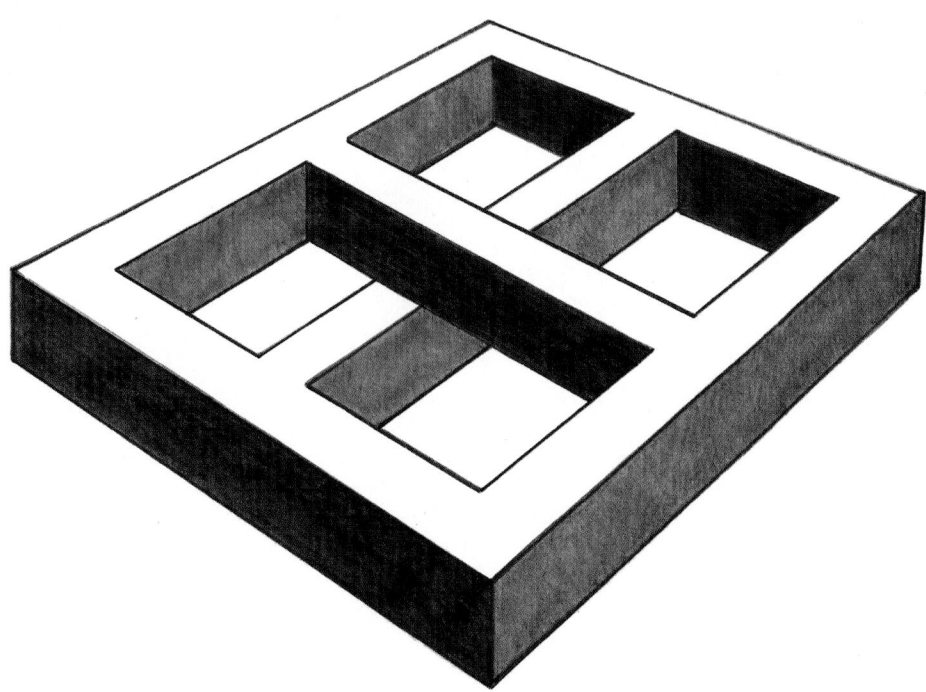

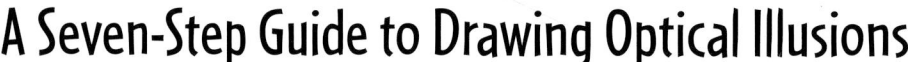

A Seven-Step Guide to Drawing Optical Illusions

Drawing optical illusions can be rewarding and challenging in equal measure. Here's a simple guide to help you begin:

1. Pick Your Subject: Choose what kind of optical illusion you want to draw.

2. Look Closer: Look at the finished image and notice the number of shapes and the angle of the lines. First, make some small thumbnail sketches to determine how the shapes work together.

3. Basic Shapes First: Draw the basic shapes lightly so they are easy to erase. Use light, loose lines at this stage; precision can be added later.

4. Define Your Lines: Make your lines look neat and confident. Use a black pen or a sharp pencil to refine the outlines of your drawing.

5. Add Shading: Keep to three tonal values if you want your image to "pop." Consider using a graded tonal value for a curved surface. When pencil shading, use a blending stump to smooth the tonal values. You could add some colors to your drawing. If using color, consider which three color combinations would best enhance your optical illusion.

6. Background: Use an eraser to clean up the background of your optical illusion. For best results, use the side of a clean plastic eraser or a soft putty eraser.

7. Know When to Stop: When you can see nothing to improve, stop your drawing. Notice what you did well and what you can improve next time. Keep and number or date all your drawings so you can learn from your progress.

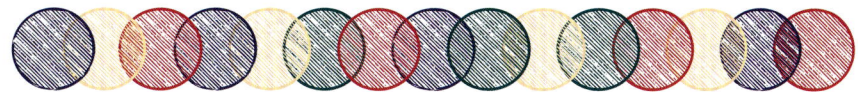

TWO

Introduction to Impossible Shapes

Impossible shapes are optical illusions that challenge our perception of reality. These images appear realistic initially but prove impossible to exist upon closer observation. They question our ability to perceive the world accurately by playing tricks on our perception of depth and form.

Impossible shapes are optical illusions that trick us into seeing realistic-looking shapes that are impossible to construct as three-dimensional objects. Although impossible shapes can't be made as three-dimensional objects, we can draw them as realistic-looking three-dimensional objects.

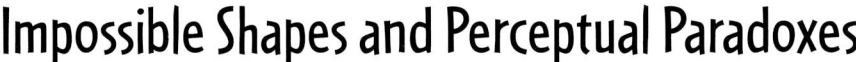

Impossible Shapes and Perceptual Paradoxes

All impossible shapes have a spatial contradiction. They do not follow the laws of geometric space. Impossible shapes defy the rules of geometry and spatial logic. All impossible shapes are impossible to be made as three-dimensional objects. However, we can draw them as visually fascinating optical illusions that create a paradox: We see a shape that cannot exist.

Impossible shapes, such as the Impossible Triangle, are geometrically impossible to exist in reality due to inherent contradictions in their spatial relationships. Impossible shapes contradict our intuitive understanding of space and form.

The ancient Greek mathematician Euclid developed the math that explains much of the two-dimensional surfaces and three-dimensional spaces we see. Impossible shapes break the rules of Euclidean geometry and our inner sense of what is geometrically possible. Drawing an impossible shape is a trick that holds a profound visual and mathematical fascination.

Understanding the Impossible Triangle

All triangles have three straight sides, making a closed loop with three inner angles. These three inner angles have a persistent geometric quality, 180 degrees. This is known as the triangle angle sum theorem and is a constant in Euclidean geometry.

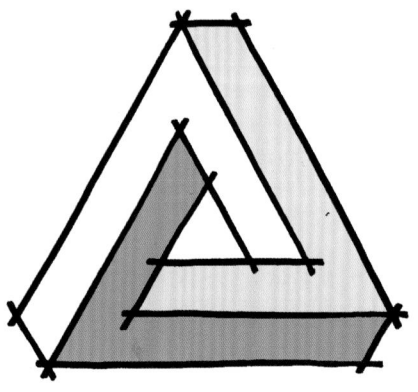

When we look at the impossible triangle, each of its three corners looks solid and real. We seem to be seeing three right angles that create a closed loop.

Three right angles cannot create a closed loop; you need four right angles to create one. But if we look at the impossible triangle more closely, we can notice no true right angles in the image.

This visual illusion contradicts the mathematical principle governing triangles and our intuitive understanding of how forms in space behave. For this reason, impossible shapes are impossible as 3D shapes in space, but we can draw them as realistic-looking 3D shapes in a drawing. Impossible shapes allow us to explore the boundary between reality and illusion. It is incredibly challenging to unsee an impossible shape, even when we know it is just an illusion.

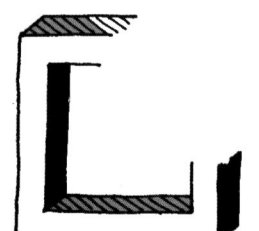

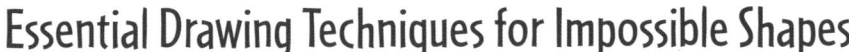

Essential Drawing Techniques for Impossible Shapes

It is best to work out drawing techniques before starting a drawing. Allow yourself time to experiment with drawing tools and mark-making to discover what will work best for the optical illusion you are drawing. Practice allows you to master techniques and minimize errors, resulting in a more realistic and precise optical illusion, creating a powerful image.

Precision and Accuracy

Use a steady hand or a ruler to draw straight lines, consistent angles, and precise measurements. Attention to detail is crucial when creating illusions that depend on the viewer's perception.

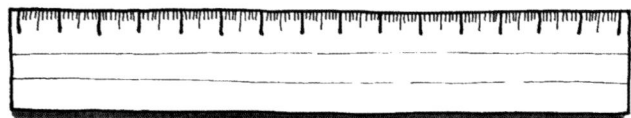

Overlap and Interlocking Shapes

Impossible shapes often involve elements that appear to overlap or interlock in physically impossible ways. Notice how each shape in the image connects to the other shapes you see. Therefore, identify and count the number of shapes in the image before you start your drawing. Get to know the shapes within the illusion.

Practice sketching the key shapes first as small thumbnail studies of the image, as this will help you know how the shapes link together to create the optical illusion. If you keep questioning what you see, you will find that the image will reveal its secrets to you.

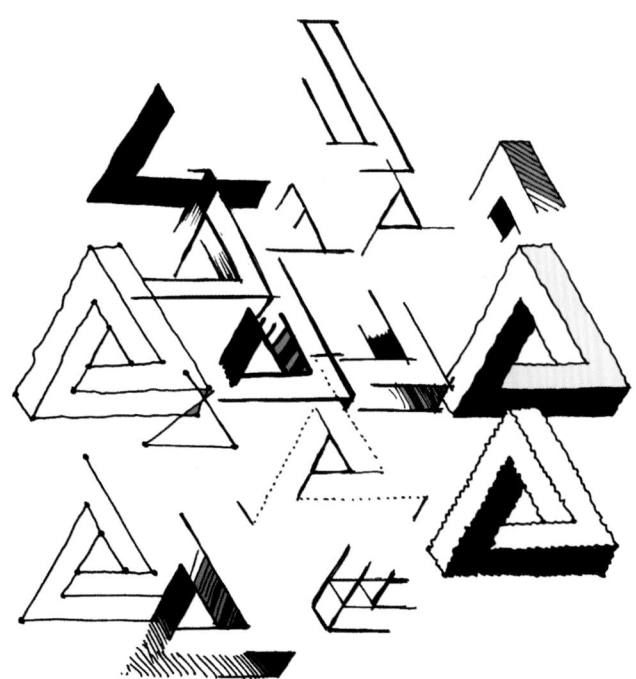

Shading Techniques

It is useful to be able to draw flat even tonal values when drawing optical illusions. When pencil shading a flat tonal value, it can often appear uneven due to inconsistent pressure, irregular marks and gapes left between the areas shaded.

To achieve a successful flat tonal value, use a consistent pressure and uniform marks using the side of the pencil point. Build up the tonal values with a small circular motions over time, starting with light tonal values and then slowly increase the pressure of the marks to darken the tone. Don't rush your shading, as neat and accurate shading will greatly enhance your tonal optical illusions.

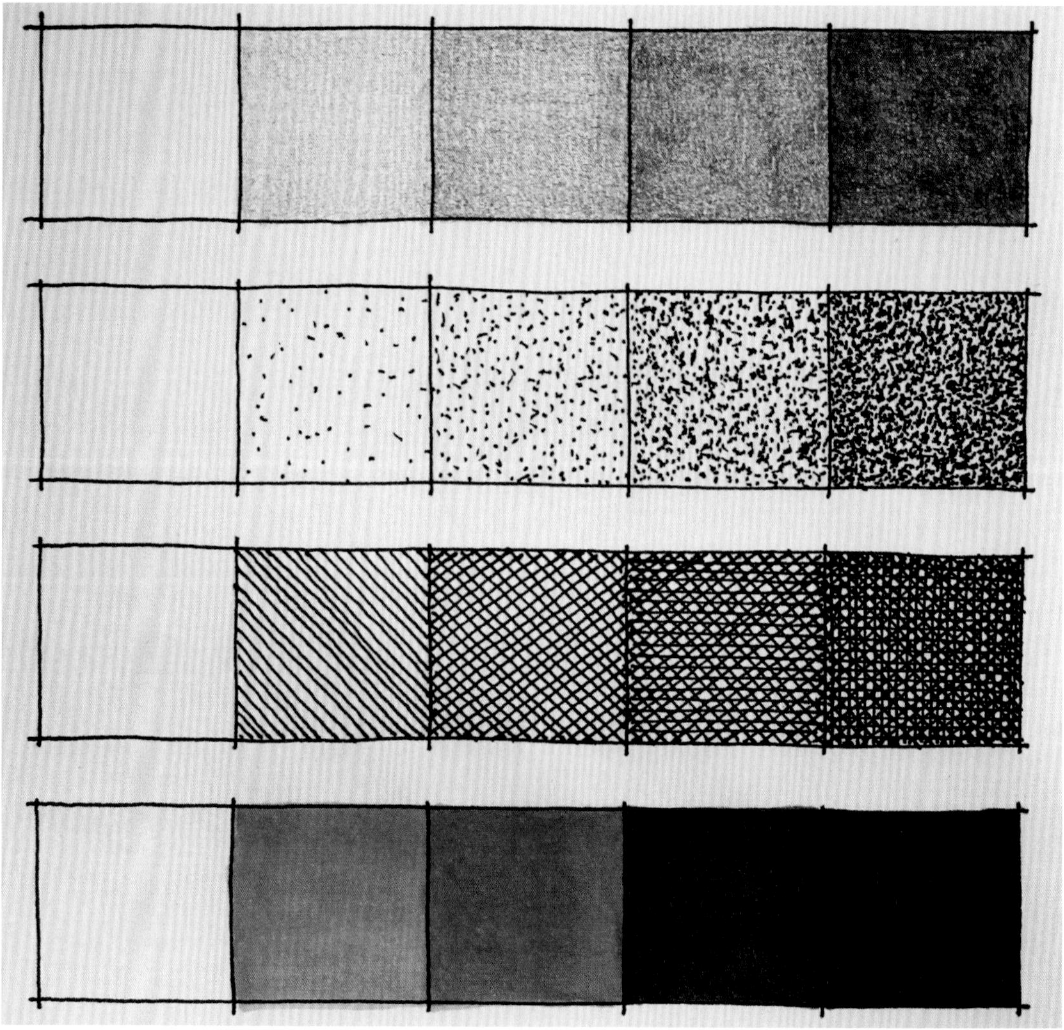

Overview

Practice regularly. Repeat the shape as a small thumbnail sketch until you understand the shapes you see and how they relate.

Learn from your drawing, from the drawings that work and those that don't work so well. You can see what works best and then do more of that.

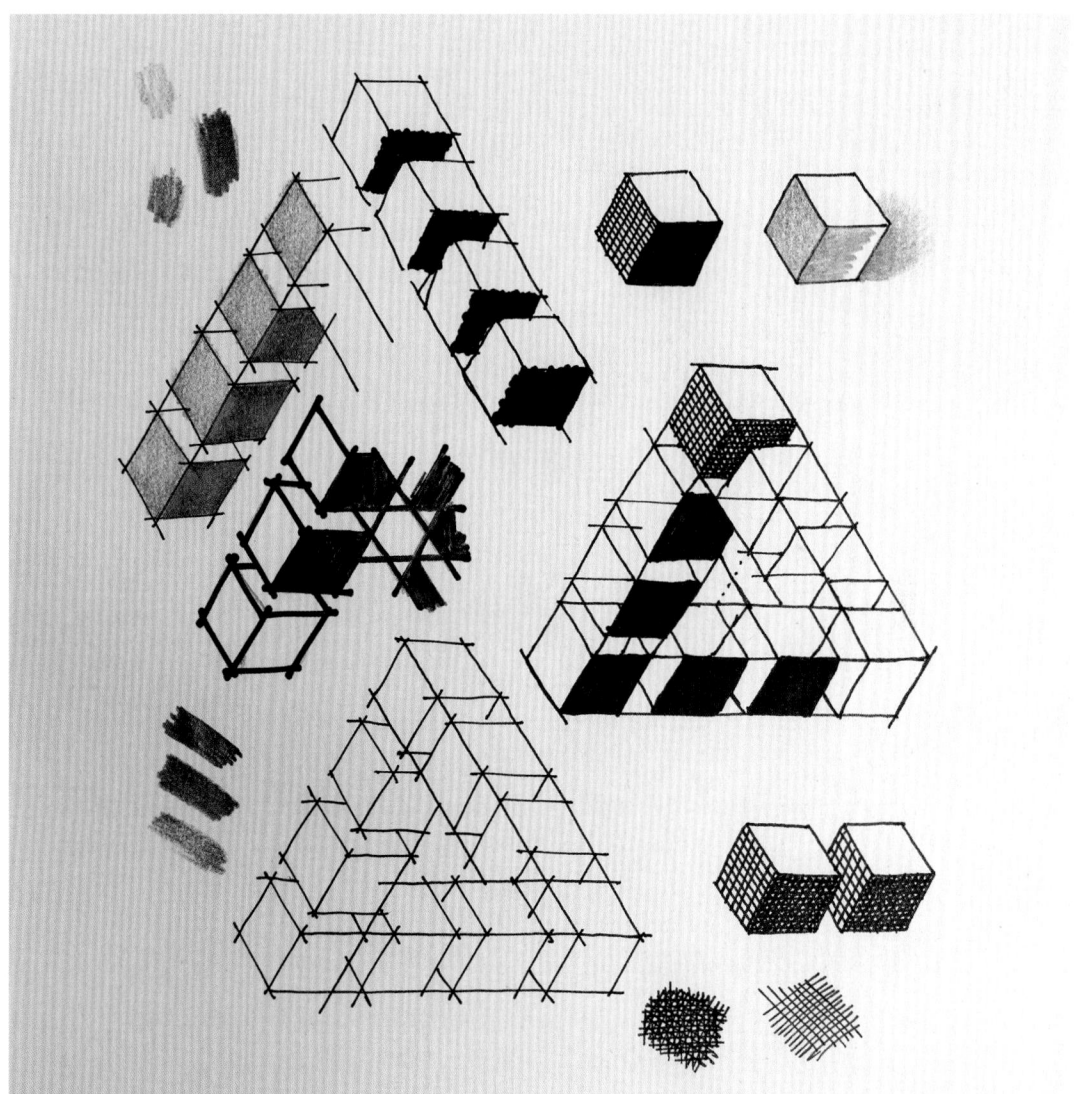

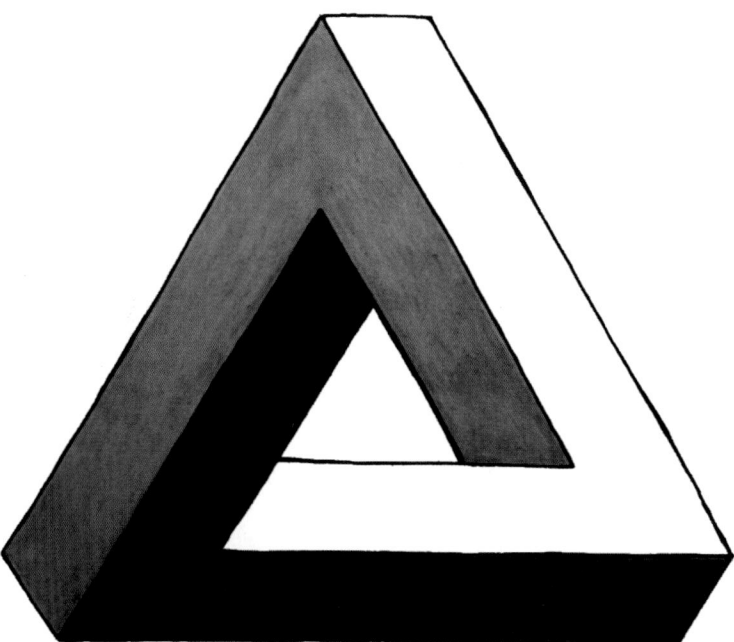

2.1 Impossible Triangle

The Impossible Triangle (also known as the Penrose Triangle or Penrose Tribar) is the most famous example of an impossible shape. The mathematician and physicist Roger Penrose popularised it in the 1950s.

HOW TO DRAW THE IMPOSSIBLE TRIANGLE

Drawing tips: Look closely and notice the number of shapes that create this illusion.

Draw each stage as a quick sketch and repeat the steps until you can draw the illusion with muscle memory and create your main drawing.

STEP 1

Draw a small equilateral triangle in the middle of your paper. An equilateral triangle has sides of equal length.

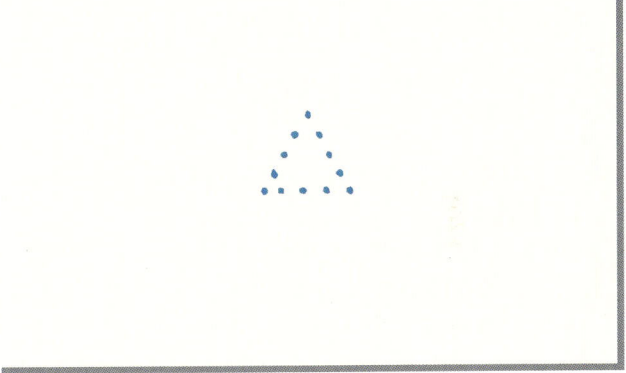

STEP 2

Draw three extension lines, each slightly longer than the sides of your equilateral triangle, from the three corners of the triangle.

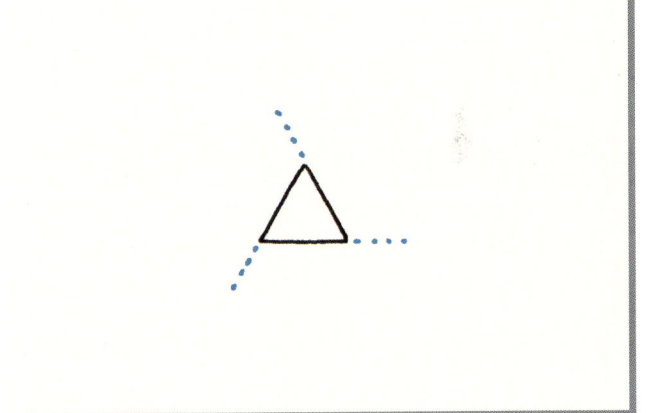

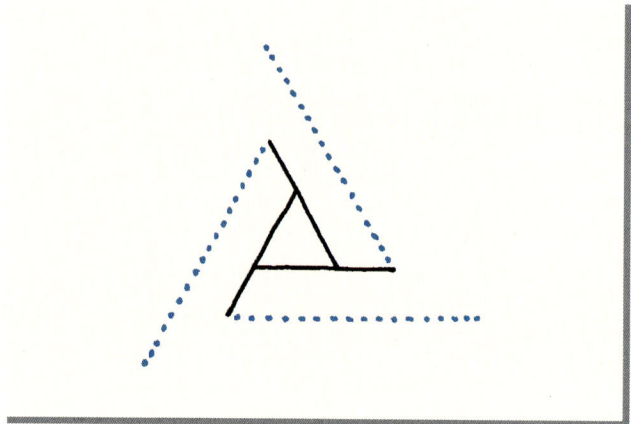

STEP 3

Draw three more lines, starting at the ends of the extension lines we just drew. Each new line is parallel to a side of the triangle and extends beyond the parallel line nearest it.

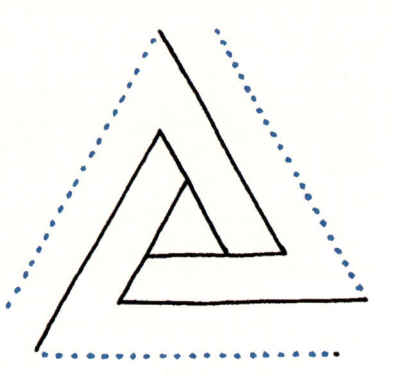

STEP 4

Using the same process, draw three more lines from the point of the recent extension lines parallel to the edge of the triangle. This time, stop the lines short of the nearest parallel line.

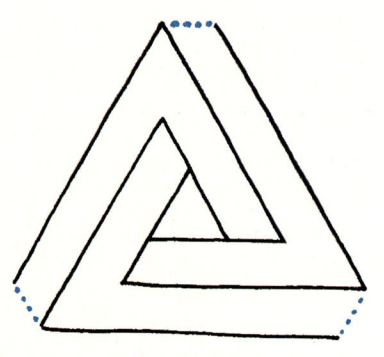

STEP 5

To complete the impossible triangle, draw three short lines connecting the longest lines to their nearest corner. Try to make these three new lines parallel to the farthest opposite side of the original equilateral triangle.

STEP 6

Look at your completed impossible triangle and consider if you could improve anything. Check what needs doing before you correct it. Now erase the part that needs changing and fix it with a confident line at the correct angle.

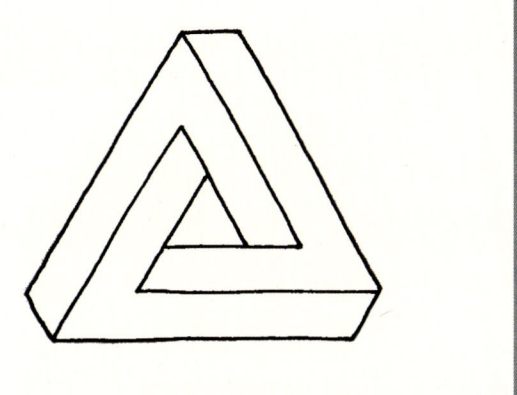

STEP 7

Once you have rechecked and corrected your drawing, it is time to add some shading. Shade one of the three areas with a solid, dark tonal value. Shade a second area with a mid-tone value, something between black and white. Leave the third area unshaded.

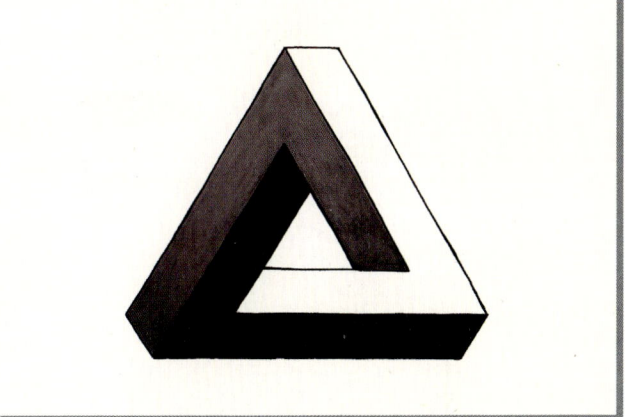

DRAWING WORKSHOP

- Enhance your drawing by adding accurate, dark outlines for your final image.
- Consider using graded shading for each of the three shapes within this illusion to make the image pop when complete.
- Enhance your drawing by adding accurate, dark lines for the final image and then adding shading with crisp, clear tonal values.

EXTRA

There is another interesting version of the impossible triangle you can draw. See Impossible Triangle with Cubes (2.5).

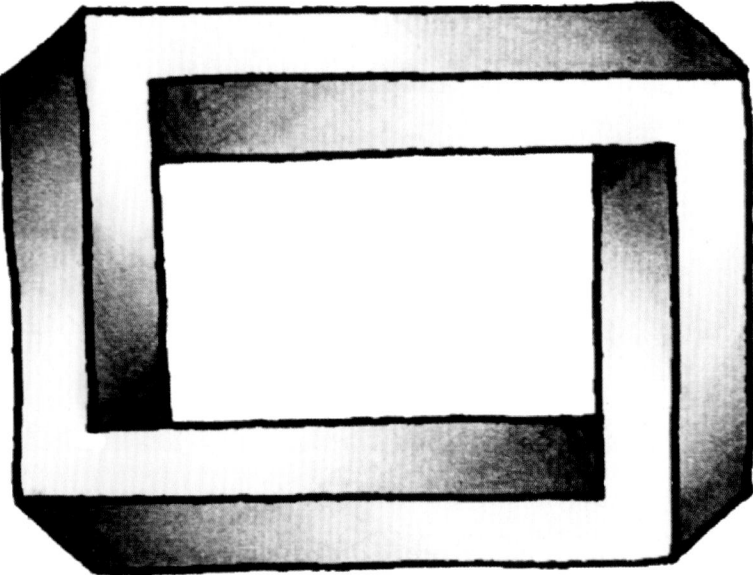

2.2 Impossible Rectangle

The Impossible Rectangle is an optical illusion that appears solid with four right angles. Still, when we look more closely, we can see that the angles and lines do not connect in a way that would be physically possible.

HOW TO DRAW THE IMPOSSIBLE RECTANGLE

Drawing tips: Draw soft guidelines as you complete each step in your drawing. Before you start, look closely and notice how each line is linked to the next.

STEP 1

Draw a simple rectangle wider than it is tall. This rectangle will become the hole in the center of the impossible rectangle.

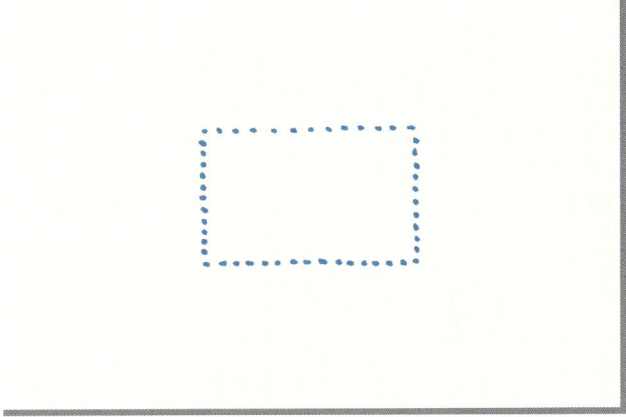

STEP 2

Extend the four sides of the rectangle at the four corners by drawing a series of short, equal-length lines.

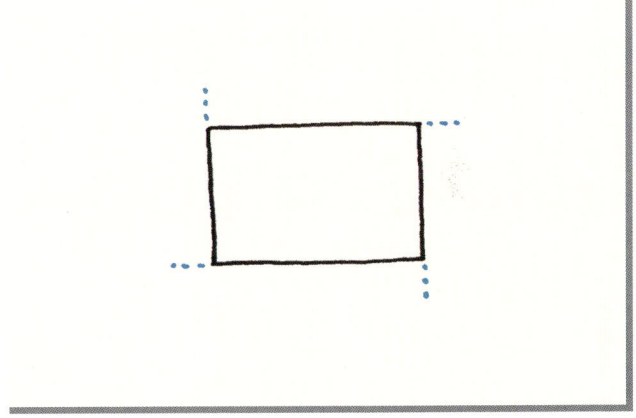

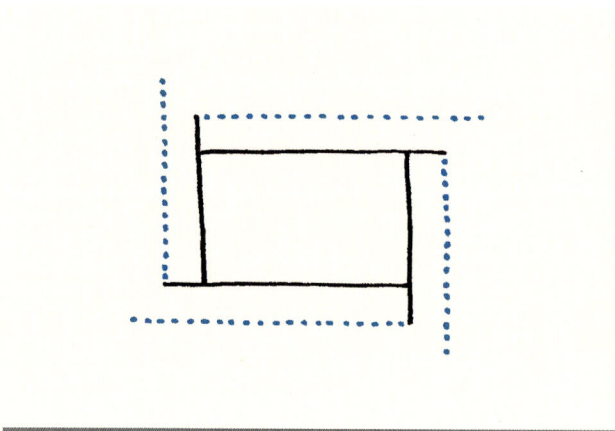

STEP 3

From the ends of the short extension lines, draw four longer lines parallel to the original rectangle we drew from the ends of the short extension lines. Each new line needs to extend past its nearest parallel line by the same length as the short lines we drew in Step 2 of this drawing.

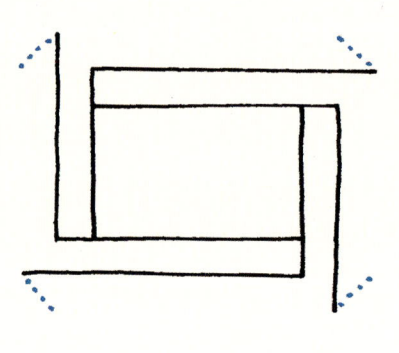

STEP 4

From the ends of the new lines from Step 3, draw four short, equal-length lines at a 45-degree angle.

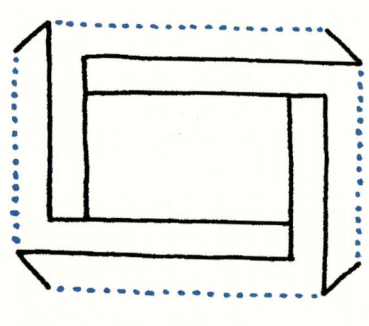

STEP 5

To complete the illusion, draw four more parallel lines connecting each end of the lines drawn in Step 4.

STEP 6

Effective shading will add the final touch for a convincing optical illusion. There are just four right-angle shapes in this impossible rectangle. Shade the ends of each right angle with a graded tonal value at each end to achieve a 3D appearance.

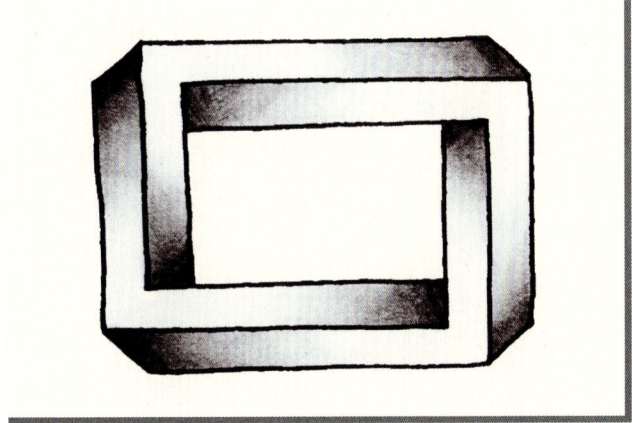

DRAWING WORKSHOP

- Consider alternative shading methods, such as flat tonal values or adding color to your drawing.
- Consider drawing textural marks to add the illusion that the shape is made of stone, with some fine cracks and small chips on its surface.

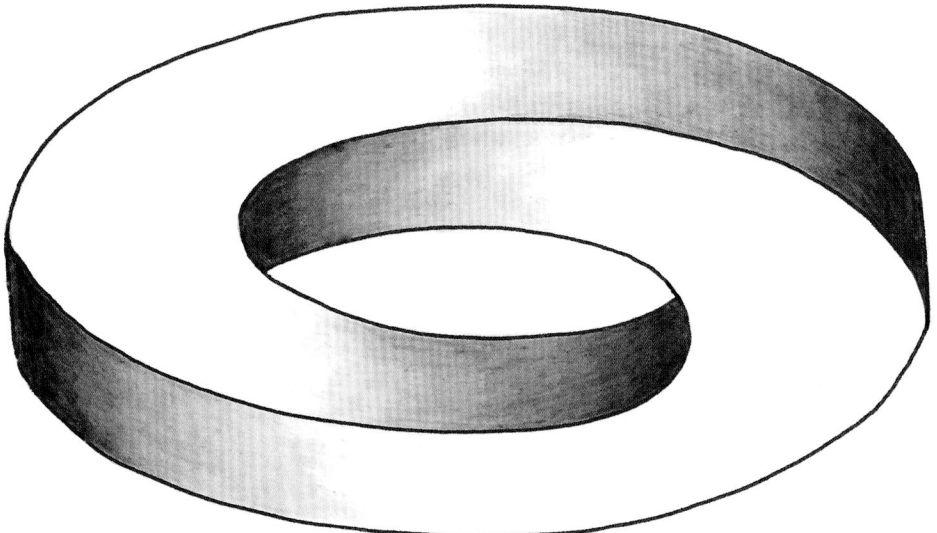

2.3 | Impossible Oval

The Impossible Oval is a deceptively simple shape. It might take a moment to realize it is impossible, but as we study it, we see that it would be impossible to construct due to its inherent geometric contradictions. We are looking down at the oval on the left side but up at the oval on the right side. In reality, it would be impossible to see both the top and bottom simultaneously.

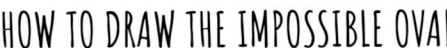

HOW TO DRAW THE IMPOSSIBLE OVAL

Drawing tips: The first time you draw this illusion, sketch each step briefly until you can easily draw the image.

Your ability to draw the required smooth curves will improve as you practice this drawing.

STEP 1

Draw a thin, narrow, oval shape with pointed ends.

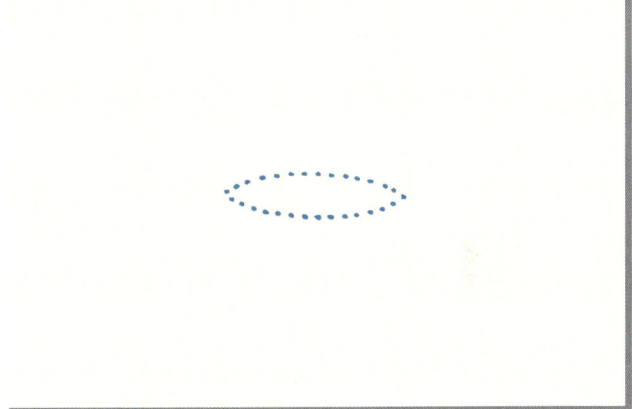

STEP 2

Imagine a horizontal line extending through the two pointed ends of your oval shape. Draw a short vertical line on the left, spaced away from the left point of your oval, that goes down from your imaginary horizontal line. Then, on the right side of your pointed oval, draw a line of equal length to the short line on the left, which goes up from your imaginary horizontal line.

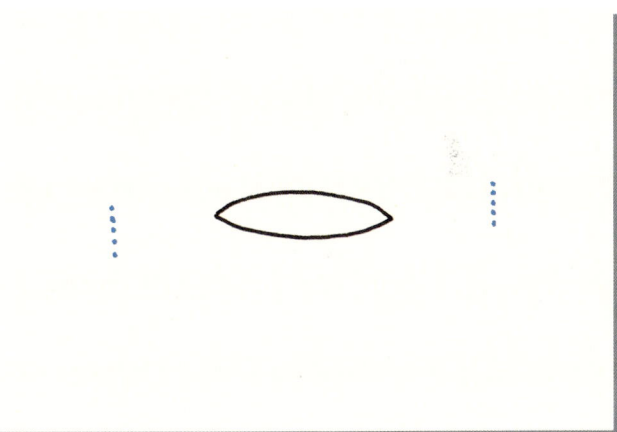

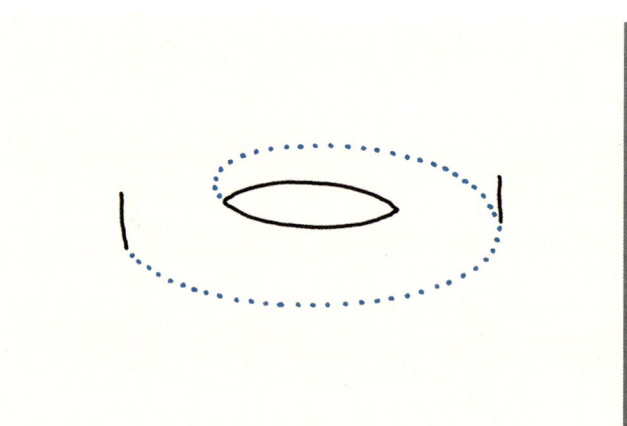

STEP 3

Before drawing the next line, visualize where the line will start and stop in your drawing. Once you are ready, draw a curved line starting at the left side point of the original pointed oval from Step 1. Allow the curve to come back on itself, curve to the base of the vertical line on the right, and then end at the base of the vertical line on the left. Don't worry at this stage about how smooth the curve is; try to get the curve to start and stop in the correct places, and have it touch the base of the right-hand vertical on its journey.

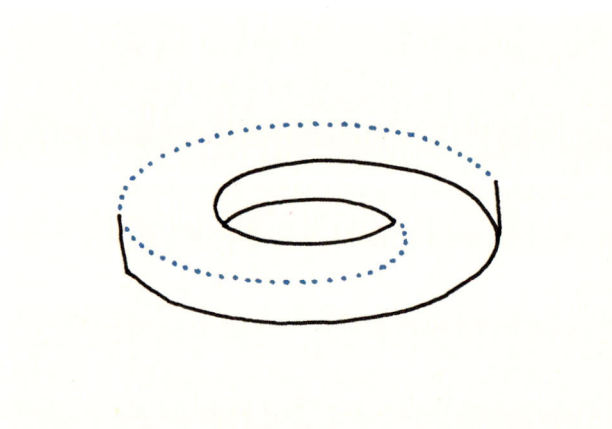

STEP 4

This step is like an upside-down version of Step 3. Start drawing the curve at the right-hand point of the original oval, continue the curved line past the top end of the vertical line on the left, and then allow your curve to arrive at the top of the vertical line on the right.

STEP 5

The impossible oval has just two positive shapes. You could shade the ends of each shape with a graded tonal value, starting with a very dark tone and slowly getting lighter.

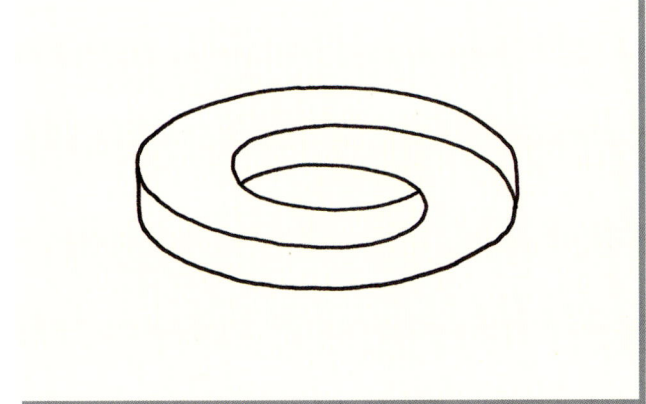

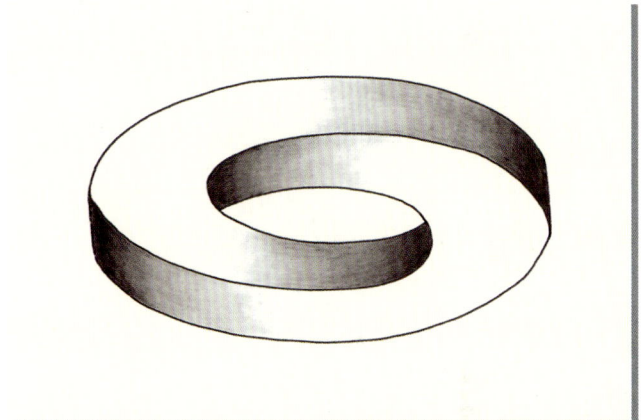

DRAWING WORKSHOP

- Experiment with drawing different shaped ovals using the same drawing techniques.
- Consider filling each of the two shapes with different colored dots.

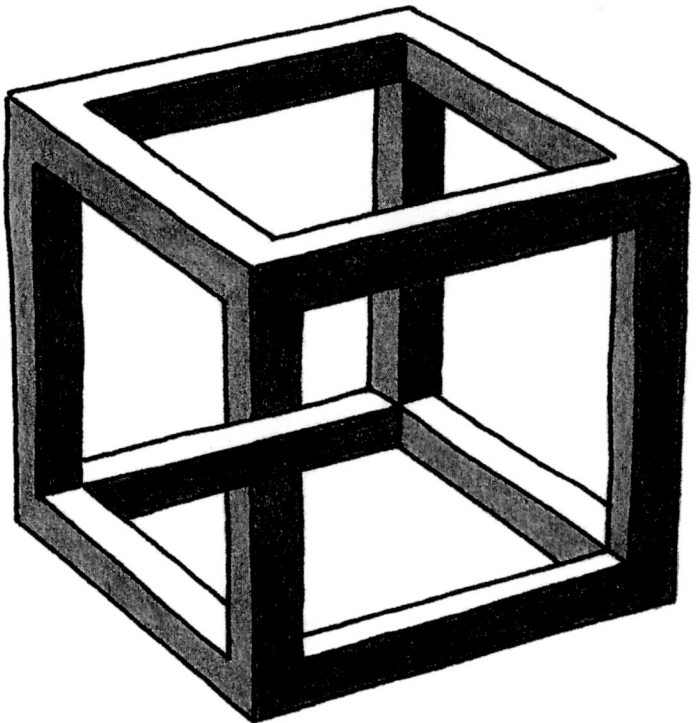

2.4 Impossible Cube

The Impossible Cube is an optical illusion depicting a three-dimensional cube made from solid bars. It has a little trick: one of the horizontal bars overlaps a vertical bar, which would be physically impossible in the three-dimensional world.

Remember that creating an optical illusion like this takes practice to get the lines and angles right. Keep going even if it doesn't look perfect on your first attempt. Your lines need to be easy to erase and correct as you draw, so use soft lines at first by applying slight pressure on the point of your pencil. In this way, you can alter and correct your drawing as you notice precisely how each line needs to be drawn for the illusion to work.

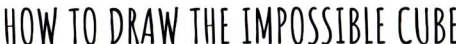
HOW TO DRAW THE IMPOSSIBLE CUBE

Drawing tips: Look carefully at each corner of the cube and notice how the lines connect to form solid-looking shapes.

Observe the lines of the cube and pay attention to where these lines overlap.

STEP 1

Draw a cube using very soft guide-lines, as you will need to erase a small part later. Start by drawing the diamond shape at the top of the cube. Notice how the top of the diamond shape is to the right of the middle, and the bottom is to the left of the middle. Next, draw three equal-length vertical lines: one from the bottom-middle point of the diamond and two at the ends of the diamond. Next, draw two lines to complete the cube. These two lines are at the same angle as the two lines of the base of the diamond shape. Leave a gap in the middle of the closest vertical line.

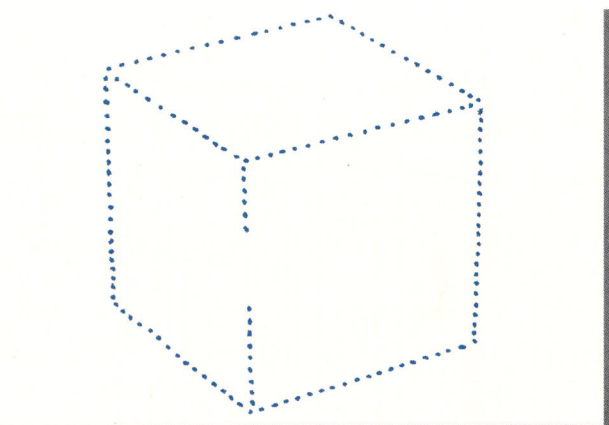

STEP 2

Draw an inner line to the top of the cube and then add a short vertical line below the middle point, and then draw two more lines to create a thickness to the two most distant parts of the top of the cube.

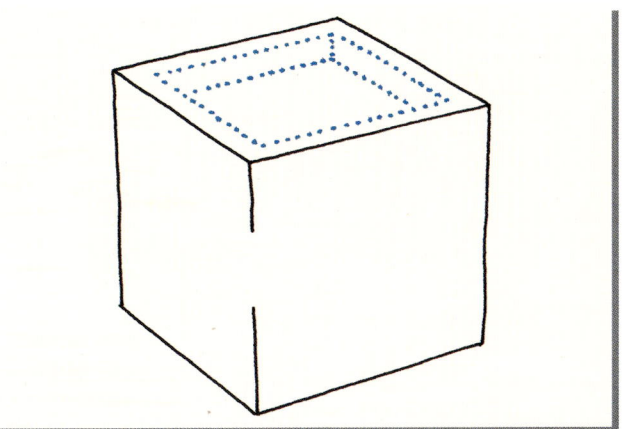

45

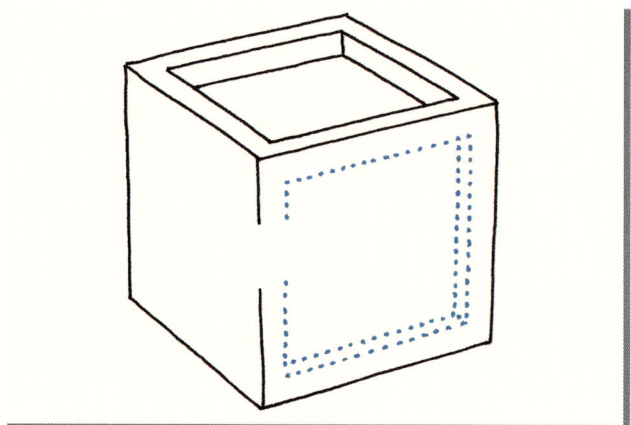

STEP 3

Repeat Step 2, but this time on the cube's right side. Continue to leave a gap in the nearest vertical line.

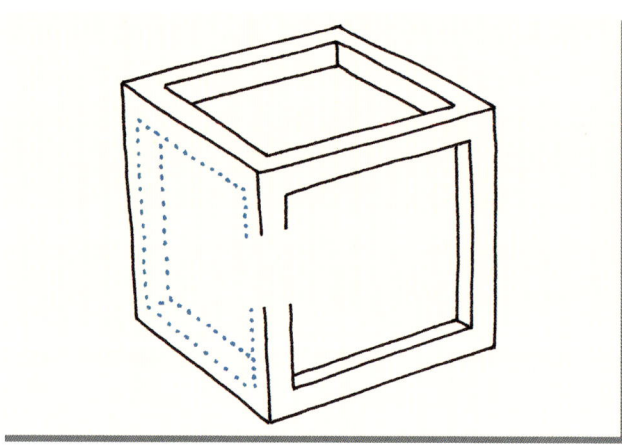

STEP 4

Repeat Step 2 on the cube's left side. Continue to leave a gap in the nearest vertical line.

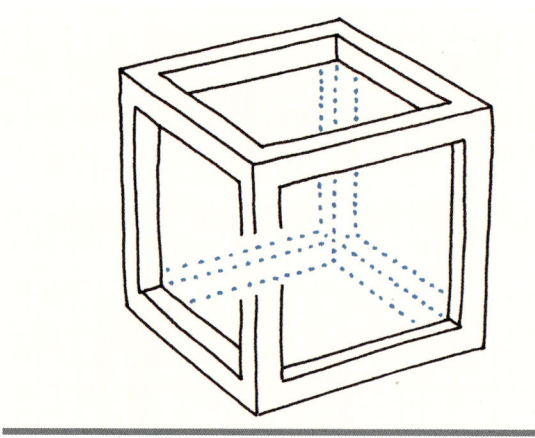

STEP 5

Draw the interior back of the cube by drawing three parallel lines from the top-middle area and the base area of the left and right verticals of the cube. Notice how these three sets of parallel lines meet at a point where the middle lines cross. Check the lines you have drawn and, when ready, darken the guidelines to create the illusion.

STEP 6

Shade one side of the cube with a dark, flat tone; shade another side as a mid-tonal value; and the third side can be left unshaded.

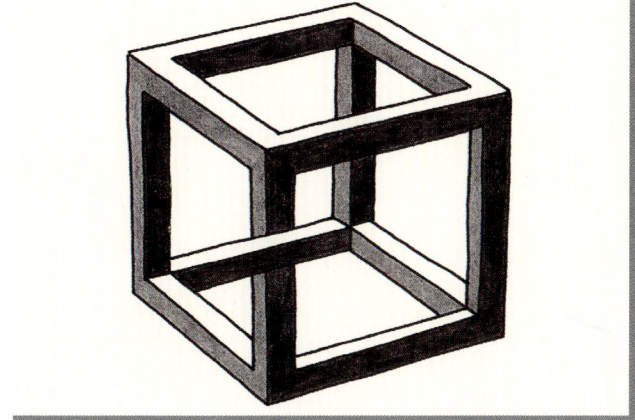

DRAWING WORKSHOP

- Consider using a different area of overlap to make a variation on the impossible cube.
- Consider adding color values rather than tonal values of the grayscale to your drawing.

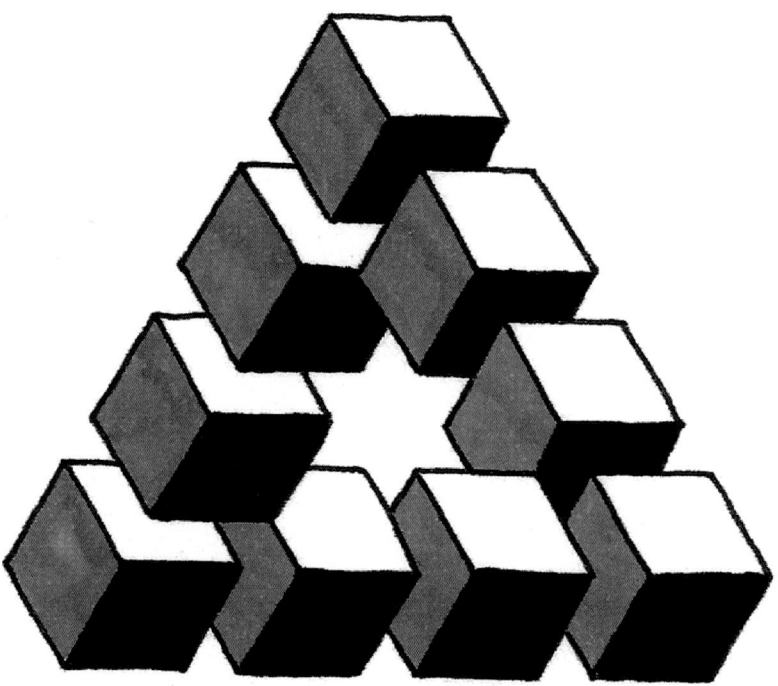

2.5 ▌ Impossible Triangle with Cubes

The *Impossible Triangle with Cubes* is a version of the *Impossible Triangle*, but in this version, the sides of the triangle are made up of cubes. Notice how some of the cubes appear to overlap others, contributing to the illusion of a continuous triangular shape.

To create this illusion, you will need to discover the exact placement and position of each cube before you fix the lines for the finished stage of the fascinating illusion.

This drawing is an alternative version of the *Impossible Triangle* (*See* 2.1).

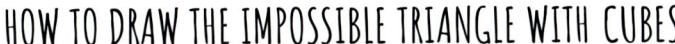

HOW TO DRAW THE IMPOSSIBLE TRIANGLE WITH CUBES

Drawing tips: Observe the position and angle of the cube outlines before you start to draw them. Notice how the angle of the cube outlines follows the angles of the impossible triangle.

STEP 1

First, draw the basic Impossible Triangle by following the steps above (*See* 2.1).

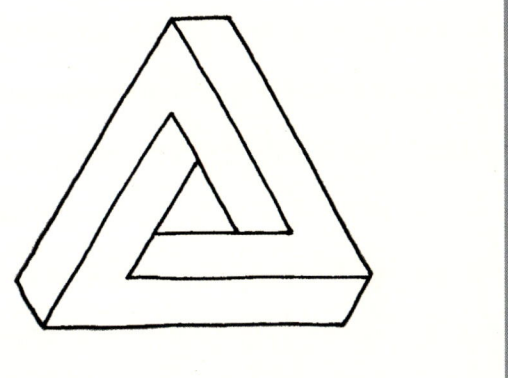

STEP 2

Draw three pairs of lines on each of the outside edges of the *Impossible Triangle*, creating four even gaps between the three narrow pairs of lines.

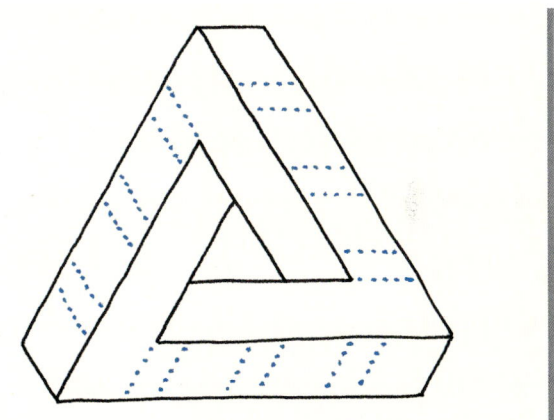

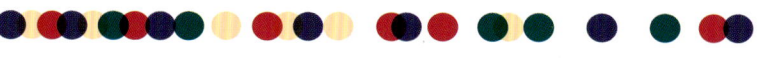

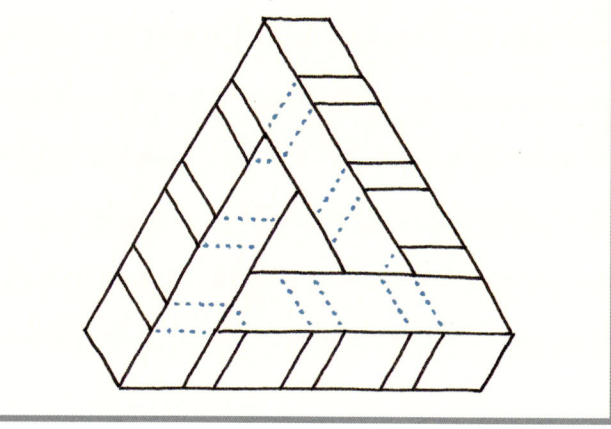

STEP 3

Draw five lines on each of the inner sides of your *Impossible Triangle*, continuing the lines from Step 2 and following the direction of the adjacent side angle.

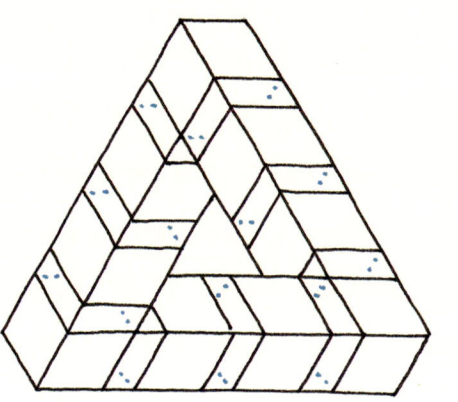

STEP 4

Draw three short lines from the outside edge on each side of the triangle and two short inner lines to create four cubes with parallel lines on each side of your triangle.

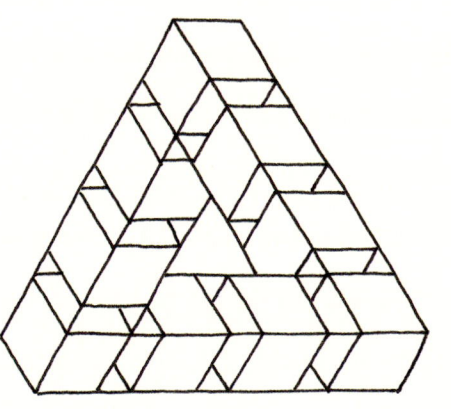

STEP 5

Look carefully at the finished example and then erase the cubes' connecting lines as they are no longer needed. Notice how the negative triangle in the center of the drawing has become a six-point star.

STEP 6

Once you have mastered the lines needed to create the *Impossible Triangle with Cubes*, shading will add depth and a sense of solidity to the illusion. Shade one side of each cube with a dark tonal value, one side with a mid-tone value, and one side can be left unshaded.

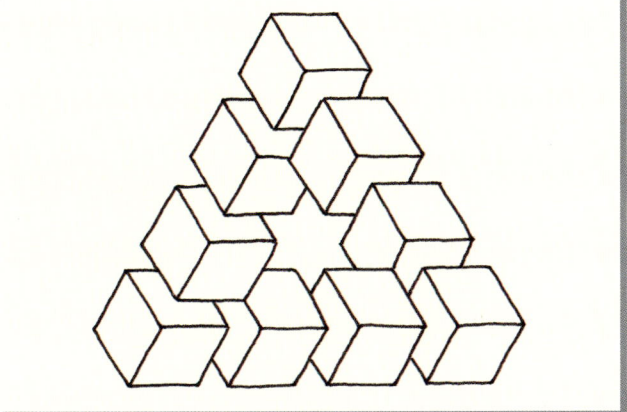

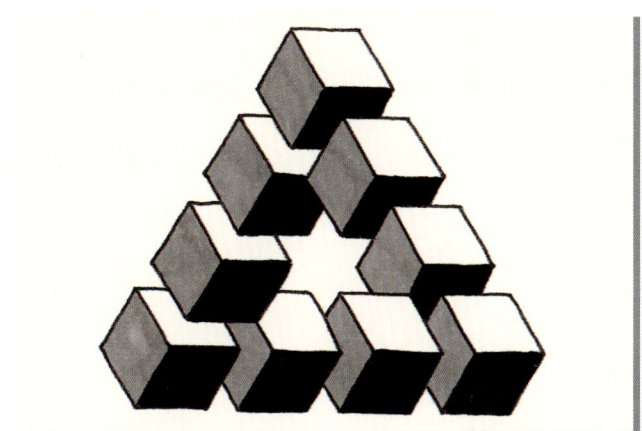

DRAWING WORKSHOP

- Consider adding color to your drawing.
- Consider coloring different cubes in different colors.

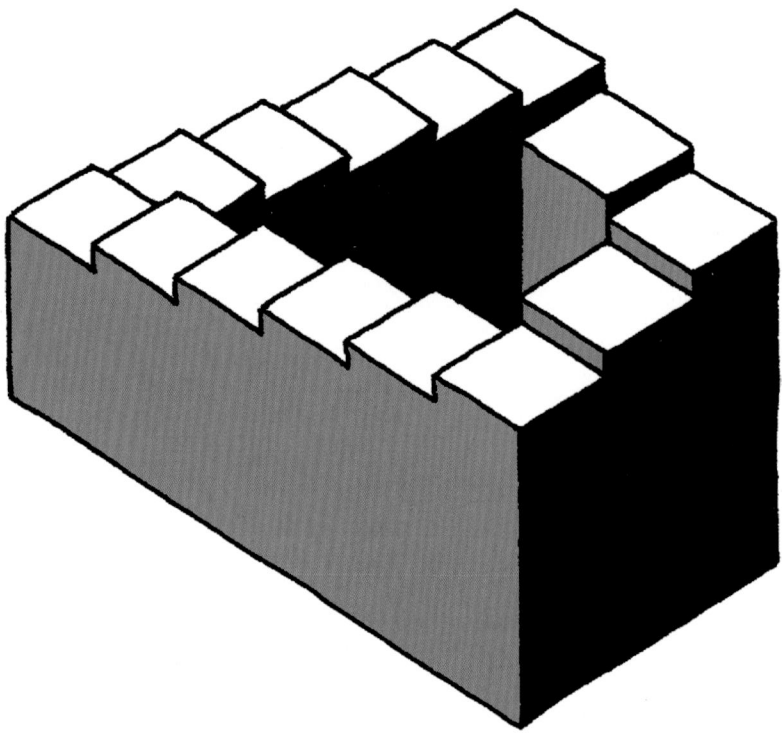

2.6 | Endless Steps

The Endless Steps optical illusion, also known as the Penrose Stairs, is a subtle depiction of a continuous loop of ascending or descending steps.

The illusion gives the impression of an endless staircase, where one can continuously move upward or downward without ever reaching an endpoint. However, the structure is physically impossible to construct in three-dimensional space.

Lionel and Roger Penrose first introduced the illusion in the 1950s, and it has since become a classic example of visual trickery.

HOW TO DRAW THE ENDLESS STEPS

Drawing tips: Look at each step's corners and analyze what you can observe.

You might have needed to add more steps to make your drawing work. That is fine to do. It can take time to see how each step relates to all the other steps in the drawing.

STEP 1

Draw a small diamond, wider than it is tall.

STEP 2

Draw two more diamonds of the same size and shape, stepping up to the right of the first diamond. Then draw four short vertical lines to connect the three steps with risers.

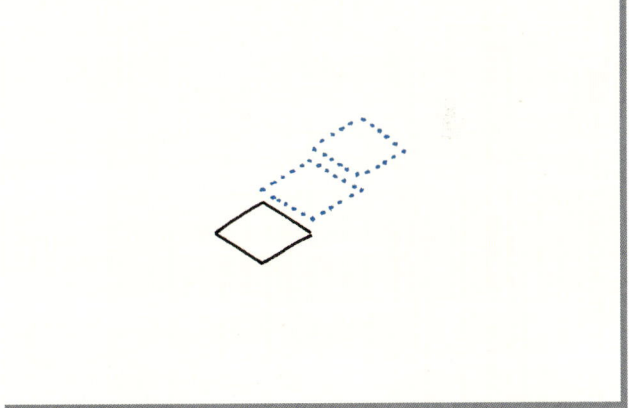

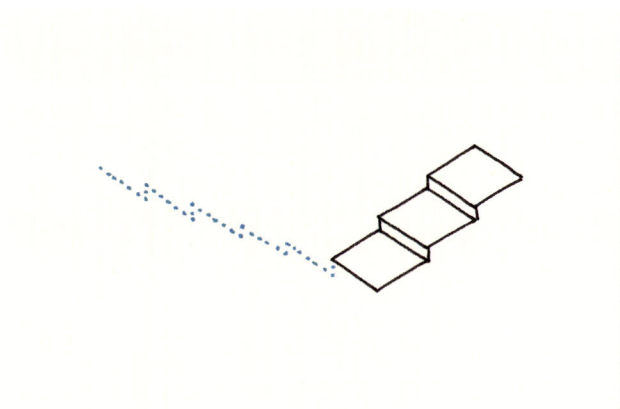

STEP 3

Draw the side outline edge of five steps toward the left from the original diamond. The end of this line of steps should be at the same height as the farthest point of the third step on the right.

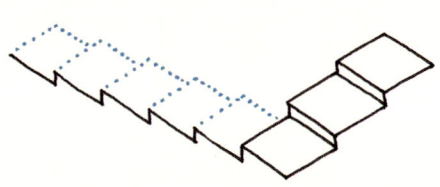

STEP 4

Draw the surface of the five steps on the left as they seem to step downward, but remember they need to stop on the left at the same height as the top point of the step on the far right.

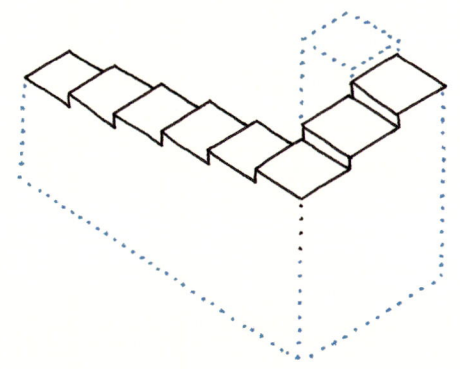

STEP 5

Draw one new step on the right, up and toward the left. Draw a vertical line downward from the left-hand side of this new step. Then, add three downward vertical lines and two bottom edge lines so that the steps look like they are at the top of a wall.

STEP 6

Draw the outline of five more steps, starting from the middle of the second step on the far left to just above the step on the top right. Look carefully at how these new steps link with the steps we have already drawn.

In this drawing, there are only three types of lines, all with fixed angles: vertical lines that are parallel to each other, diagonal lines toward the left at a consistent fixed angle, and diagonal lines toward the right at a fixed, consistent angle.

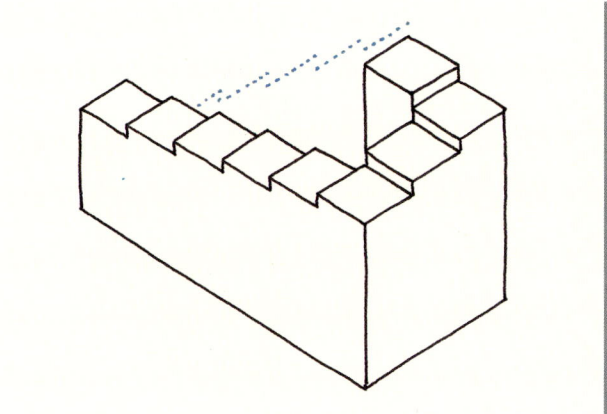

STEP 7

Draw the top surfaces of the last five steps. Although they might look like they are going downward, from left to right, each step is actually angled upward.

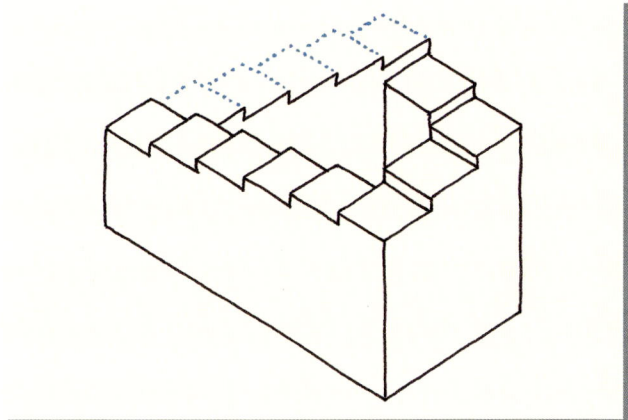

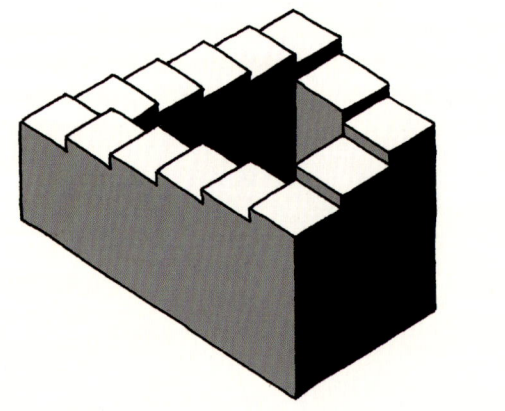

STEP 8

There are just three different surface directions in this drawing. Shade one surface direction with a dark tonal value, another with a mid-tone value, and the third surface direction can be left unshaded.

DRAWING WORKSHOP

- You could draw tiny people walking up or down the steps at a distance.
- You could add extra buildings behind the steps, using the same outline angles as you used in the main shape of the steps.

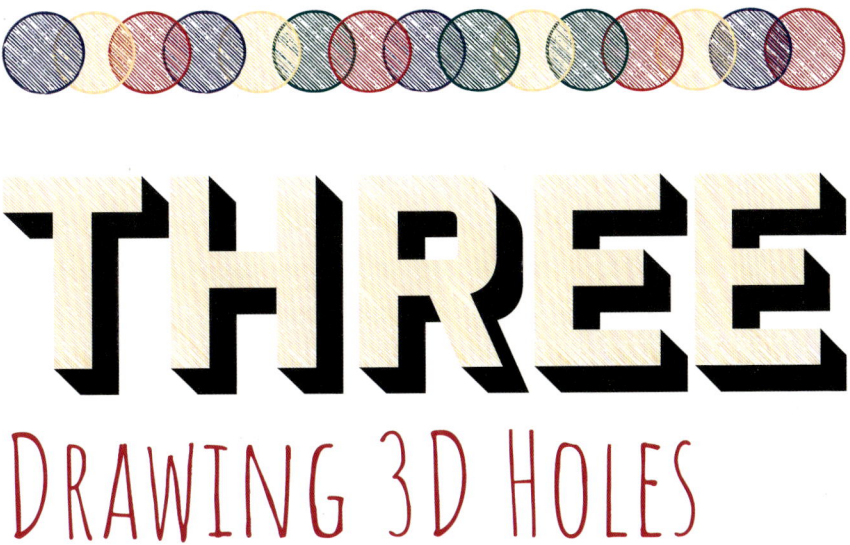

THREE
Drawing 3D Holes

3D Hole Optical Illusions

3D hole optical illusions are visual illusions that trick the viewer into perceiving a hole in the surface of the image that does not exist. When drawing 3D holes, you can imagine a three-dimensional void within the paper's surface.

There are two main types of 3D holes: trompe l'oeil illusions and dramatic fantasy illusions.

Trompe L'oeil 3D Holes

The French term "trompe l'oeil" means "deceive the eye." A trompe l'oeil optical illusion gains its power by tricking the eye into thinking that the illusion is real. Trompe l'oeil hole illusions need meticulous attention to detail at the hole's horizon so that the hole and the surface upon which it is drawn are seamlessly integrated into a realistic-looking environment.

To trick the eye into seeing the edge of a hole as natural, creating a blend of illusion and reality, you will need to use precise rendering, crisp, lifelike shadows, and textural details to make the illusion indistinguishable from a genuine hole in the surface of the paper.

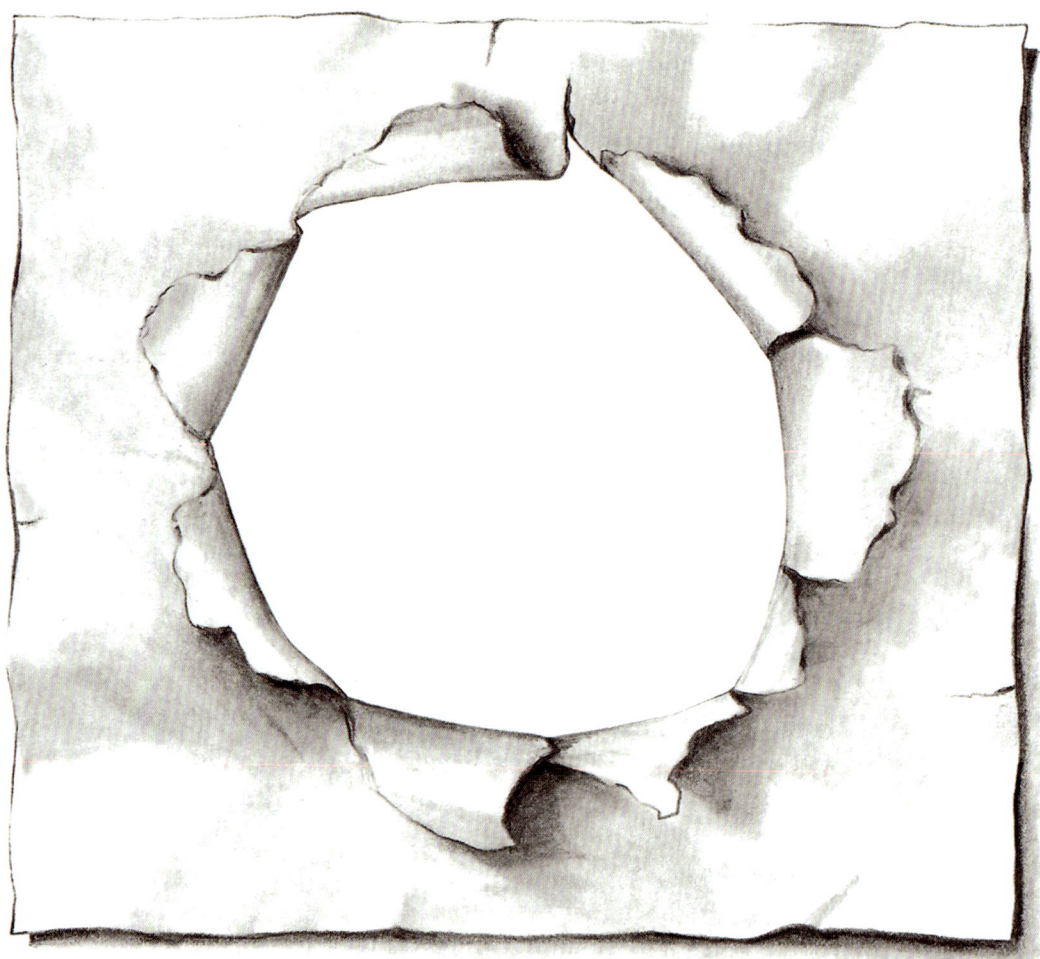

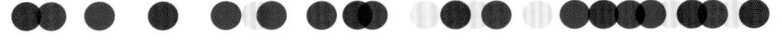

Fantasy 3D Holes

In contrast, fantasy 3D hole optical illusions take a more imaginative and dramatic approach. The aim is to draw a creative fantasy that allows for experimentation. For example, an earthquake's crevasse appears on the paper's surface, or a range of city buildings appears to rise from a deep hole. Both 3D hole optical illusions aim to trick and challenge our perception of space.

Depth perception plays a crucial role in our eye-brain partnership. The realistic depiction of shadows will significantly reinforce the eye-brain partnership's interpretation of a genuine spatial hole.

Essential Drawing Techniques for 3D Holes

Here are some essential skills for drawing three-dimensional holes.

Anamorphic Perspective

Anamorphic perspective is a form of optical illusion in which the drawing is deliberately distorted but will reveal itself as a realistic representation when viewed from a particular viewpoint above the anamorphic dot.

This distortion is essential for the illusion to achieve its intended effect when seen from a particular point of view.

Anamorphic perspective adds an extra layer of complexity and realism to 3D hole optical illusions, enhancing their visual impact, and is a fundamental technique for creating ambitious and convincing 3D holes.

Manipulating Shadows

We can use shading techniques to accurately represent the play of light and shadow on the surfaces within the void, enhancing the illusion of depth. By skillfully blending tonal values, we can adjust the intensity of shadows and create a real sense of the existence of a hole on the paper's surface.

When shading clear cut edges it is helpful to use just three tonal values; a light tone, a medium tone, and a dark tone. If the illusion is depicting a dark void a range of tonal values which get gradually darker as they recede below the surface of the illusion will work best.

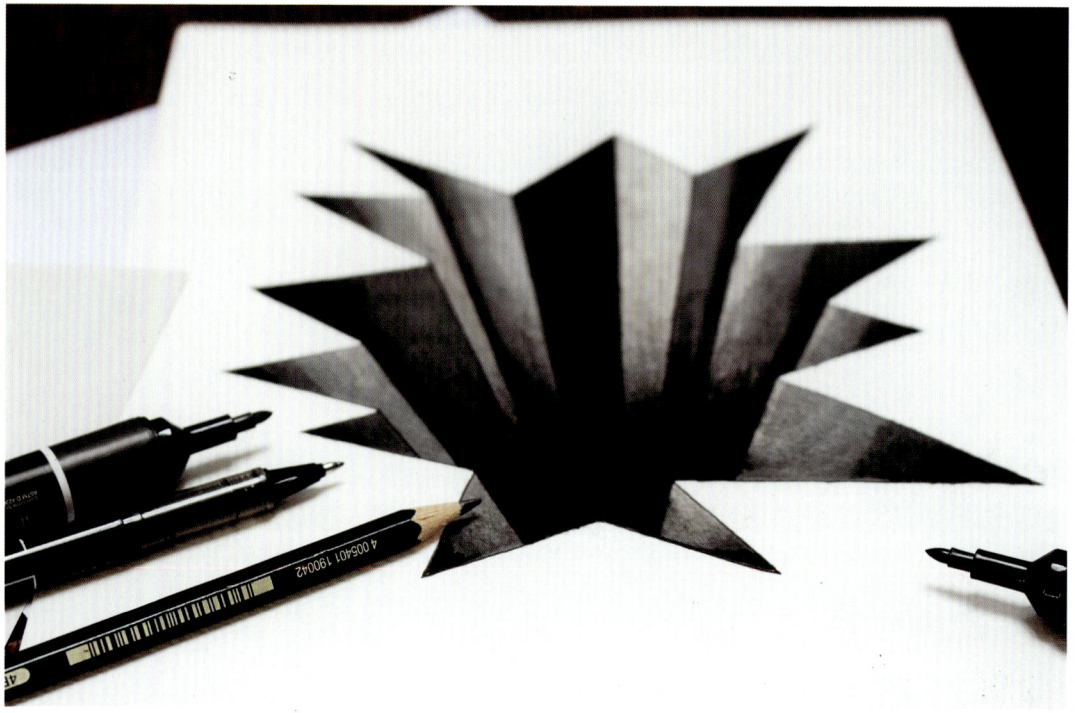

3.1 Deep Hole Star

To create the illusion of a deep hole in a star shape, we need to use sharp angles and dramatic shading to give the impression of a seemingly bottomless hole into the darkest void when seen from one fixed viewpoint.

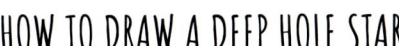
HOW TO DRAW A DEEP HOLE STAR

Drawing tips: View your drawing from a low angle directly above the cross you drew to see the illusion at its optimal perspective. All anamorphic illusions must be viewed from one specific viewpoint for the distortion to reveal itself as an optical illusion.

Use a sharp pencil or pen and a crisp line to keep the edges of your main shape as sharp as possible.

STEP 1

Draw a clear zigzag outline of a star shape that is taller than it is wide.

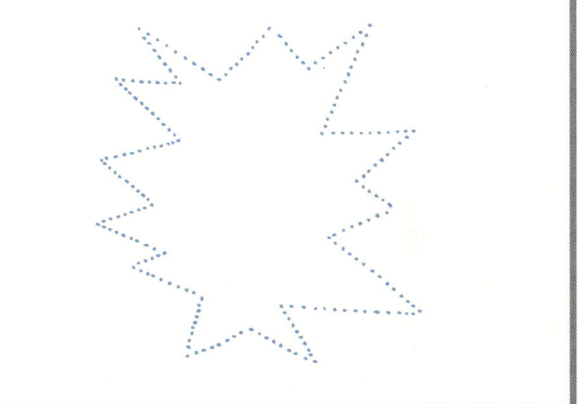

STEP 2

Draw a dot directly below the base of your zigzag star shape. This represents your anamorphic dot, marking the point above which your drawing should be viewed.

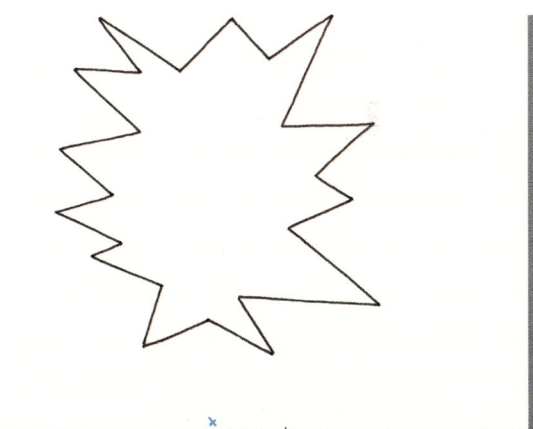

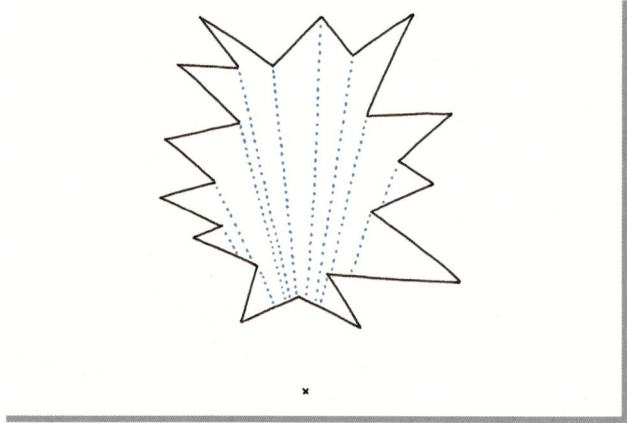

STEP 3

Draw a series of straight lines from the interior points of the star towards your anamorphic dot. Each straight line stops at the star's edge.

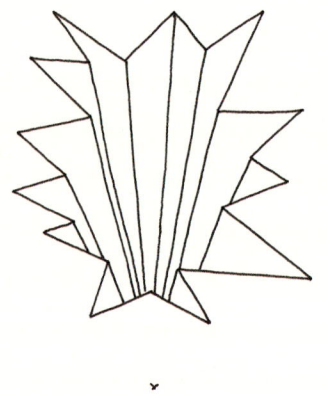

STEP 4

It is best to alternate the tonal values of each of the star's interior surfaces. One surface can have a mid-tone value, the next a darker value, and then repeat.

As the hole recedes, the tonal values should become as dark as possible. Try to create a darkness that is not shiny. If you shade with pencils, try using the softest, darkest pencil for the darkest part of the hole.

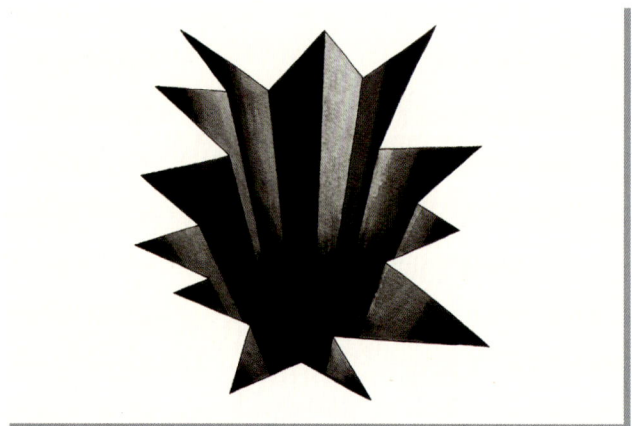

DRAWING WORKSHOP

- Explore drawing holes of different zigzag shapes and find the shape you think works best when viewed above the anamorphic dot.
- Consider adding a flat color to the area surrounding the hole.

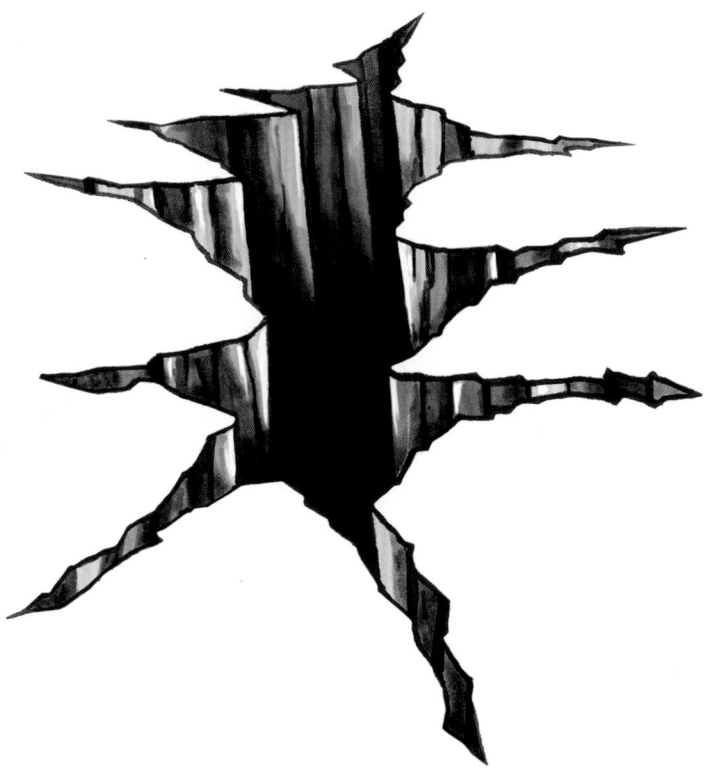

3.2 Earthquake Hole

An earthquake illusion depicts a dramatic hole created by fracturing the paper's surface.

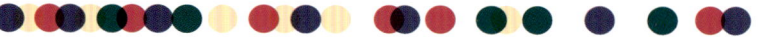
HOW TO DRAW AN EARTHQUAKE HOLE

Drawing tips: Keep your lines sharp and straightforward to help create a dramatic illusion.

Consider extending the earthquake's cracks into your paper's surrounding area.

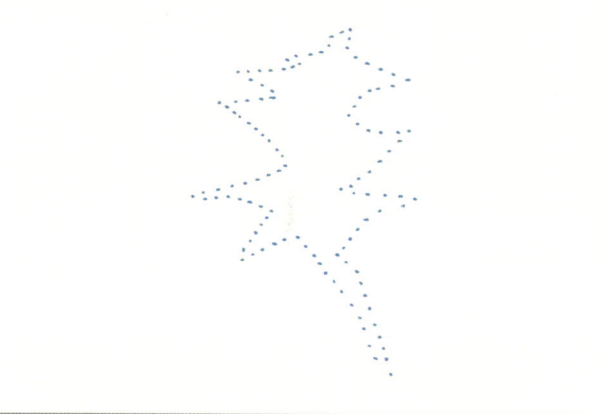

STEP 1

Draw a spiky, creative outline of an earthquake hole. Ensure the outline you draw has a zigzag edge and an interesting shape.

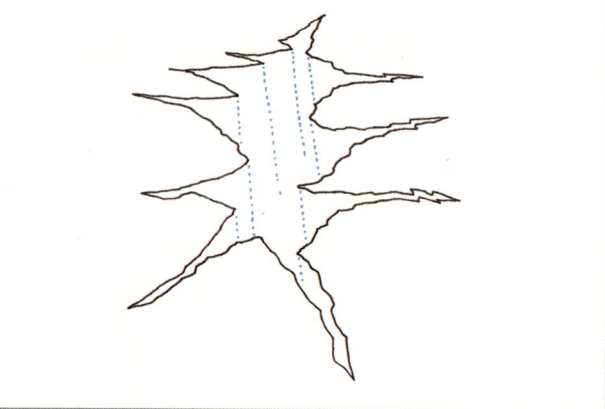

STEP 2

Draw a series of vertical lines from the interior points of your outline that stop at the base edge of the outline.

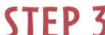

STEP 3

Try extending the points of the earthquake to create a more subtle image.

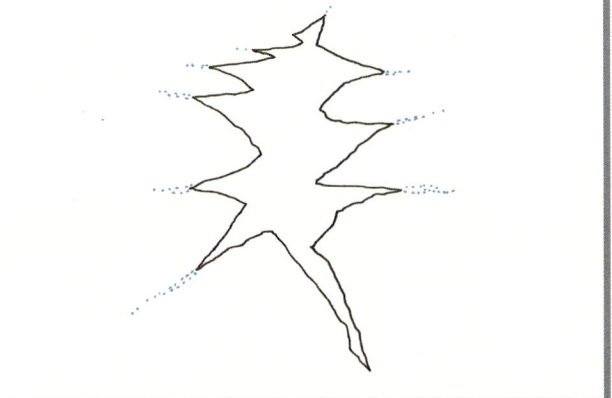

STEP 4

Add some shading to your drawing using a range of tonal contrasts to the receding edges of the earthquake, darkening progressively with depth.

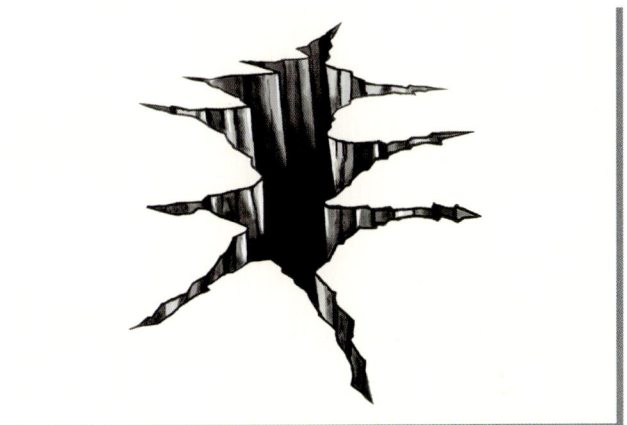

DRAWING WORKSHOP

- Consider adding details outside the rim of your earthquake, such as rocks, small buildings, and roads seen at a distance.
- Consider contrasting the dramatic, dark monochrome of the earthquake with a colorful, peaceful landscape in the surrounding areas.

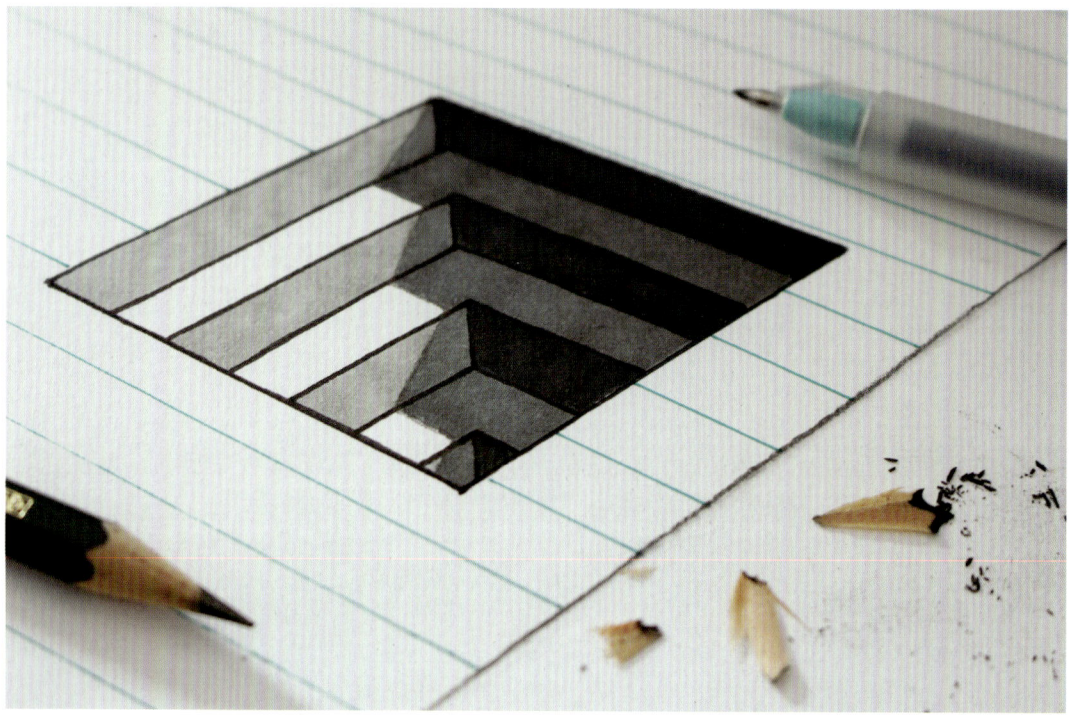

3.3 3D Steps in a Hole

The *3D Steps in a Hole* optical illusion is a simple yet powerful image that uses our eye-brain partnership to see steps receding away from us, the viewer. We can combine this instinct to see steps with the trick of anamorphic projection to create a convincing optical illusion.

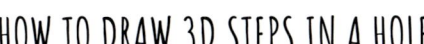

HOW TO DRAW 3D STEPS IN A HOLE

Drawing tips: Ensure that the steps are drawn consistently in terms of size and spacing.

Use shadows to strengthen the three-dimensional form of the steps.

STEP 1

Draw a diamond shape that has opposite points in line with each other.

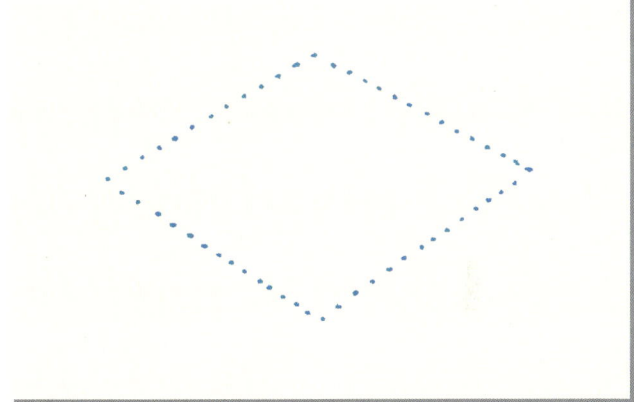

STEP 2

Draw a short vertical line down from the top to the base point of the diamond, and then draw two lines on either side, parallel to the nearest edges of the diamond.

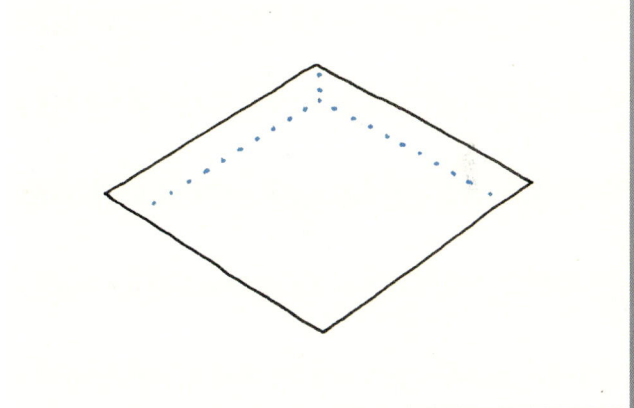

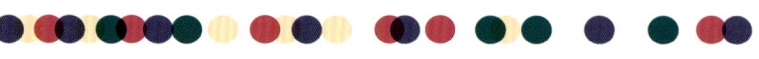

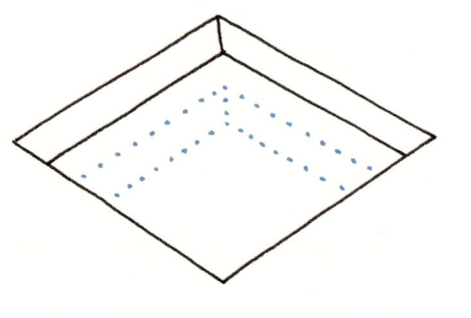

STEP 3

Leave a gap below the vertical straight line you drew. The gap should be the same length as the vertical line. Next, draw a new vertical line and two parallel lines on either side.

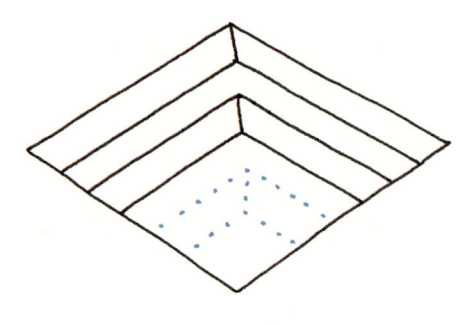

STEP 4

Repeat Step 3.

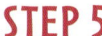

STEP 5

Repeat Step 3 to have a series of evenly spaced steps in a diamond-shaped hole.

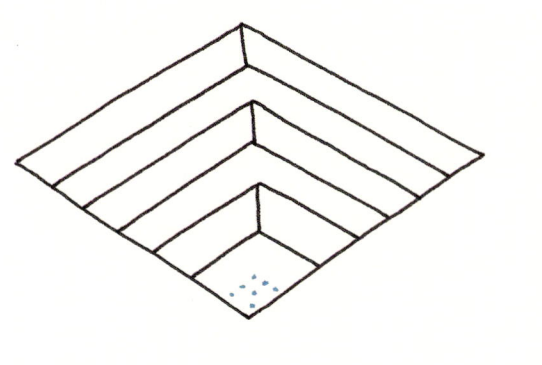

STEP 6

Draw a diagonal line in front of the top inner point of the diamond toward the left. When this diagonal line meets a step line, change its direction so it runs parallel to the bottom-left angle of the diamond. Repeat this process for each of the steps we are drawing. This line represents the edge of a cast shadow as it recedes down the steps.

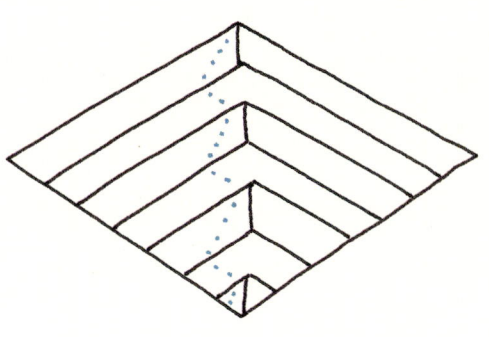

STEP 7

Add shading using flat tonal values to create a solid 3D effect. Start by drawing a light tone on the tread of each step. Then, add a slightly darker tone on the area of each tread that is in shadow. Next, shade the risers of the steps with a dark tonal value.

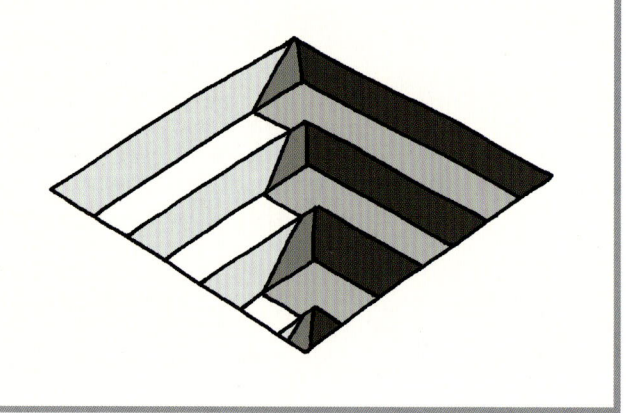

DRAWING WORKSHOP

- Consider adding subtle details such as cracks and chips to make the steps more realistic.
- Consider adding a drawing of an object to one of your steps, such as a ball on a step or a book slightly overlapping one of the steps.

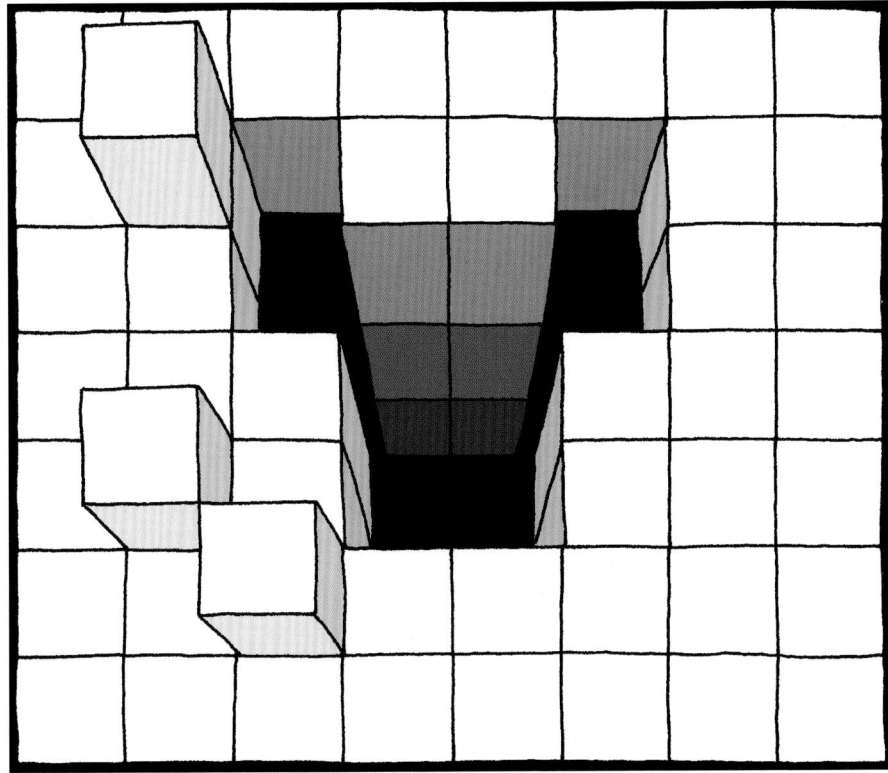

3.4 | 3D Falling Cubes

Drawing 3D falling cubes creates the illusion that cubes appear to be descending or floating in midair when seen from a fixed viewpoint.

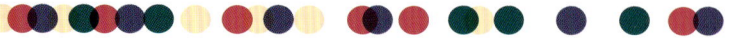

HOW TO DRAW 3D FALLING CUBES

Drawing tips: Practice drawing cubes from different angles to create solid-looking cubes.

To create a greater sense of depth, overlap or stack the cubes with each other.

STEP 1

For this drawing, you need to use graph paper or, even better, draw a square grid on plain paper using a pencil to create your graph paper. It is best to draw your grid, as you can later erase the areas that are not needed; however, graph paper is fine to use as long as the printed grid is pale. If you draw a grid, spend some time and use a ruler and a soft pencil.

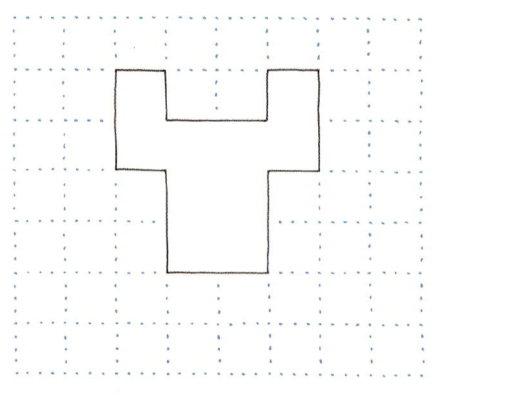

STEP 2

Draw an outline of the hole in the middle of your paper, following the grid lines to create the hole's shape.

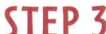

STEP 3

Draw a cross below the center of the hole you drew. Draw straight lines from the interior edges of the grid that point toward your cross below. Draw vertical and diagonal lines to create a sense of depth for the squares at the hole's edges. You could add extra cubes behind the first cubes of the grid.

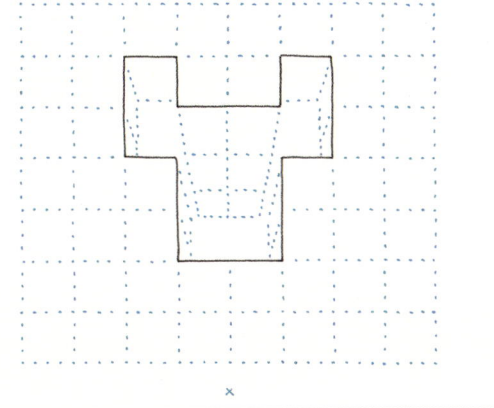

STEP 4

In the area of the grid, outside the hole, you can draw straight lines from the direction of your cross to create cubes on the surface of your grid. Just join the three diagonal lines from the cross that go through the corner of the grid with a new square. This new square will be slightly larger than the squares in your grid, as it is nearer the viewer of the image.

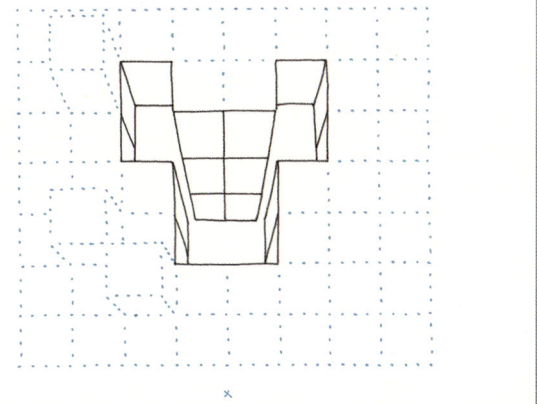

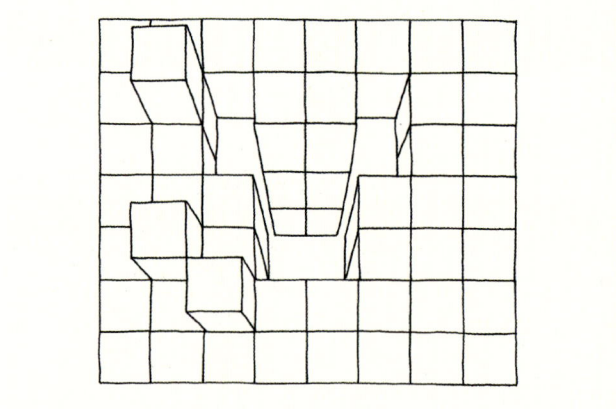

STEP 5

Shading your drawing neatly and simply: Shade each of the three sides of the cube surface: one side with a mid-tone value, one with a light value, and one side unshaded. Shade the hole with the darkest tonal value you can make.

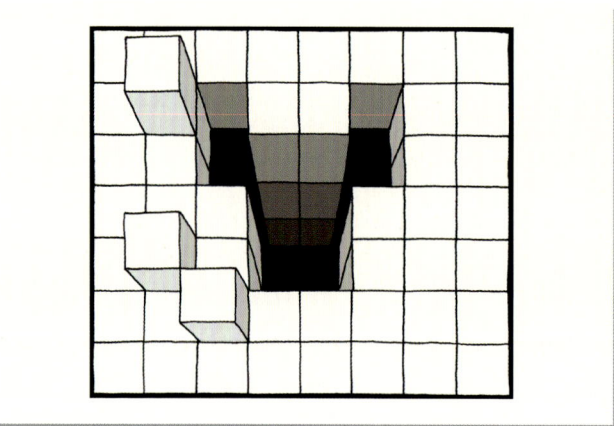

DRAWING WORKSHOP

- Consider drawing a trompe l'oeil edge around the hole.
- Consider adding textures or reflections to make your cubes look more realistic. Be careful not to add too much detail, as it can distract from the overall illusion.

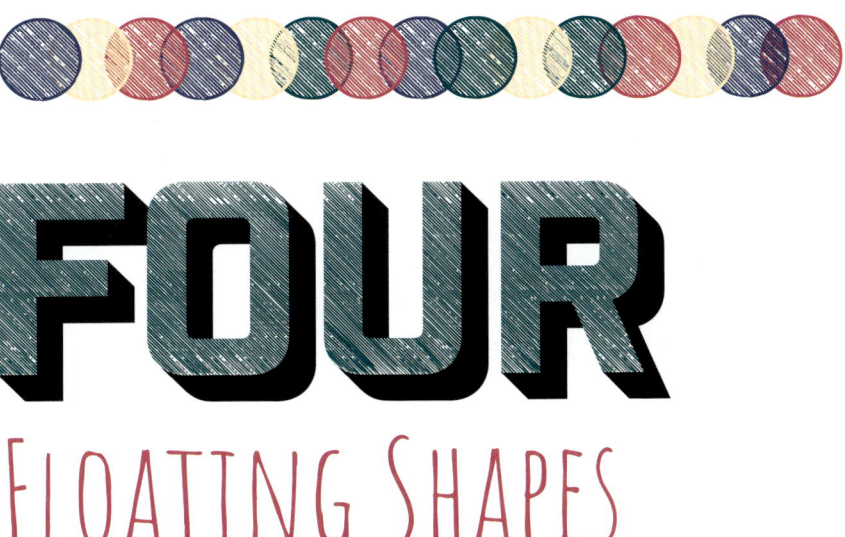

FOUR
Floating Shapes

Floating shapes are a deceptively simple visual illusion designed to make an object appear as if it is floating above the paper upon which it is drawn, defying the force of gravity.

When drawing floating shapes, it is useful to place a cast shadow to emphasize the sense that the shape is floating above the surface upon which it is drawn.

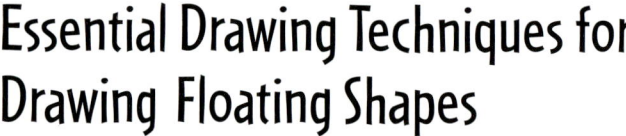

Essential Drawing Techniques for Drawing Floating Shapes

These are some essential lessons for drawing floating shapes.

Cast Shadows and Drop Shadows

A cast shadow is created when an object blocks light rather than appearing on the object's surface as a form shadow.

A drop shadow is a type of cast shadow that helps an object stand out from its background. It is often underneath the object depicted and offset to one side. If the drop shadow is far from the object rather than behind it, an impression of a floating object can be created.

Floating Shapes and Anamorphic Perspective

We can heighten and emphasize the illusion of floating shapes by drawing the object and its shadow in an anamorphic perspective. This perspective makes the image appear distorted unless viewed from a fixed viewpoint. When viewed correctly, the floating object should pop out of the page with a heightened sense of three-dimensional realism, creating a realistic representation. The anamorphic perspective will add to the illusion of depth, challenging the viewer's interpretation of the optical illusion they see and tricking their sense of spatial reality.

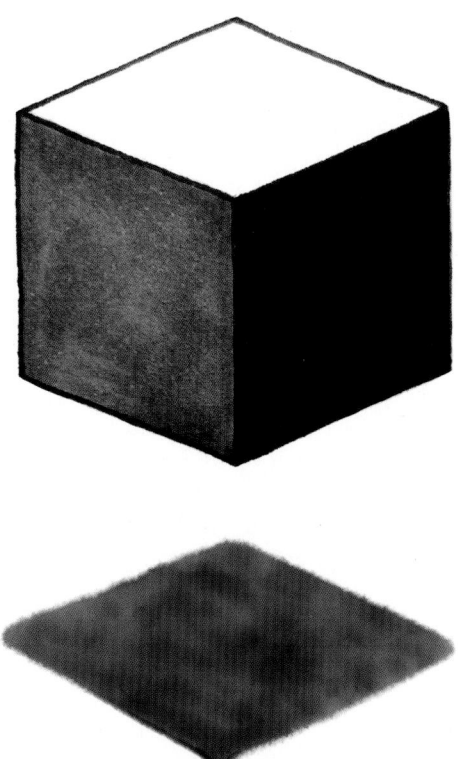

4.1 Floating Cube

A floating cube is a simple but effective optical illusion depicting a cube that appears to float when seen from a fixed viewpoint.

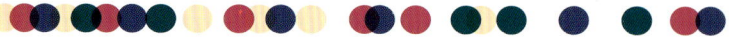

HOW TO DRAW A 3D FLOATING CUBE

Drawing tips: Draw your lines as soft guidelines to help maintain symmetry and proportionality in your distortion of the cube.

Observe and analyze the shapes of the edges and corners you will need to draw to make your illusion more convincing.

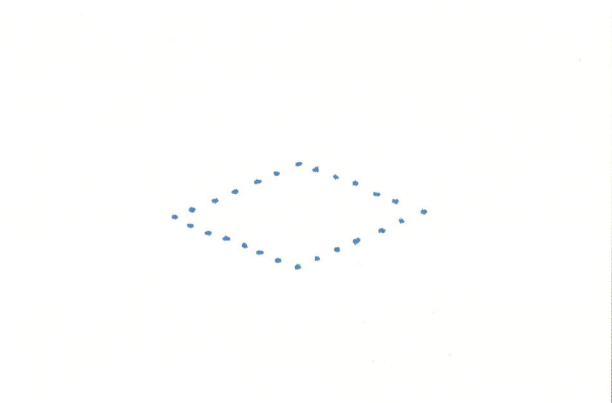

STEP 1

Draw a diamond shape for the top surface of the cube. The outline of the diamond should be the same length on each side.

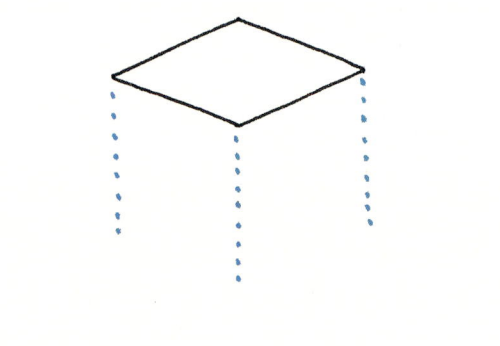

STEP 2

Draw three equal-length lines going downward from the base of the diamond shape. Each of these lines should be parallel and the same length as the sides of the diamond.

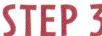
STEP 3

Draw two lines to make the base of the cube. Note that these two lines are the same length as all the other lines and mirror the angles of the two baselines of the diamond shape. Now, we have a simple cube.

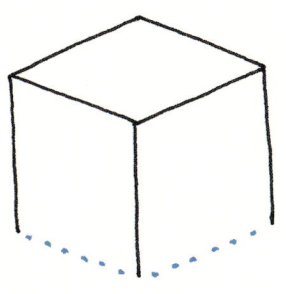

STEP 4

Shade one surface of the cube with a dark tonal value and one with a mid-tone value, leaving one surface unshaded. Next, draw a drop shadow in the shape of a slightly smaller diamond directly below the cube.

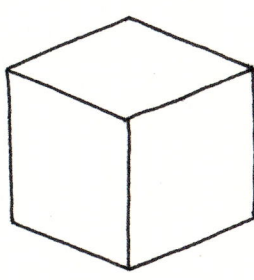

DRAWING WORKSHOP

- To heighten the illusion, consider cutting out the top part of the background and then placing the drawing on a dark table.
- Consider drawing a piece of paper below the cube to look like it is floating above a piece of paper, and the cast shadow is on the paper below.

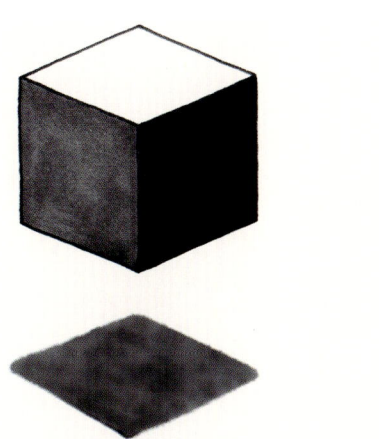

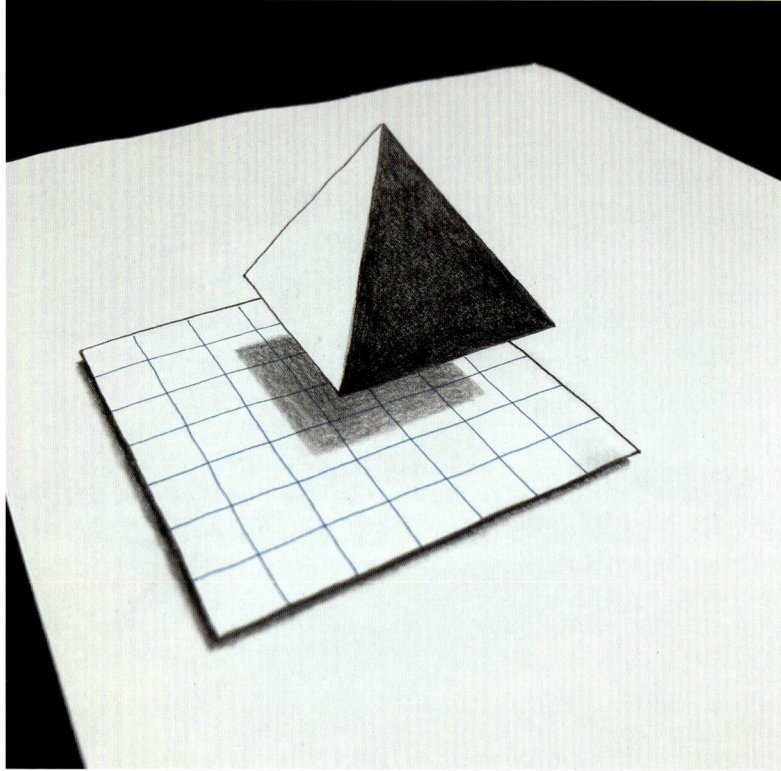

4.2 Floating Pyramid

A square-based pyramid is a three-dimensional geometric shape with a square base and triangular faces that meet at a single point called the apex. We can use anamorphic perspective and a drop shadow to create the visual illusion of a square-based pyramid floating above the paper it is drawn on.

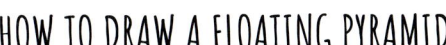

HOW TO DRAW A FLOATING PYRAMID

Drawing tips: Sketch some basic geometric pyramids first to plan your desired proportions and angles.

Use neat, sharp, dark outlines between the pyramid and its surroundings to make it appear floating.

STEP 1

Draw two lines to make a right angle for two sides of a square that will form the base of the pyramid.

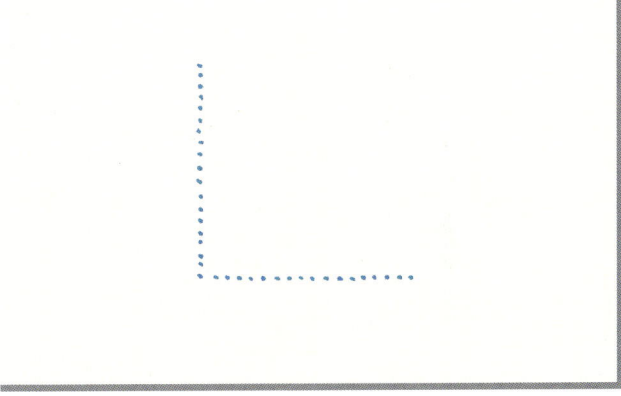

STEP 2

Draw a dot above your right angle to mark the top of the pyramid we are drawing.

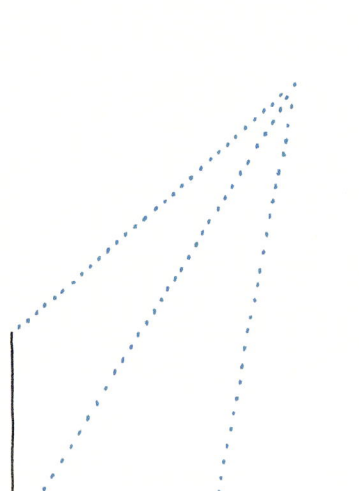

STEP 3

Draw three straight lines from the right angle to the dot to create a pyramid shape. Check your illusion every now and then, from a low angle opposite the point of your pyramid, to see how the anamorphic shape looks. The aim is that the pyramid looks much shorter, but still solid and accurate, when viewed from this low angle position.

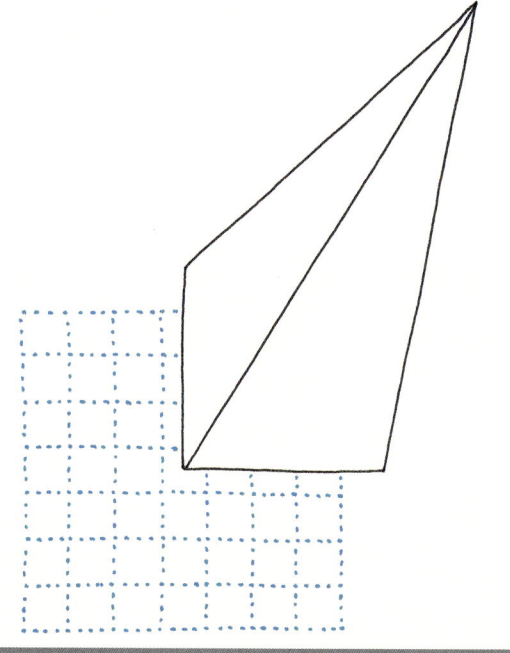

STEP 4

You could draw a grid below the pyramid using the same angles as the original right angle.

STEP 5

To complete the image, add a tonal value to one side of the pyramid and a pale drop shadow below the pyramid and in line with the grid squares. The illusion will work best when viewed from an angle below and opposite the top of the pyramid, making the pyramid seem shorter and more three-dimensional.

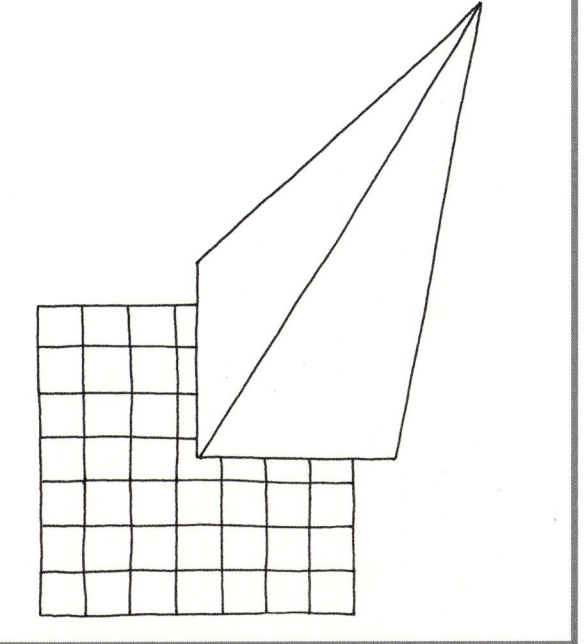

DRAWING WORKSHOP

- Consider adding textures to the pyramid's surface to make it more visually interesting.
- Consider adding graded color to the pyramid's surface. Start with lighter colors at the top and gradually darken towards the base.

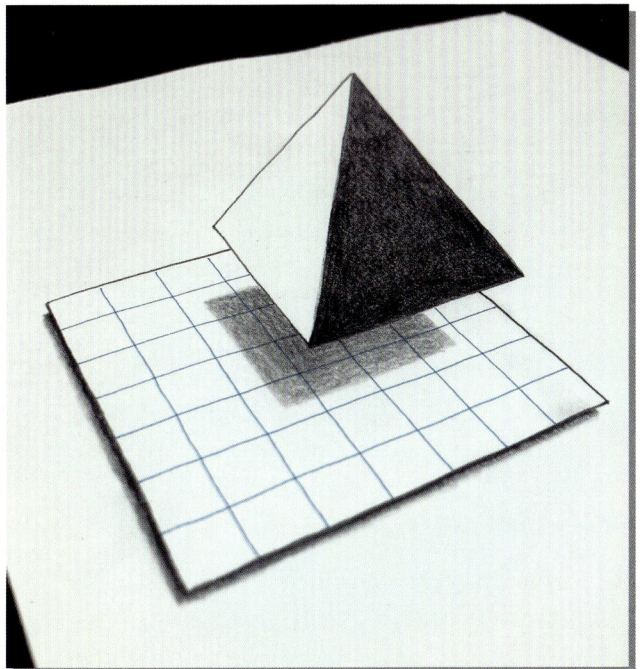

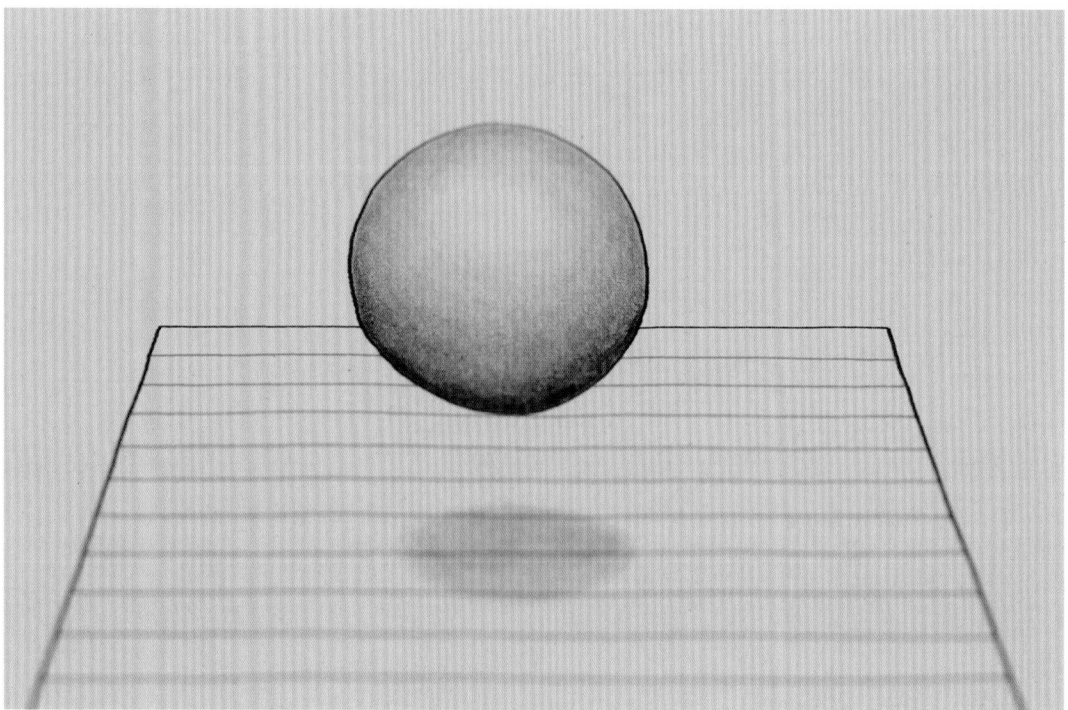

4.3 | Floating Sphere

A sphere is a three-dimensional geometric shape with all surface points equidistant from its center, forming a perfectly round object. We can draw a distorted sphere version using anamorphic perspective to create the illusion of a realistic-looking floating sphere.

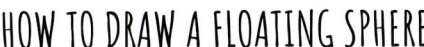
HOW TO DRAW A FLOATING SPHERE

Drawing tips: Imagine a line of symmetry through the center of your anamorphic sphere. Then, check that both halves are identical; if not, copy the better half to the other side.

Practice subtle graded shading of a circle, using the side point of a soft pencil, before you start shading the floating sphere in your illusion.

STEP 1

Draw a thin, elongated oval. Ensure your oval is symmetrical (shaped the same on both sides). Once you have drawn your oval, try to view it from a low position so that the length of the oval is in front of you. There will be a position where the oval looks like a circle. Once you have found the correct position to view your illusion, see if there are any corrections or improvements you can make to your oval so that it looks like a perfect circle when seen from the correct position.

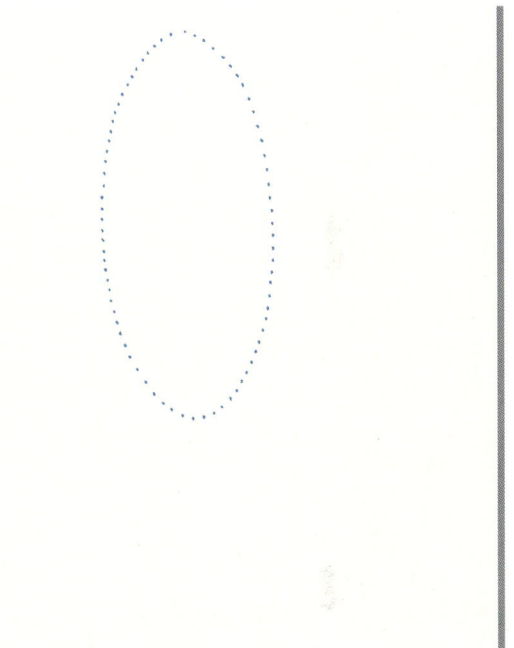

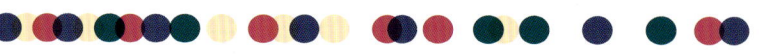

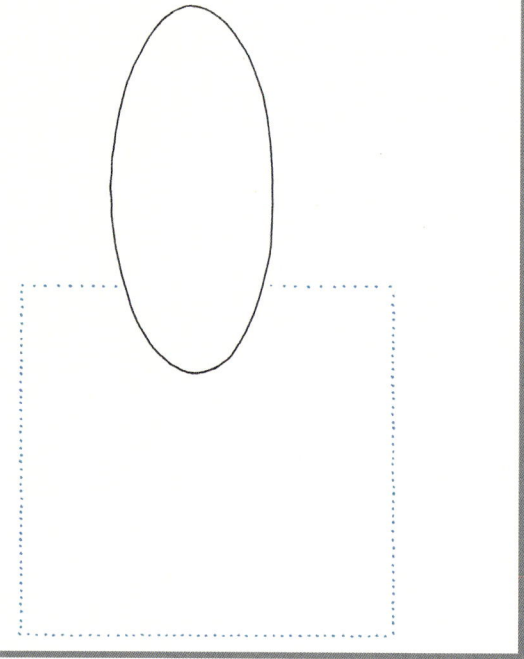

STEP 2

Draw a rectangle behind and below the oval.

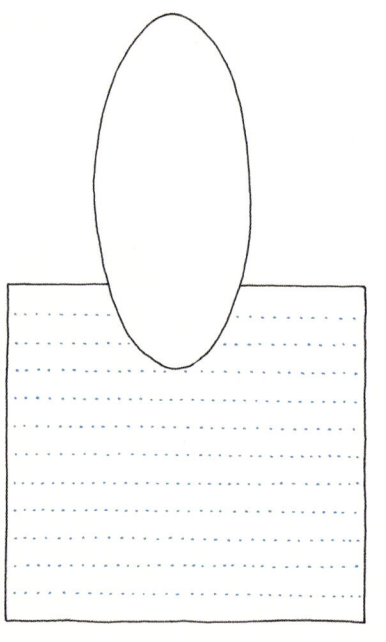

STEP 3

Draw horizontal lines on the rectangle to make it look like lined paper.

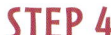

STEP 4

Carefully shade the distorted sphere with the side point of a soft pencil. The oval needs to be darkest at its edges, and then the tonal values gradually decrease towards the highlight, which is the lightest area of the sphere. Next, add a drop shadow below the oval with a soft tone and blurred edges.

STEP 5

To see where to add your drop shadow, view your anamorphic illusion from a low angle, so that the oval looks like a perfect sphere floating above lined paper. Once you can see your illusion, mark in a light outline of where you want the drop shadow to go and then gently shade it in with a soft tone and blurred edges.

STEP 6

Now that your drawing is finished, view it from the position you found in Step 1, so that the oval looks like a sphere floating above a lined piece of paper. Remember than anamorphic illusion will only ever reveal themselves from one fixed position.

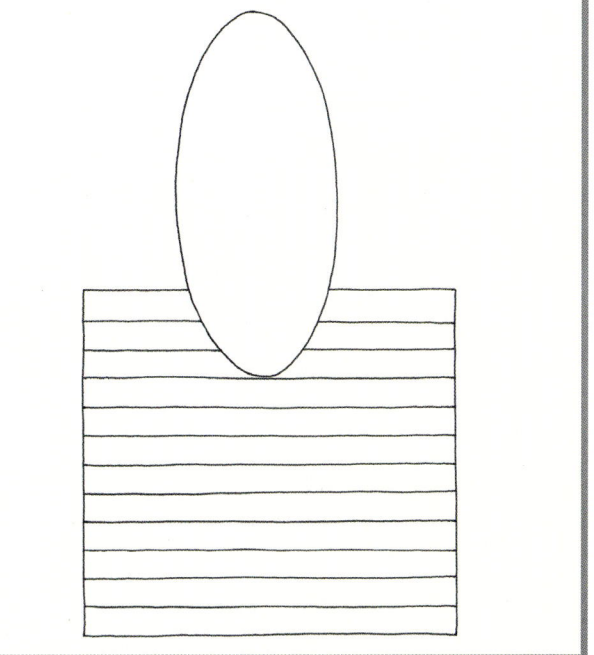

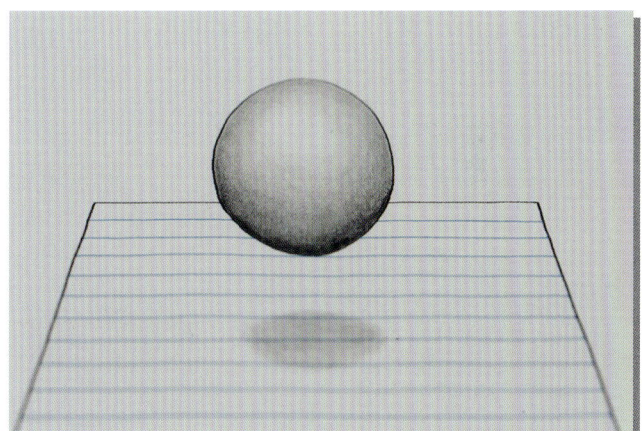

DRAWING WORKSHOP

- Experiment with different sizes of drop shadows.
- Consider drawing the outline of a piece of paper with the furthest edge behind the center of your sphere; then, you could darken the area beyond your drawing to emphasize the illusion.

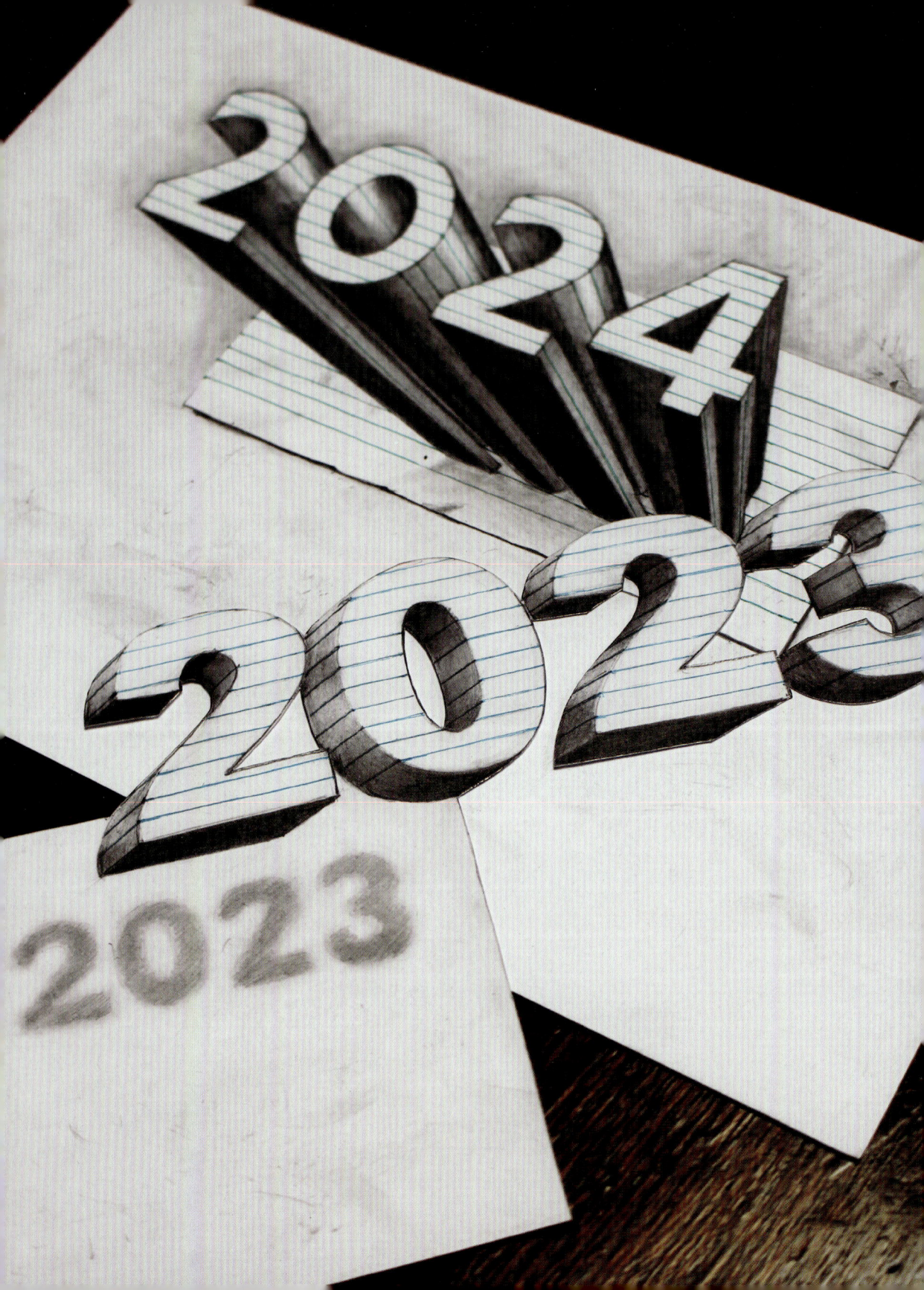

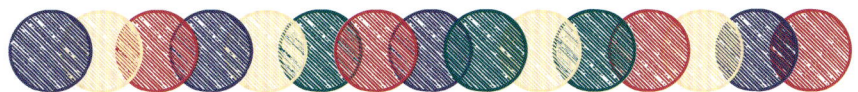

FIVE

3D LETTERS AND NUMBERS

3D letter and number optical illusions use visual tricks to create the illusion of three-dimensional depth on a two-dimensional surface. Letters and numbers are subjects suitable for 3D optical illusions, as they can be drawn in various styles that challenge our perception of depth and reality.

Floating Letters and Numbers

Typography is the art and technique of arranging letters and number shapes to make them readable and visually appealing when viewed. A good method for turning the typography of letter and number fonts into optical illusions is to depict them as three-dimensional floating shapes.

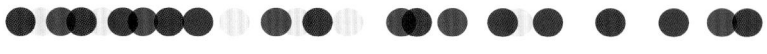

Letter and number shapes are graphic symbols we are most used to seeing as 2D-printed or written shapes. By adding depth, we create a solid 3D quality in the typography. Then, we can use a soft drop shadow to create a floating quality to the solid 3D form we are drawing. We typically see typography as flat graphic images, but by adding depth to their shapes and depicting them from an angle with a drop shadow, we can create the illusion of levitation.

Floating letters and numbers introduce a dynamic and visually striking dimension to typography, breaking away from the constraints of flat surfaces.

Curved Letters

Curved letters enhance the sense of drama in optical letter illusions and offer more depth than angular letters. To emphasize the curve, apply gradient shading to the letter and soft, flat shading for its shadow. Curved letters inject energy into your illusions, turning simple letters into dynamic optical illusions.

Solid 3D Typography

Solid 3D typography emphasizes the tangible depth and volume of letter forms, creating a three-dimensional solidity that rises from the paper upon which they are drawn. We can draw short words, numbers, and year dates as solid 3D forms in such a way as to emphasize the inherent power of the shapes used.

Drawing 3D letters and numbers can be as simple or complex as possible, depending on your artistic skill, time, and creative mood. Practice and experimentation will help you improve your technique to create convincing illusions.

Essential Drawing Techniques for Drawing 3D Letters and Numbers

More Anamorphic Perspective

Anamorphic perspective is a technique in which a deliberately distorted drawing appears normal when viewed only from a specific angle. It is crucial when drawing floating and curved 3D letters and numbers, enabling you to create powerful optical illusions that feel separate from the paper upon which they are drawn. You can also add an element of anamorphic perspective when drawing 3D words or dates as solid blocks, as it will add to the drama of the optical illusions you create.

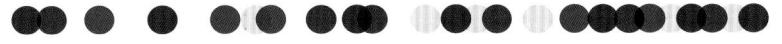

Size and Proportion

When drawing letter and number forms, carefully consider the size and proportion of all the elements within and around each shape. Typography is created by the balance between the positive shapes of letters and numbers and the negative space of the background around them.

Ensure consistency in size to maintain a cohesive look to each letter form. Adequately sized and proportioned letters and numbers are essential when drawing successful typographical illusions. Consider using soft guidelines to map out the proportions of each letter or number before you commit to the shapes you are drawing. Well-proportioned shapes can greatly enhance spatial depth perception in your 3D typographical optical illusions.

Shading and Highlights

Careful shading techniques will add dimension to your 3D letters and numbers. Apply light and shadow to simulate how light interacts with three-dimensional forms. On a flat surface, the shading may be smooth and even, but on a curved surface, the shading is likely to be graded from dark to light.

Practicing your graded shading techniques as small sketches separate from your main drawings. Add shading to your optical illusions only after you have practiced and mastered the particular shading needed for the drawing you are creating. This will help you see faster improvements in your ability to create realistic and convincing optical illusions.

Try to emphasize the contrast between light and dark areas in your drawing, amplifying the 3D effect. Use shadows strategically, placing them below and around letters to enhance the appearance of solidity and depth. When a tonal value stops at an edge, keep the edge as clean and precise as possible. Use a scrap of paper on the edge line to mask the non-shaded area of your optical illusion. Then, use an eraser to clean up any areas that must be white and pristine. The greater the contrast between the shading of the letter and the unshaded background, the more the illusion will visually pop, creating a dynamic and powerful image.

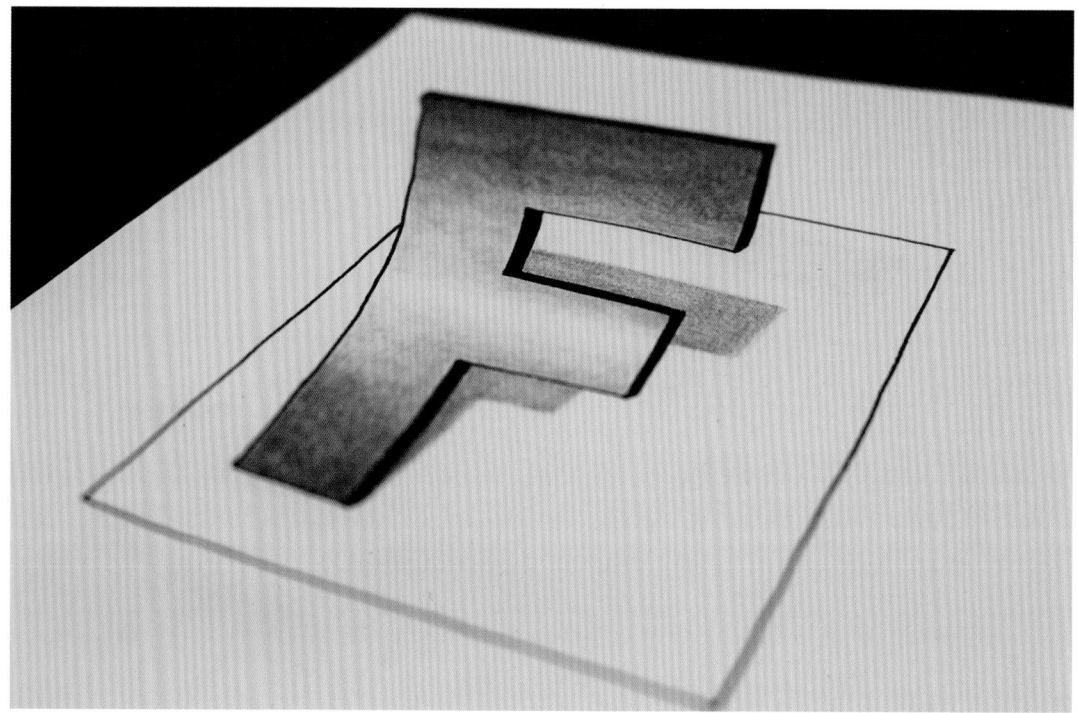

5.1 Curved "F"

The capital letter "F" has only straight lines, so it is an excellent letter to draw first when learning the art of 3D curved letters. This drawing will need careful and dramatic shading to make the final image pop, so take your time.

HOW TO DRAW A CURVED "F"

Drawing tips: Start by sketching the letter "F" a few times to get used to the shape as a letter block.

Experiment with variations in line weight to emphasize certain parts of the letter "F" to create a more dynamic optical illusion.

STEP 1

Start sketching the capital letter "F" with a solid curvature to enhance its curving illusion. Make sure the "F" curves from its base and gets much larger as you draw the shape higher toward the top.

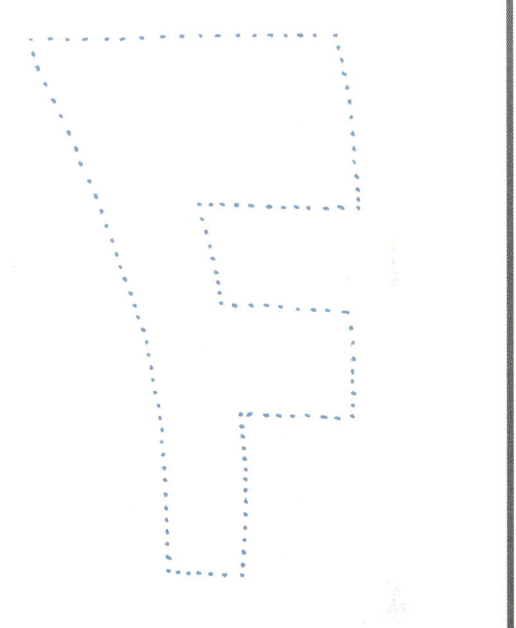

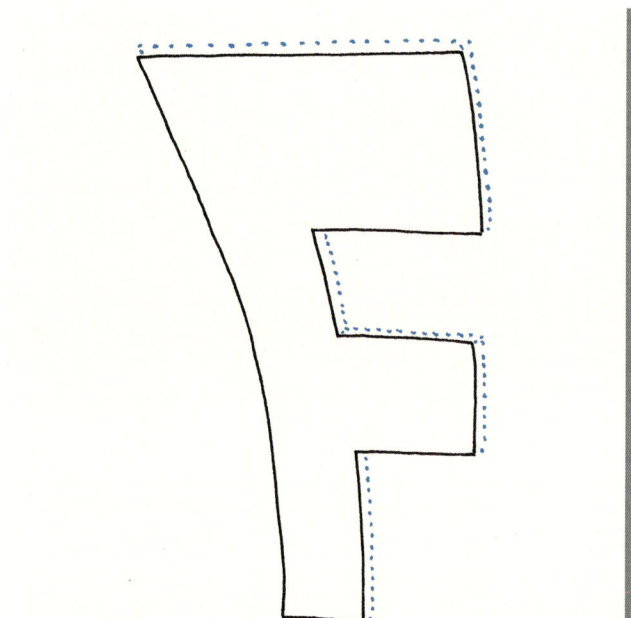

STEP 2

Draw a thickness on the right and tops of each part of the "F" shape. Make sure the "F" thickness is deeper at the top than at the bottom.

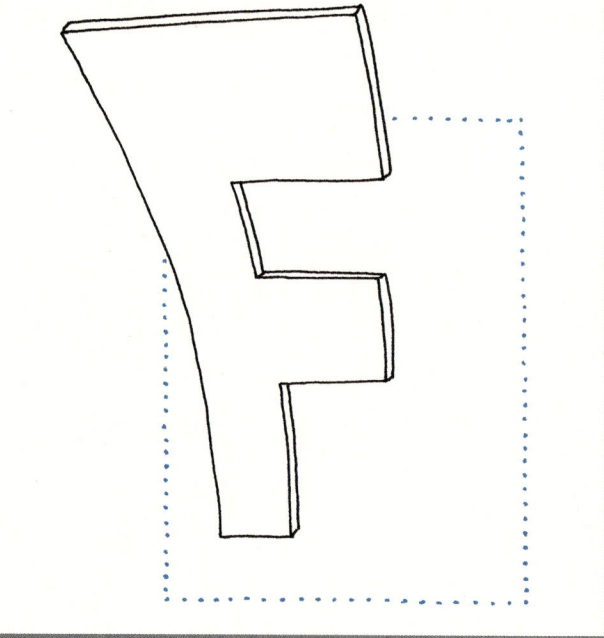

STEP 3

Draw a rectangle behind the "F" shape.

STEP 4

Start shading where the edge of the curve begins using a dark tone. Gradually change the pressure on the pencil point so the shading gets lighter as it moves away from the curve. This graded shading will give a strong illusion of a curved surface. Darken the vertical thickness of the "F" and then add a delicate cast shadow with soft edges.

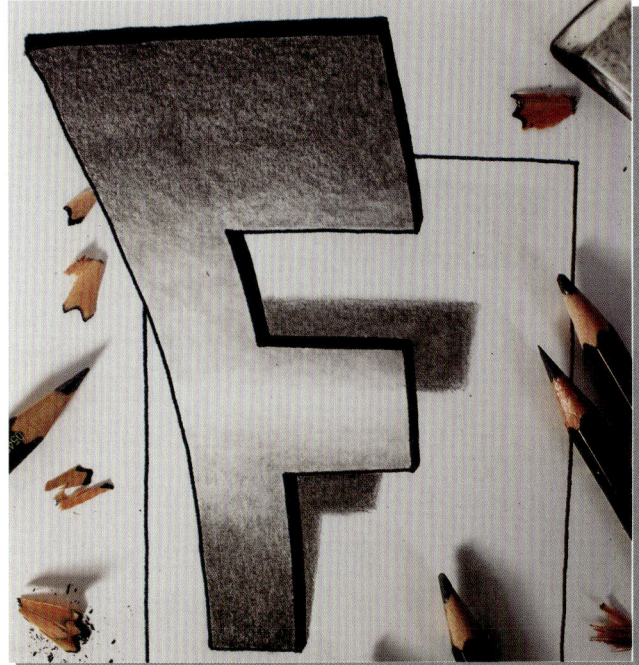

STEP 5

The last step is to view your anamorphic illusion from the best height and angle so that the curved letter seems to rise from the paper.

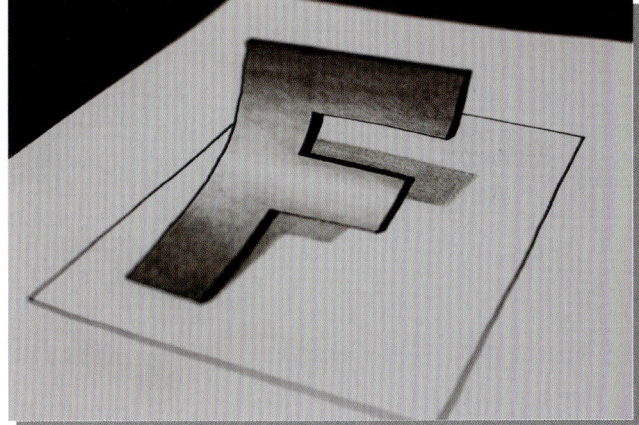

DRAWING WORKSHOP

- Consider taking a photograph of your drawing, viewed from the most dramatic position you can find.
- If you add a selection of drawing tools to your photograph, position your drawing so that the shadows you drew are in line with the cast shadows of the tools.

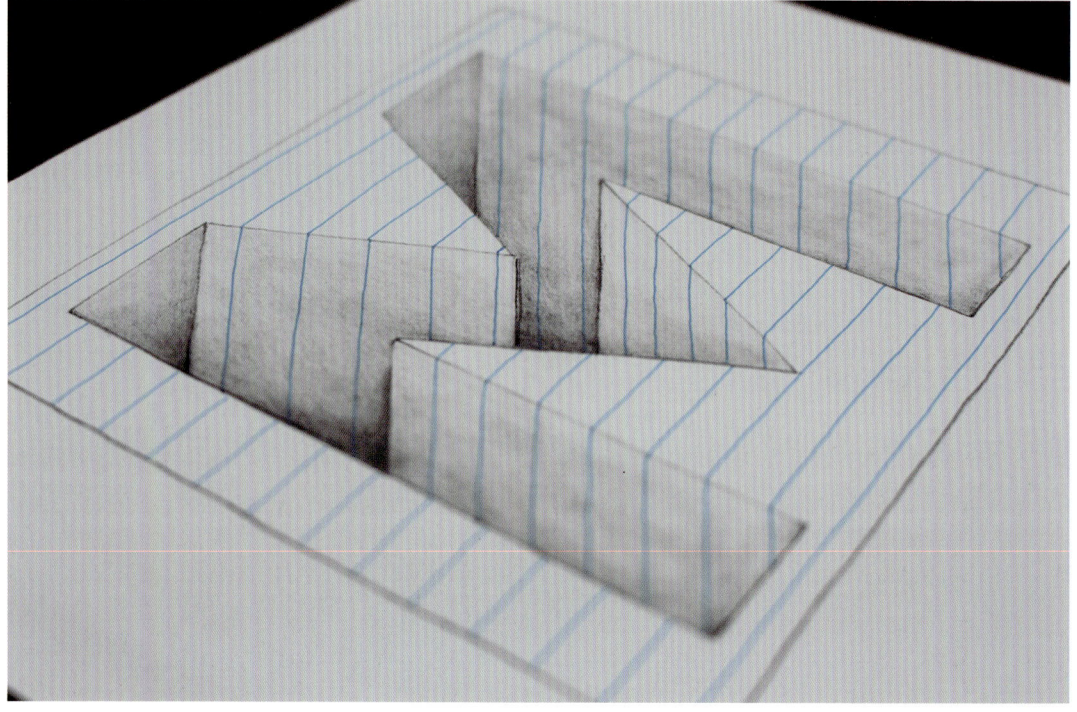

5.2 Letter in a Hole: "M"

We can draw the capital letter "M" as a hole in a piece of paper. If we draw lines on the paper we can add to the power of this simple optical illusion, when it is viewed from an angle.

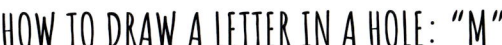

HOW TO DRAW A LETTER IN A HOLE: "M"

Drawing tips: To draw the letter "M" as a block letter, draw a line drawing of the capital letter and then draw around your line drawing at an even distance to create a block letter.

Consider using a soft pencil for your early lines so that the edges don't dominate your drawing, and then you could use a colored fine-liner pen of green or blue to add color to your paper lines.

STEP 1

Draw a capital letter "M".

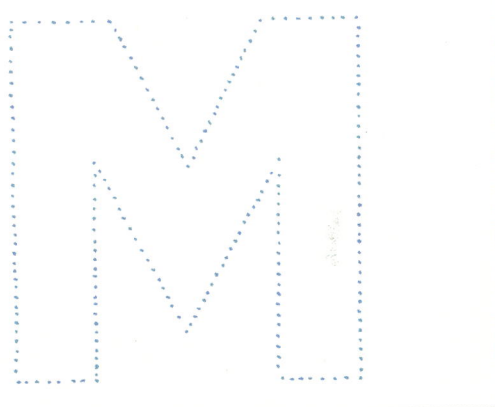

STEP 2

Draw a rectangle around your letter shape.

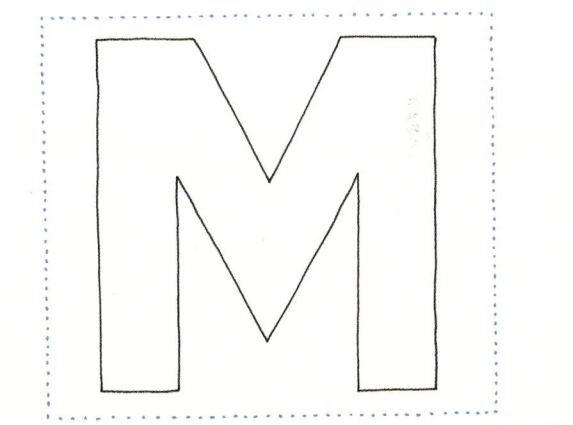

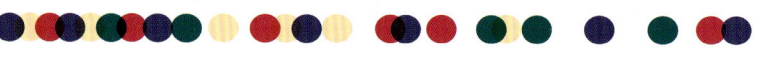

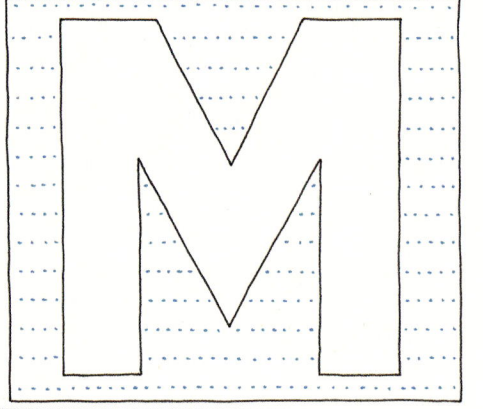

STEP 3

Draw a series of horizontal lines on the surface of the rectangle to create lined paper.

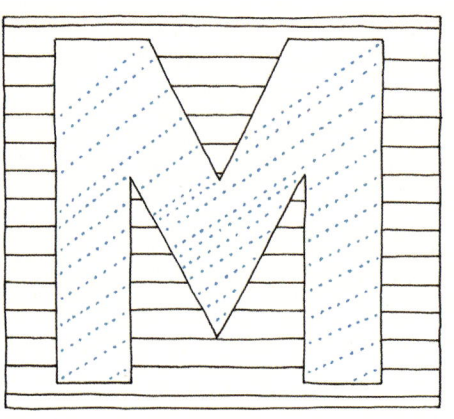

STEP 4

Choose a set angle and then draw a series of parallel lines from the right-hand edges of the letter toward the left of the letter shape. Continue these parallel lines from each of the right-hand sides of the lined paper.

STEP 5

It is best to leave the dark tonal values out of this drawing. Start with delicate soft shading for the different surface directions of the letter formed within the hole in the lined paper.

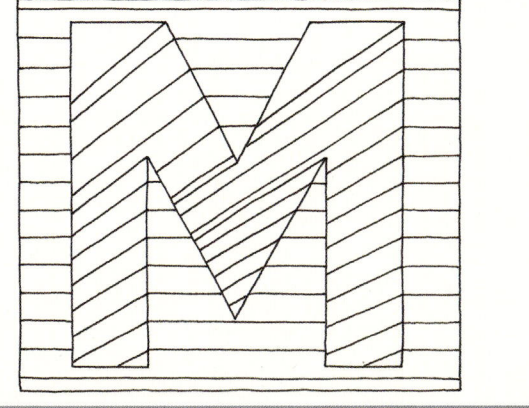

STEP 6

To reveal the illusion, view your drawing from a low diagonal angle in line with the diagonal lines within the hole.

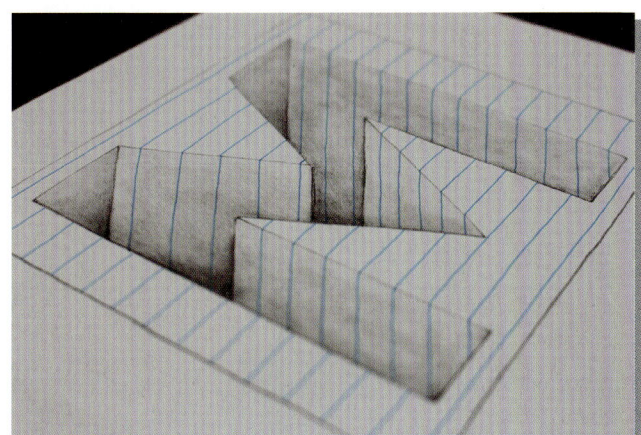

DRAWING WORKSHOP

- Consider adding additional details, such as torn edges around the hole or subtle shadows of creases in the line paper, to enhance the realism of your optical illusion.
- Experiment with additional shading around the edges of the letter hole to make it appear deeper.

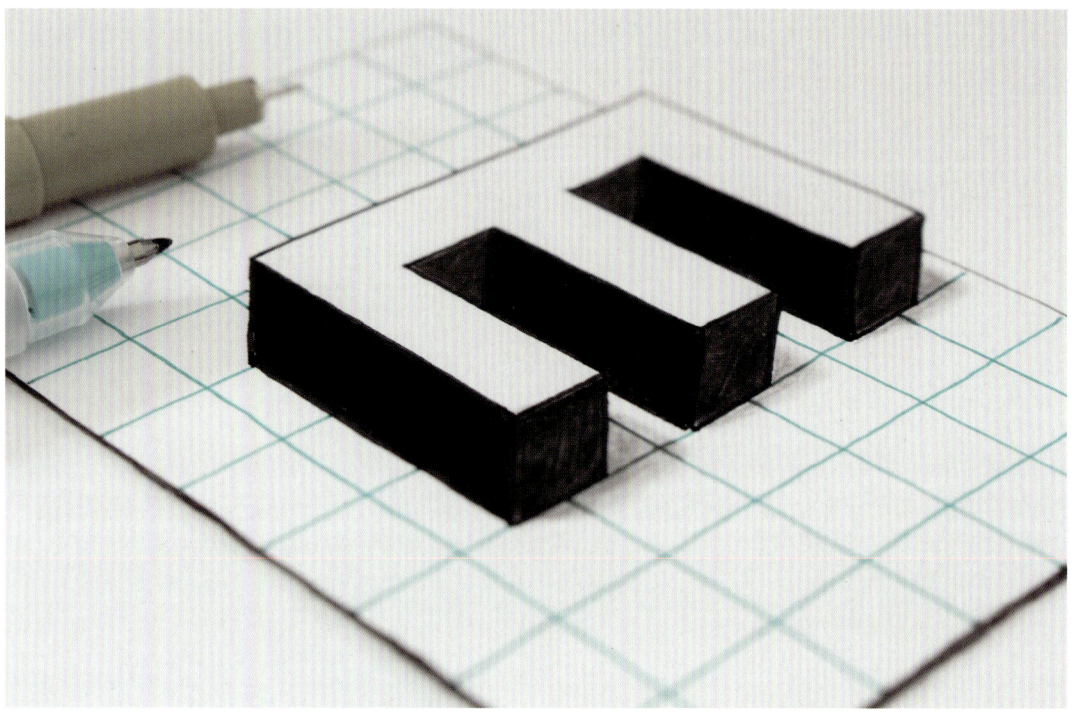

5.3 | Block "E"

The capital letter "E" is an excellent choice for creating a solid block letter on a grid or lined paper.

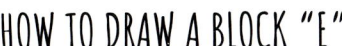

HOW TO DRAW A BLOCK "E"

Drawing tips: Before you begin the main drawing, consider making quick sketches of the letter's outline in its basic 2D and 3D form.

Experiment with different angles of your 3D letter so you can pick the angle that you think works best.

STEP 1

Draw a simple capital "E."

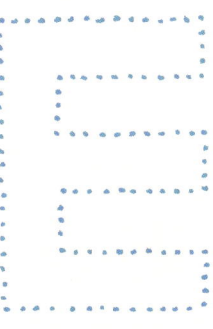

STEP 2

Draw a series of parallel lines from the letter shape's right side and lower edges. Each of these parallel lines should be the same length. Then, repeat the part of the letter shape at the ends of the parallel lines, making a simple 3D "E" letter.

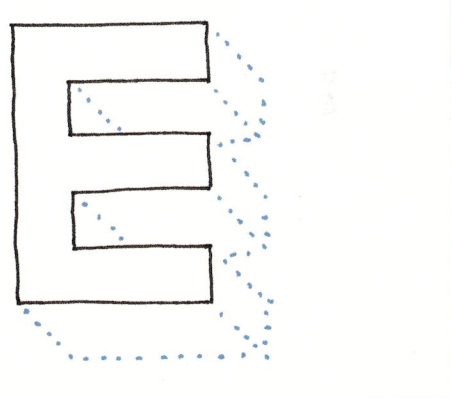

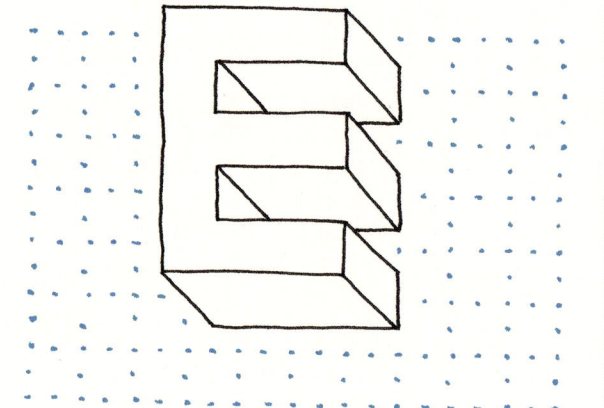

STEP 3

Add a grid or draw lined paper behind the 3D "E" you drew.

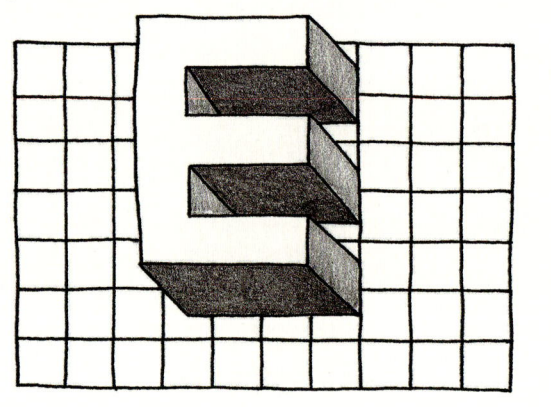

STEP 4

Add shading using a dark tone to the base shapes of the letter and a mid-tone to the right-hand parts of the letter.

STEP 5

Once you have completed your drawing view it from the best angle so that it looks solid and 3D.

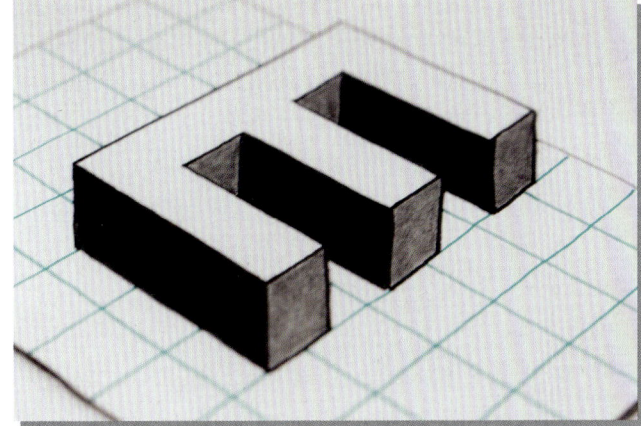

DRAWING WORKSHOP

- Consider adding reflections or highlights on the surface of the letter to make it appear shiny or metallic, further enhancing the 3D effect.
- Consider adding color to the grid lines to create a contrast between the tonal shading of the letter form and the color of the grid.

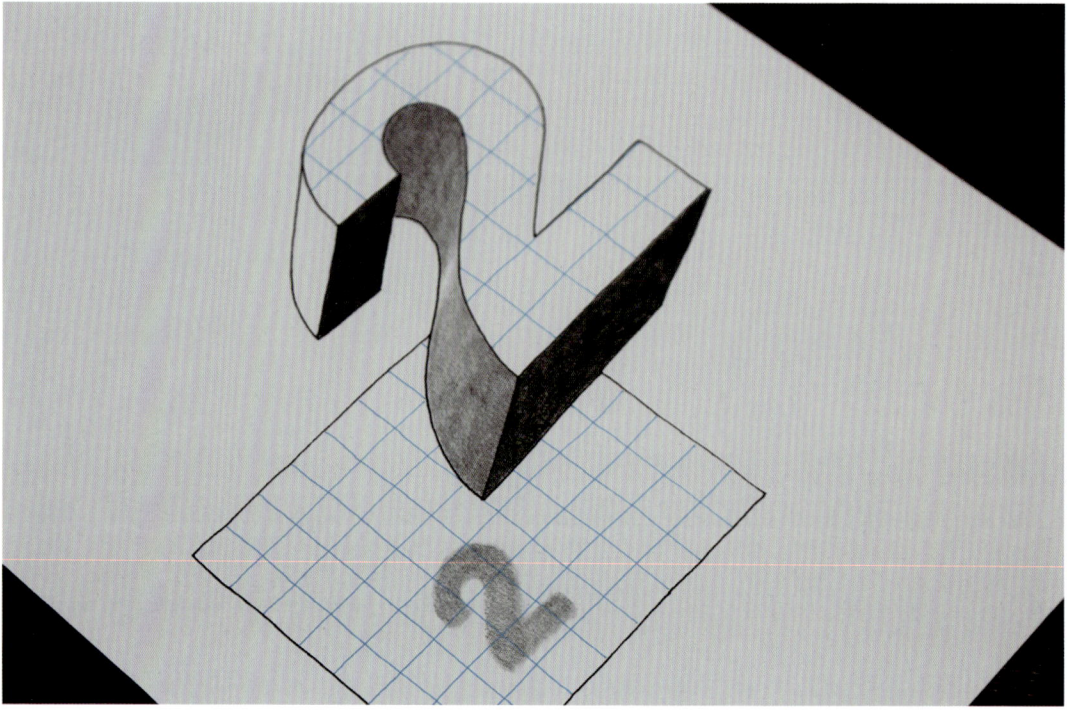

5.4 Floating "2"

The optical trick of floating letters can be achieved using anamorphic perspective, a good understanding of shapes, and careful shading. For this drawing, we shall draw the number "2" floating at the corner of the drawing when seen from a single fixed viewpoint.

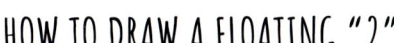

HOW TO DRAW A FLOATING "2"

Drawing tips: Explore some different topographical shapes and designs for the number you are drawing.

Explore different angles and orientations for the number "2" to create a dynamic composition.

STEP 1

Draw the number "2" as a 2D shape with an even thickness.

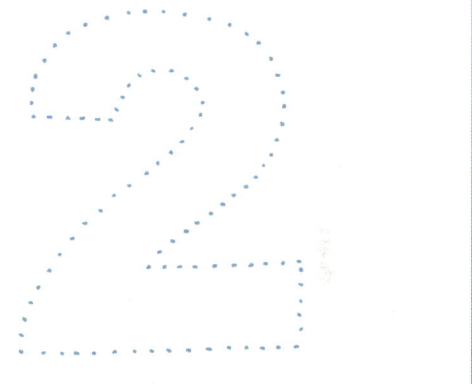

STEP 2

Draw a series of parallel lines of the same length from the left-hand edges of the number shape. Then, draw the shape of the number at the ends of the lines.

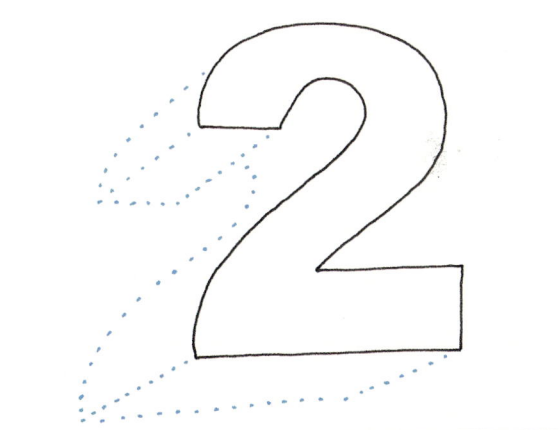

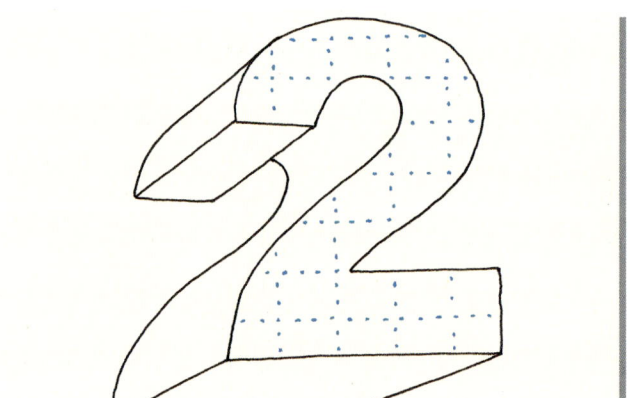

STEP 3

Draw a grid of squares on the top surface of the number.

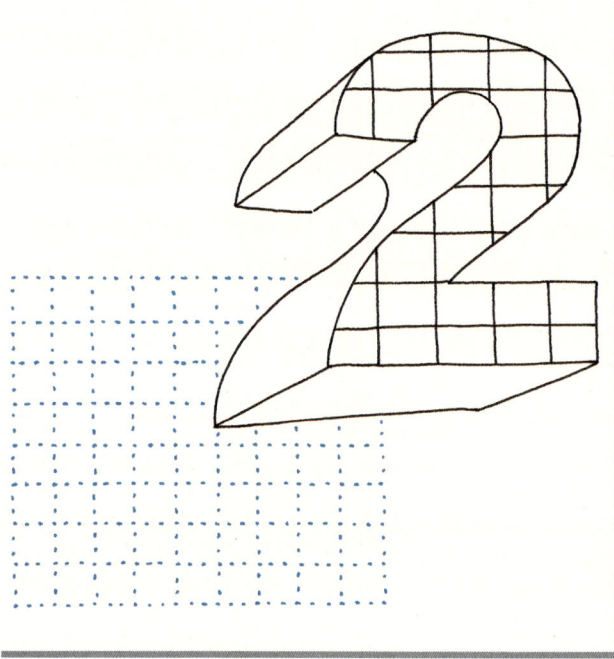

STEP 4

Draw a square with a grid behind and to the left of the number shape.

STEP 5

Add shading using a range of tonal values to the thickness of the number and then draw a drop shadow with soft edges on the grid.

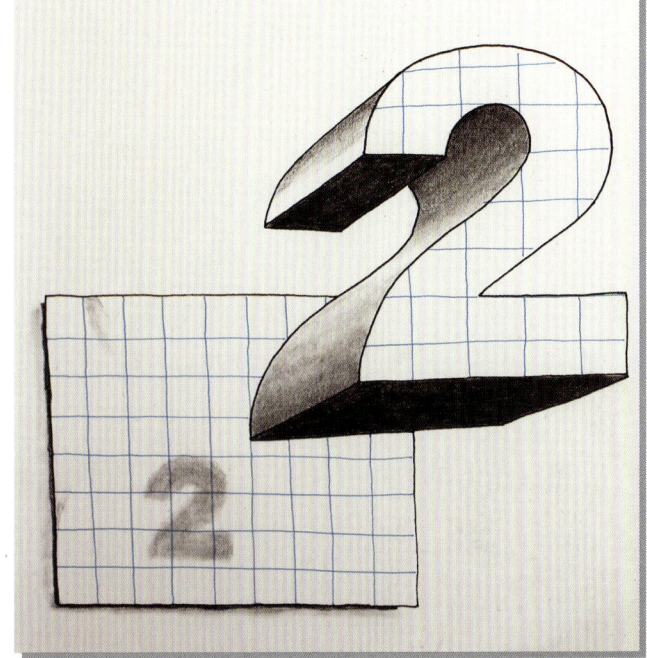

STEP 6

Once you have completed your drawing, find the position to see the illusion work well. If you take a photograph from this position, consider adding some drawing tools around the image and keep the direction of the light source at an angle so that the cast shadows of the drawing tools match the cast drop shadow in your illusion.

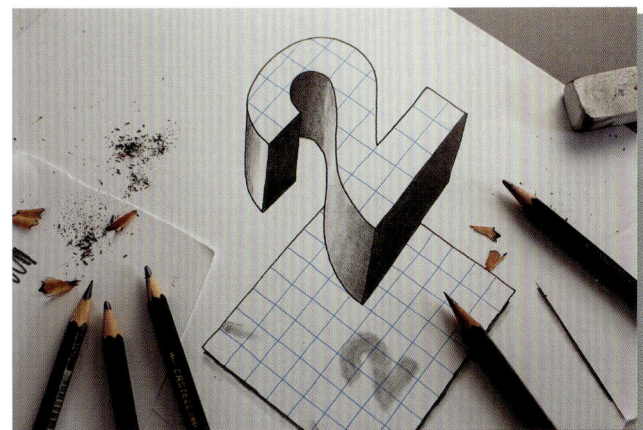

DRAWING WORKSHOP

- Experiment with wireframe or transparent sections within the number to create a layered effect, enhancing the illusion of it floating.
- Introduce motion lines around the number to imply movement and energy.

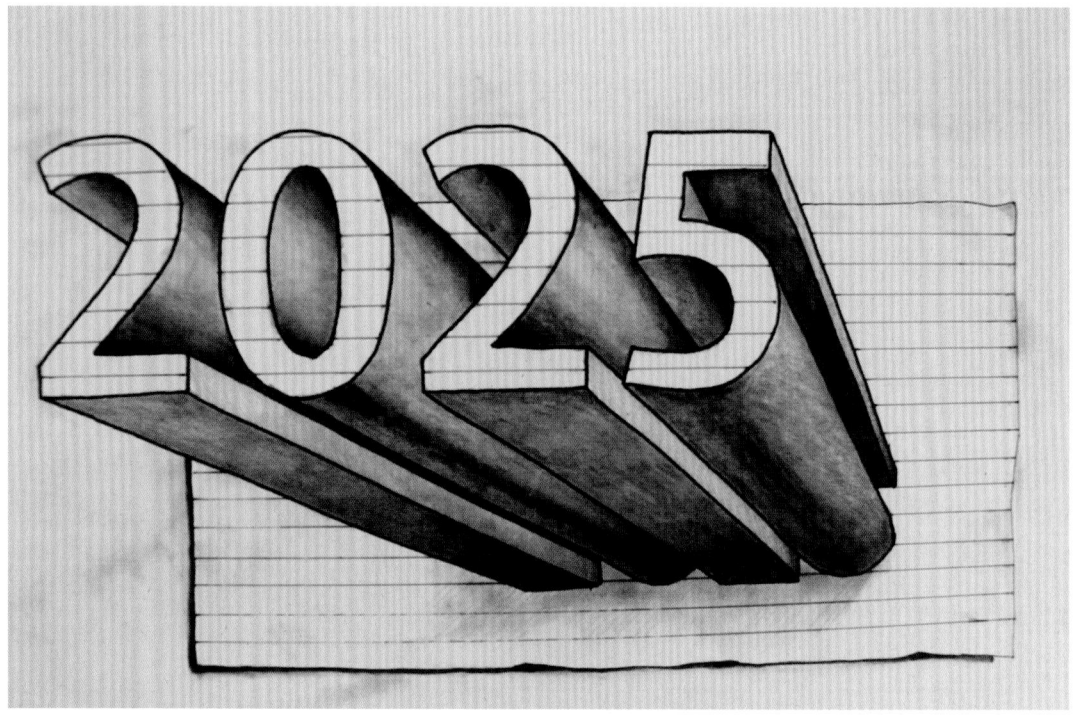

5.5   3D Years

Creating a year as a 3D optical illusion can be a creative and visually striking way to emphasize its significance or make it stand out in a design or work of art. Here is one way to draw the year "2025".

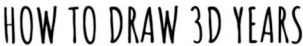

HOW TO DRAW 3D YEARS

Drawing tips: Choose a number shape with even thickness and precise lines to ensure the numbers stand out prominently.

To draw each number as a block, consider first drawing the numbers as lines and then drawing around the lines at an even distance to make block numbers.

STEP 1

Choose the year you want to draw and then draw the numbers in a row, with a simple even thickness to each number.

STEP 2

Draw a cross below and to the right of your year. Then, draw a horizontal guideline parallel to the line at the base of the numbers. Now, draw a series of guidelines from the edges of all the numbers toward your cross.

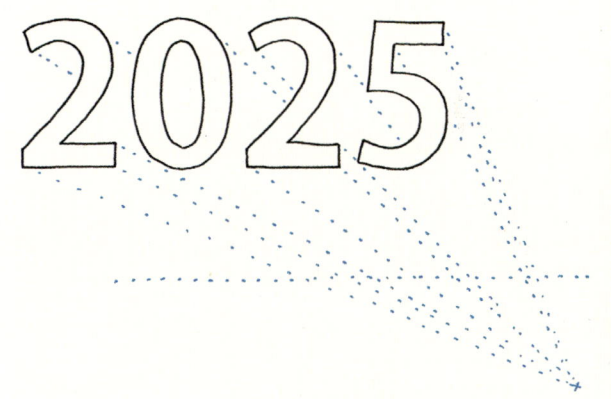

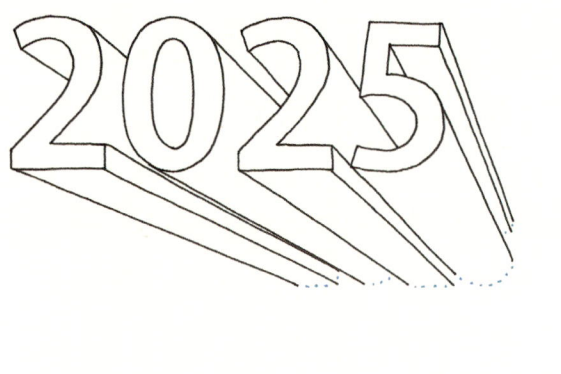

STEP 3

Using your horizontal guideline as a baseline, draw the lower parts of each number at the base of each number shape, echoing the shapes found in the numbers above.

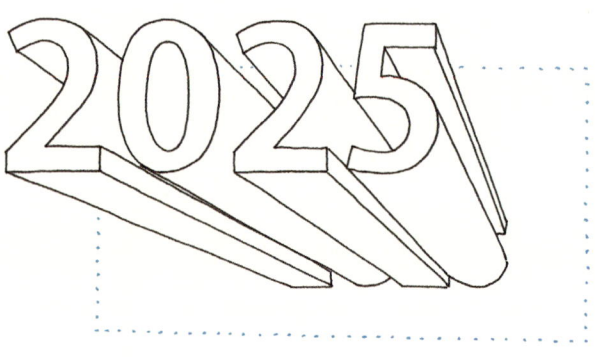

STEP 4

Draw a rectangle surrounding the 3D numbers. It is a good idea to check your illusion to make sure it pops out when seen from a low angle above your anamorphic dot. If there is some lines you can improve, now it the time to do that.

STEP 5

Shade the flat surfaces of each number with a flat tonal value and then use a carefully graded tonal range for the curved surfaces of each number. Add a cast shadow at the base of the 3D numbers. You could draw some blue lines for lined paper on the top surface of the numbers and then more blue lines on the paper the numbers are on, which are closer together as we want them to look further away.

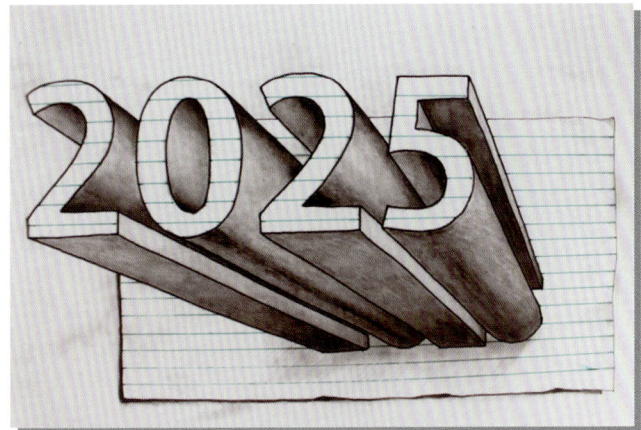

STEP 6

Once you have finished your drawing find the ideal position to see the anamorphic illusion. The best position will be at a high angle above the anamorphic dot.

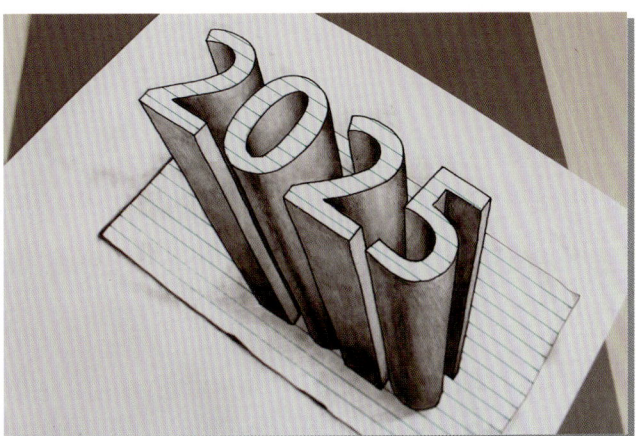

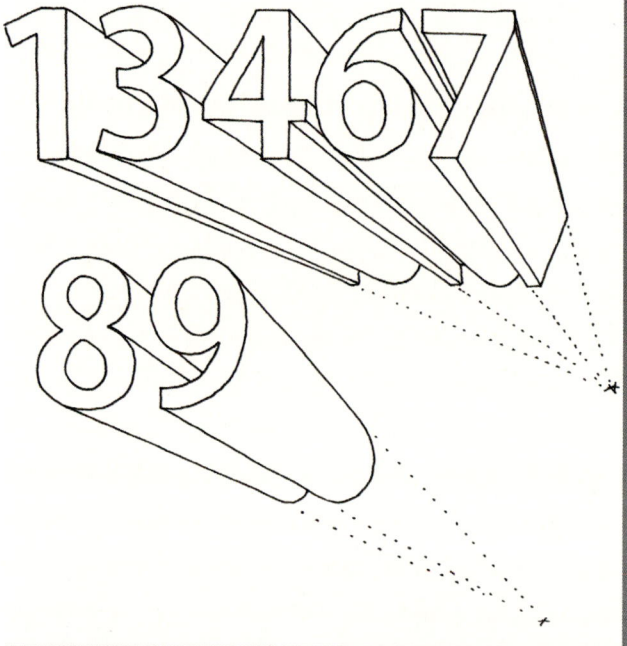

STEP 7

All numbers can be drawn using the same technique. Here are examples of other numbers.

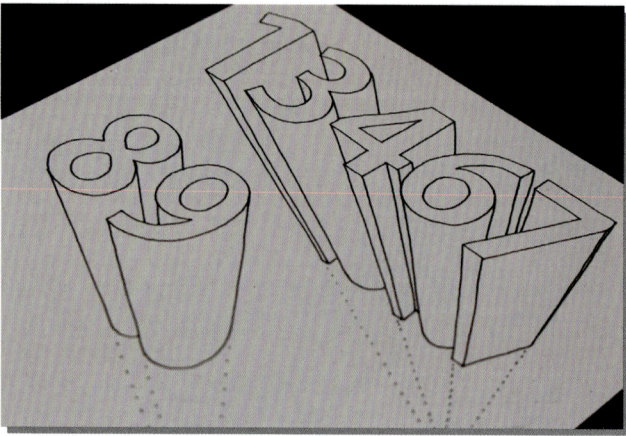

DRAWING WORKSHOP

- Consider shading the numbers with a graded tonal value, with darker tones toward the bottom of each number and lighter tones toward the top.
- Experiment with contrasting colors to enhance the illusion of depth.

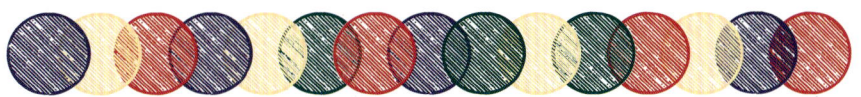

SIX

3D Buildings and Cities

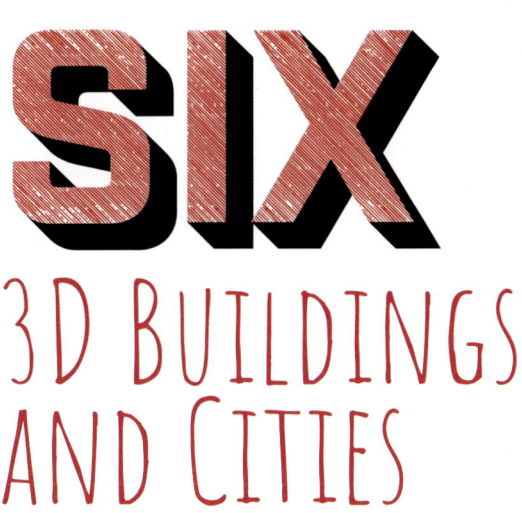

Optical illusions of 3D buildings and cityscapes use powerful visual techniques to create the illusion of three-dimensional architecture that seems to leap off the page with lifelike realism. In this section, you will learn how to use anamorphic perspective to create amazing illusions of buildings and cities.

Combining architectural details and shading techniques with accurately drawn basic shapes heightens realism and the illusion of depth. Adding details like windows and doors offers a scale reference for your drawing.

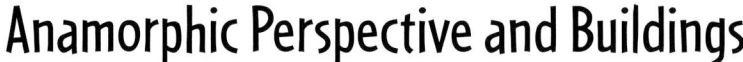

Anamorphic Perspective and Buildings

Anamorphic perspective distorts images to look normal from a particular viewpoint, a point above the anamorphic dot. When creating an anamorphic drawing of a building, selecting a suitable image of a building with simple and distinct features is crucial, as these will play a vital role in the illusion. Anamorphic perspective manipulates and defies the constraints of linear perspective, bringing structures to life with a powerful illusionary third dimension.

To achieve an optical illusion, you will create an anamorphic effect in your drawing, stretching elements of the building along the grid lines. Pay close attention to architectural details like windows and doors, ensuring they align with the grid and the single viewpoint to create a realistic distortion.

Include shading, shadows, and highlights to enhance your three-dimensional illusions. Exaggerate shadows to emphasize the altered perspective, adding depth to the anamorphic drawing.

Carefully refine your drawing to ensure clean lines and accurate distortion. Use a variety of pencils and shading techniques to add depth and realism. Regularly check that your drawing is working when viewed from a point above your anamorphic dot. Check your drawing to assess the anamorphic effect and make necessary adjustments. Achieving precision in the distortion process is critical to a successful optical illusion.

Buildings and cities can be an ideal subject for anamorphic perspective. If we take it step by step, starting with the most basic shapes, we can create dynamic and powerful 3d optical illusions.

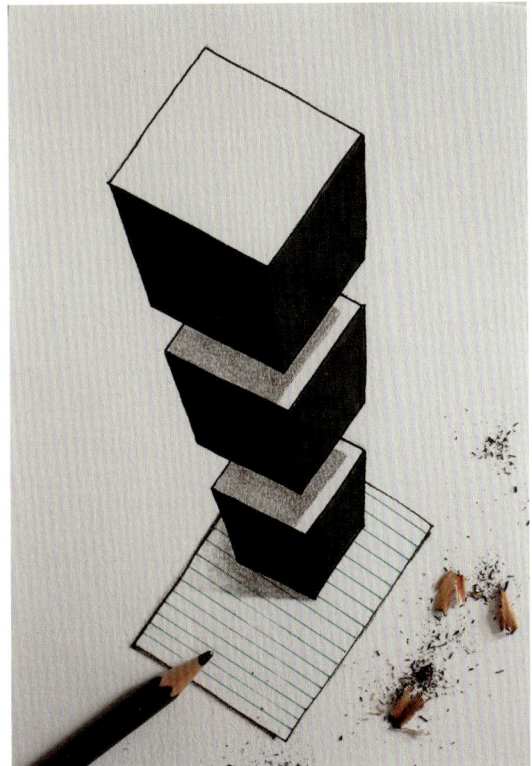

3D Building Blocks (Block of Cubes)

Creating powerful 3D optical illusions of buildings starts with drawing accurate building blocks using anamorphic perspective. Mastering the basics first will give you the skills to be truly creative in your optical illusion drawings of 3D buildings.

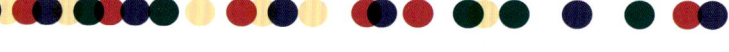

HOW TO DRAW BUILDING BLOCKS

Drawing tips: Use a sharp pencil point for your lines, and consider darkening the lines with a fine-liner pen to complete your drawing.

Notice how the angles of each cube's top and base lines are identical.

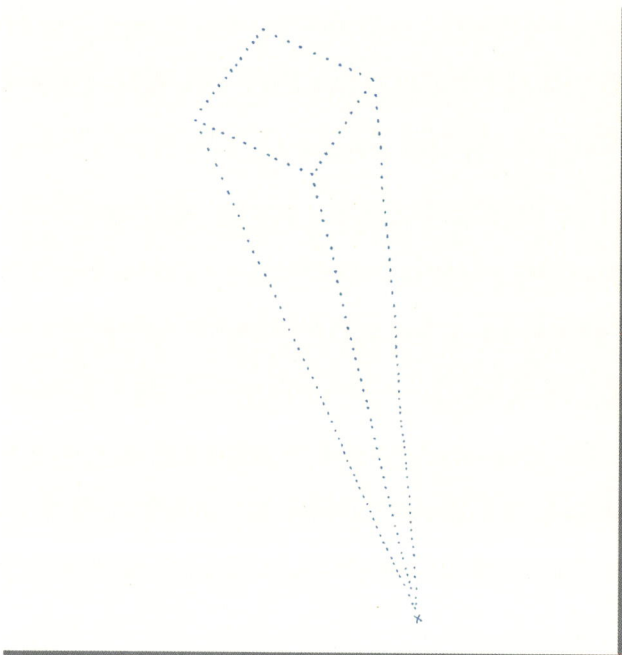

STEP 1

Draw a square at an angle so one of the corners is at the top of your drawing. Draw a long vertical guide-line below the bottom corner of your square towards the base of the paper. The point where you stop this line will be your anamorphic dot, making the fixed point to best view your finished drawing. Draw two more guidelines from the two side corners of your square to your anamorphic dot.

STEP 2

Draw three equal-length lines from the three lower points of the square's top, following the long lines from Step 1. These lines should be shorter than the square's length. Then, join these three lines with two baselines for your first cube. Next, draw four more lines on each side to create three cubes that get smaller toward the anamorphic dot.

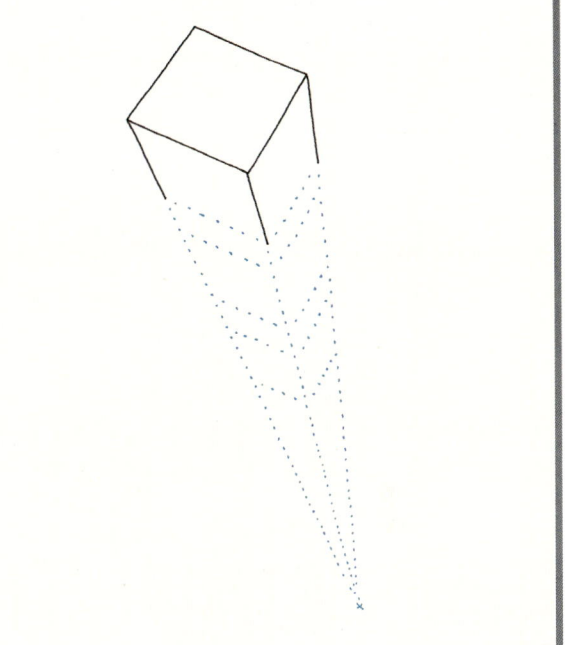

STEP 3

Draw two short, angled lines for the top left and right edges of the second and third cubes. The angles of these lines are the same as those of the top two lines of the square in Step 1.

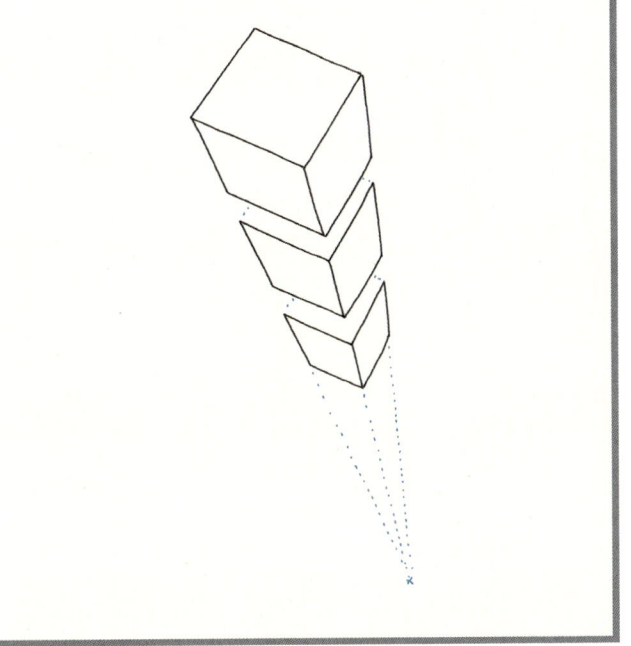

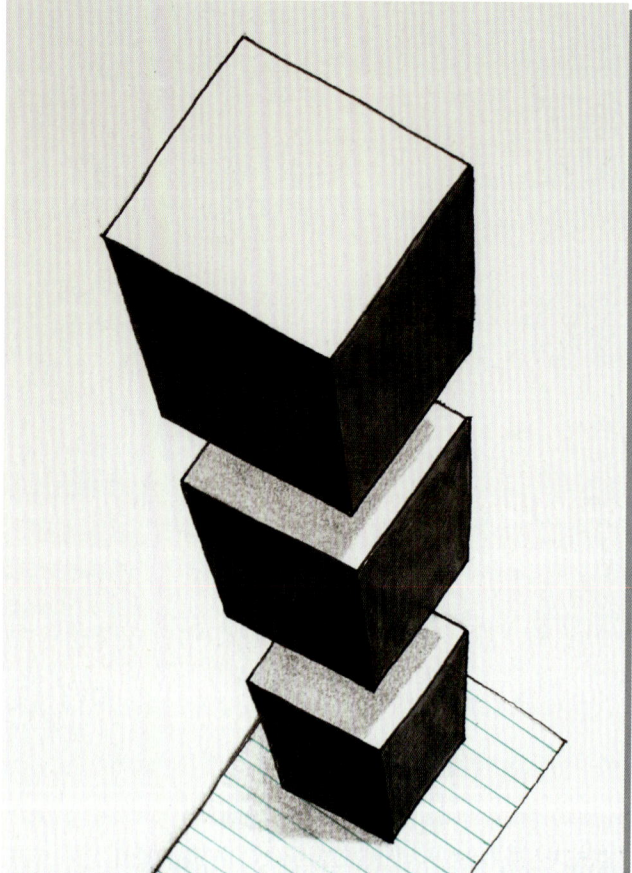

STEP 4

Erase any guidelines you no longer need. Consider darkening your lines with a fine-liner pen and shading one surface direction of the cubes with a dark tonal value and one surface direction with a mid-tonal value, leaving one surface direction of the cubes unshaded.

You could draw a small rectangle, in line with the angle of the top square, at the base of your cubes and then draw narrow lines on the rectangle to create the illusion of floating blocks on lined paper.

You now have three cubes in anamorphic perspective. To see how the image works, viewing your drawing from above the anamorphic dot is best.

DRAWING WORKSHOP

- Consider adding various colors and textures to your blocks.
- Consider adding more cubes using the same drawing technique toward your anamorphic dot.

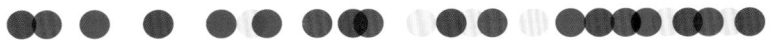

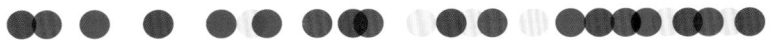

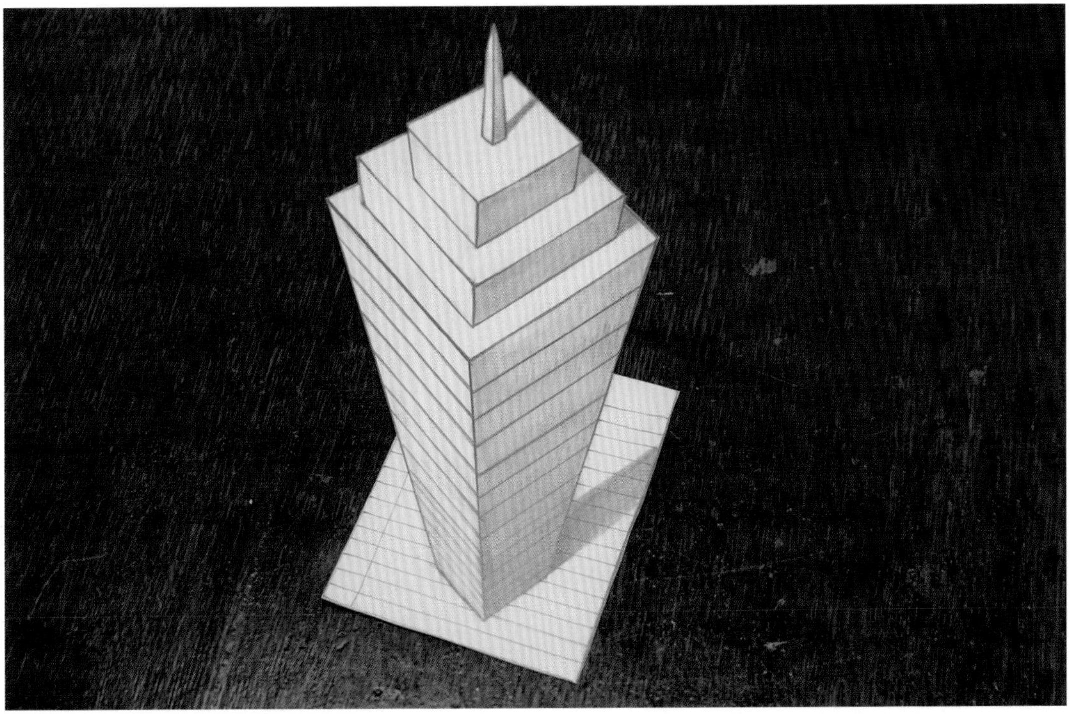

6.2 | 3D Skyscraper

Anamorphic perspective is particularly effective when applied to a skyscraper
due to its distinct, well-defined structure and towering appearance. Anamorphic
perspective is ideal for drawing tall skyscapers because it makes the image appear
to rise from the paper, when viewed from the correct position.

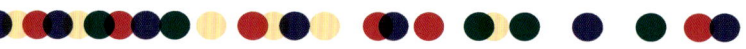

HOW TO DRAW A 3D SKYSCRAPER

Drawing tips: Keep the center line of the architectural form a straight line when seen from the anamorphic dot.

Use thinner lines for details that are nearer your anamorphic dot, and thicker lines for details and shapes that are farther away.

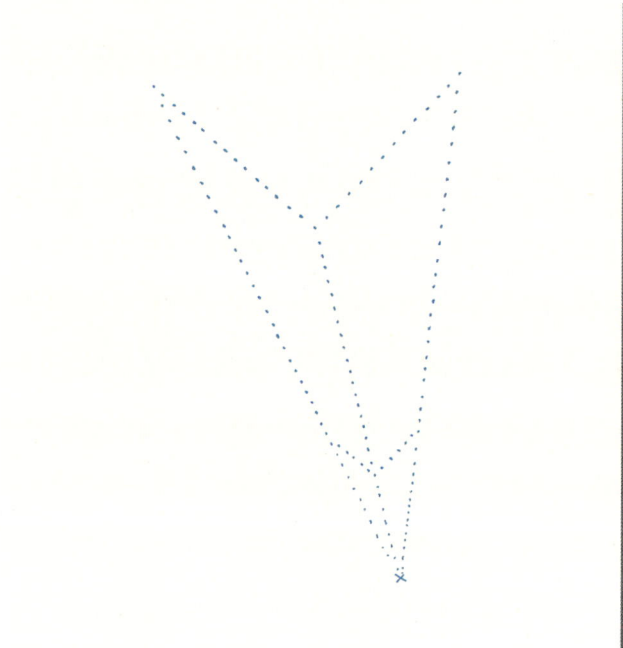

STEP 1

Study all the steps in this drawing before you start. When ready, draw a right angle for the top of the nearest largest skyscraper. Next, draw a cross near the bottom of your paper to use as a guide for the anamorphic perspective. Next, draw three lines toward the cross and two lines for the skyscraper's base using the same angles as the original right angle.

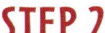

STEP 2

Draw two smaller right angles above the first right angle, then add three short receding lines to connect the two new right angles. The short receding lines should go toward the cross at the base of your drawing.

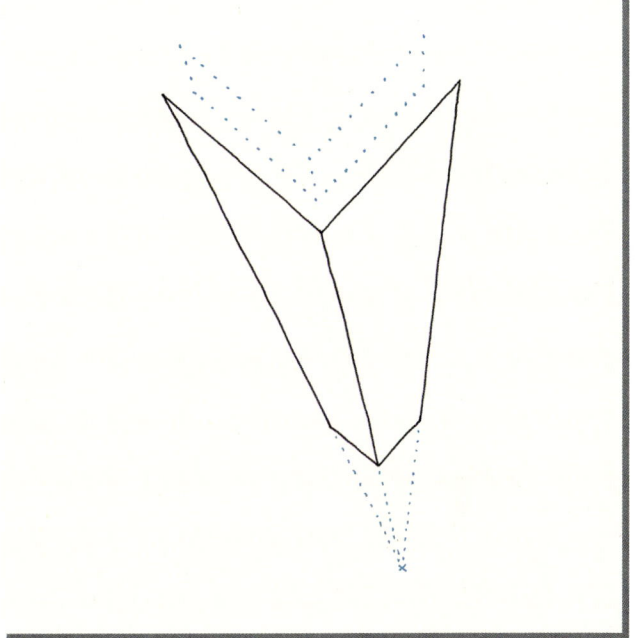

STEP 3

Repeat Step 2 with a smaller set of right angles, then draw the top angle of each of these three squares that make up the top of the skyscraper.

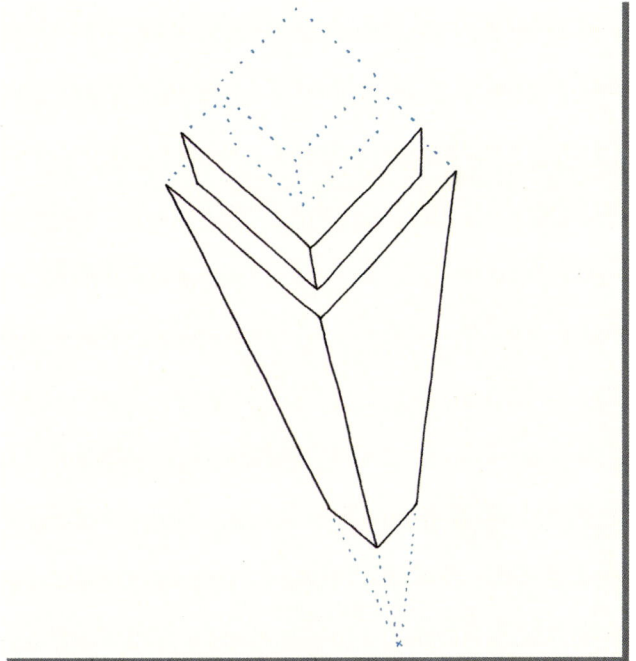

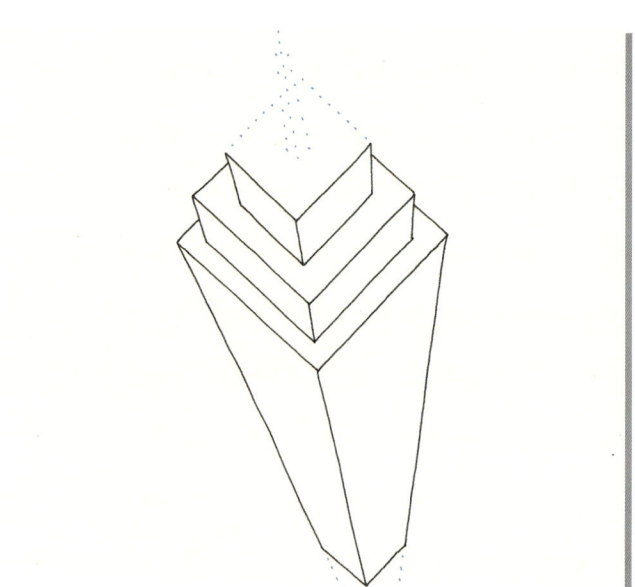

STEP 4

Draw a thin tower at the top of the skyscraper, in line with the cross at the base of your drawing.

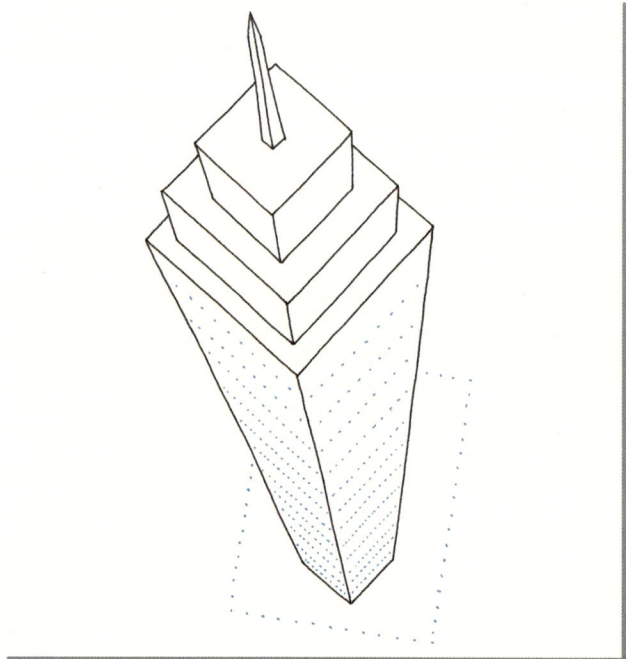

STEP 5

Draw a series of receding floors of the skyscraper using the angle of the base of the cubes. The floors will look closer to one another as they recede into the distance. Next, draw a rectangle below the base of the skyscraper.

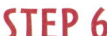

STEP 6

Shade the left base with a mid-tone that gradually grades out to the tone of the paper as it rises to the top of the skyscraper. Next shade in the right side of the structure with a simple mid-tone value. Add a cast shadow to the right. You could also draw thin blue lines on the paper below to make it look like the skyscraper is on lined paper.

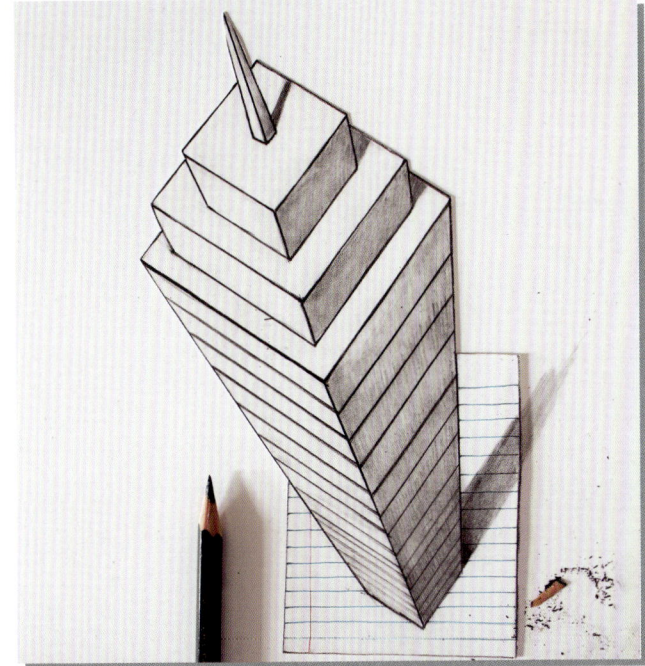

DRAWING WORKSHOP

- You could add tiny windows to each floor, getting smaller and smaller as they recede towards the direction of the anamorphic dot.
- Consider carefully cutting out your illusion so that you can place the image on different surfaces and then capture the image in a photograph taken from a high point above the anamorphic dot.

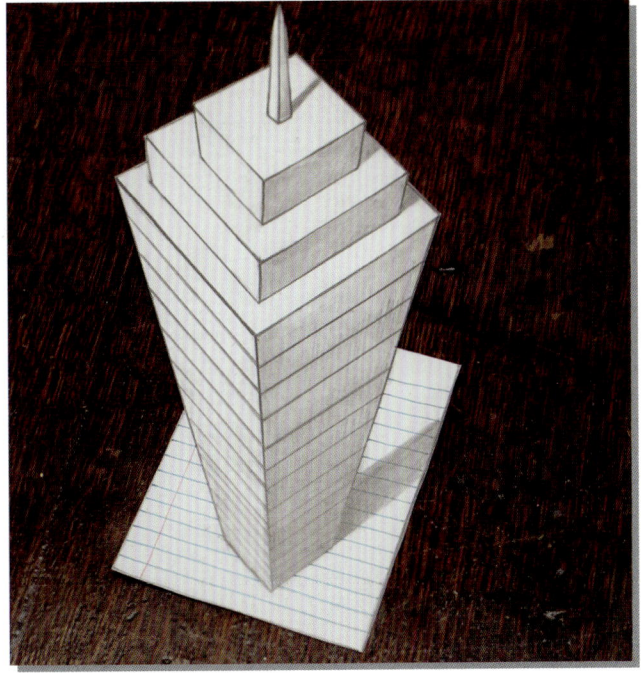

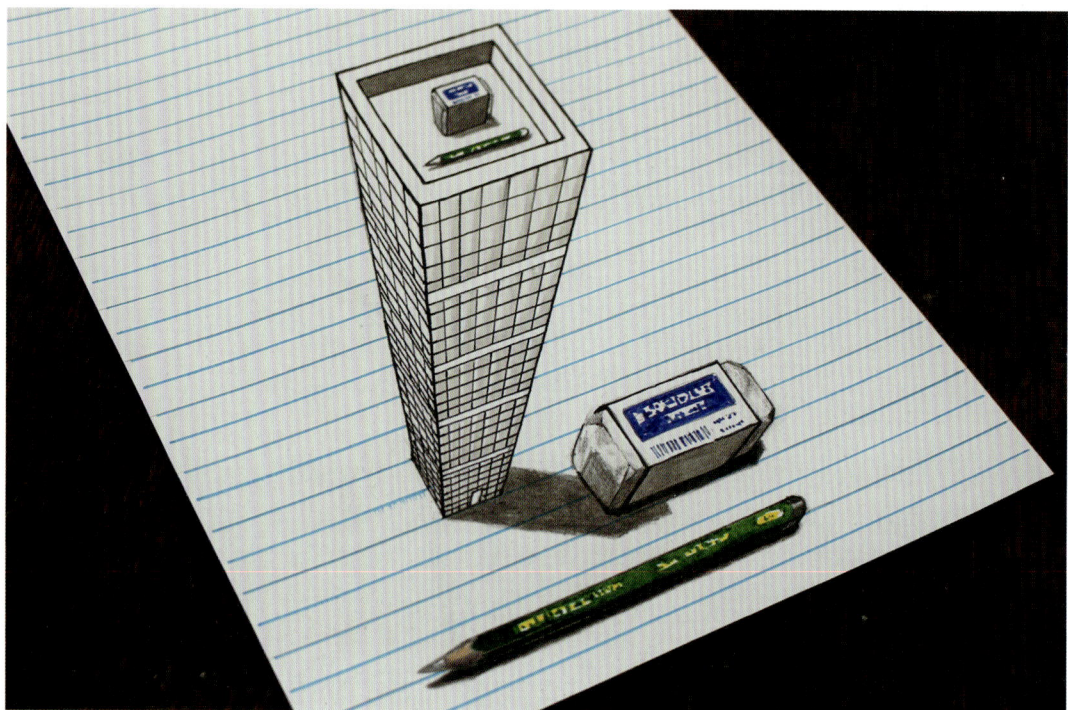

6.3   3D Skyscraper II

In an anamorphic perspective, we can add a trompe l'oel pencil or two to a 3D skyscraper.

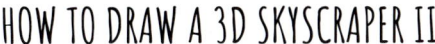
HOW TO DRAW A 3D SKYSCRAPER II

Drawing tips: Draw basic shapes first, add details later.

Check your drawing as it progresses by looking at it from slightly above your anamorphic dot.

STEP 1

First, draw a cross at the bottom of your paper, towards the left, to mark the anamorphic dot. Next draw a square for the top of the sky-scraper towards the top right. Next draw three light guidelines from the anamorphic dot to the three near corners of the square. Next draw a vertical line and a horizontal line between your diagonal lines, towards the dot. These two lines represent the base of the skyscraper.

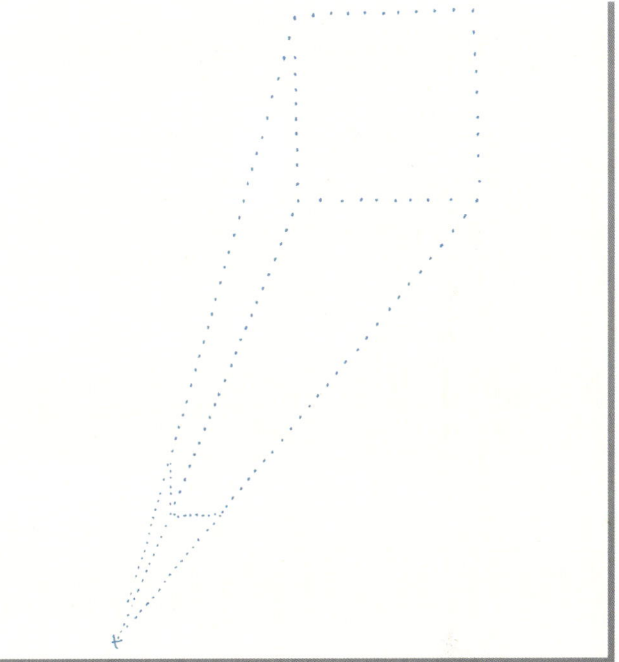

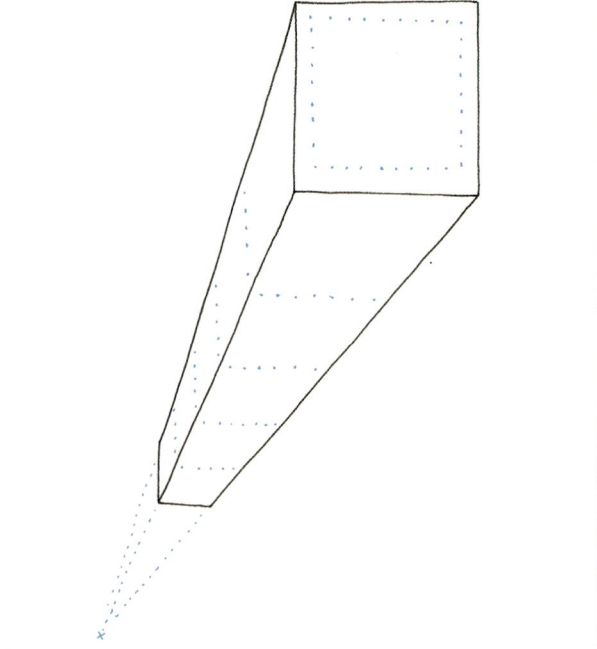

STEP 2

Draw an inner square at the top and draw four receding levels to the skyscraper that get closer together as they recede from us.

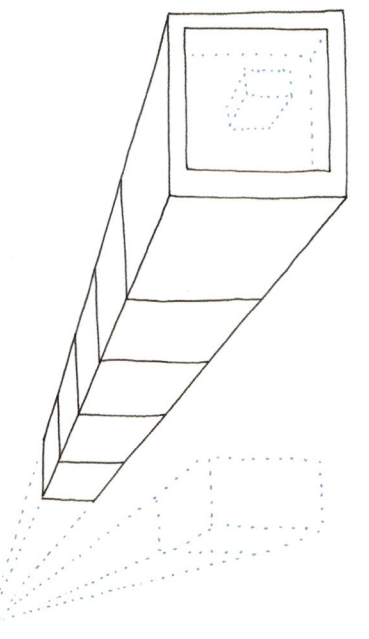

STEP 3

Draw a shallow depth to the top of the skyscraper and a small rectangle. The sides of the rectangle and the vertical line all go toward the anamorphic dot at the base of your drawing. Beside the skyscraper, draw a new rectangle in anamorphic perspective, with receding lines that go toward your anamorphic dot. This rectangle and the one on the top of the building will become the two erasers in the finished drawing.

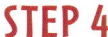

STEP 4

Draw a small pencil at the top of the skyscraper and a larger pencil directly below its base. The right-hand edge of the pencil needs to be an oval rather than a semicircle due to the distortions required for an anamorphic perspective.

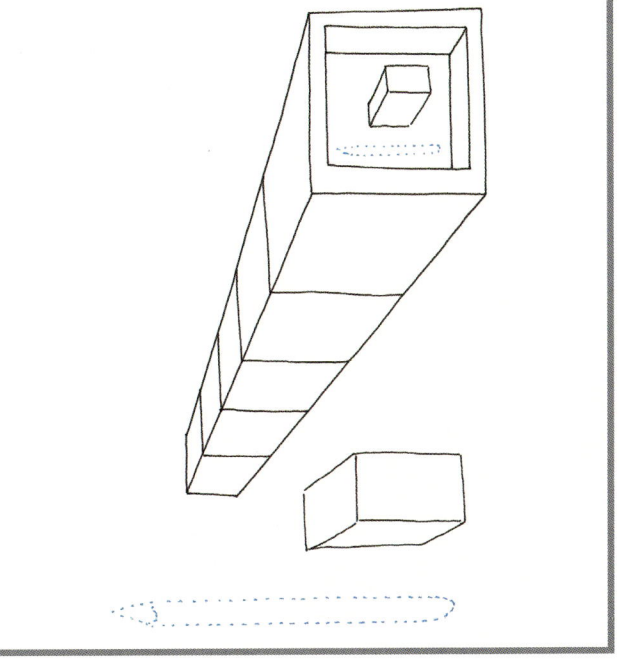

STEP 5

Now that you have completed the basic shapes for your drawing, check the accuracy of the lines when viewed from a just above the anamorphic dot. If you see something that you can improve in your drawing, when viewed from this angle, improve it, and then check your drawing again.

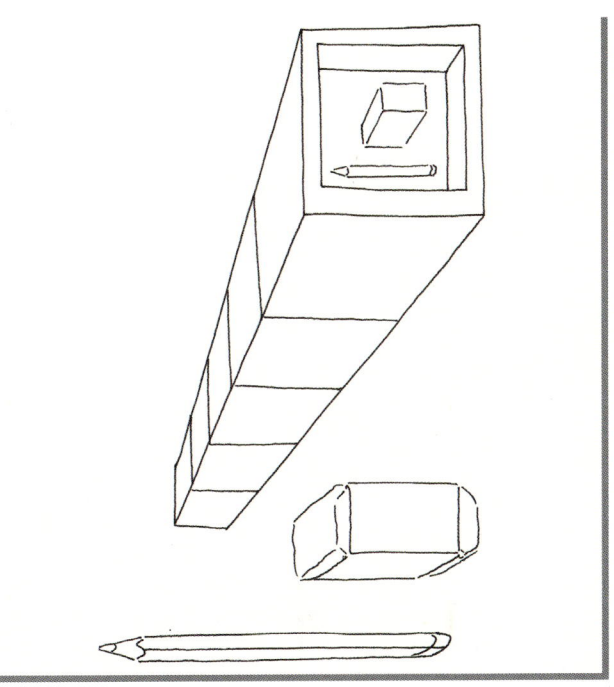

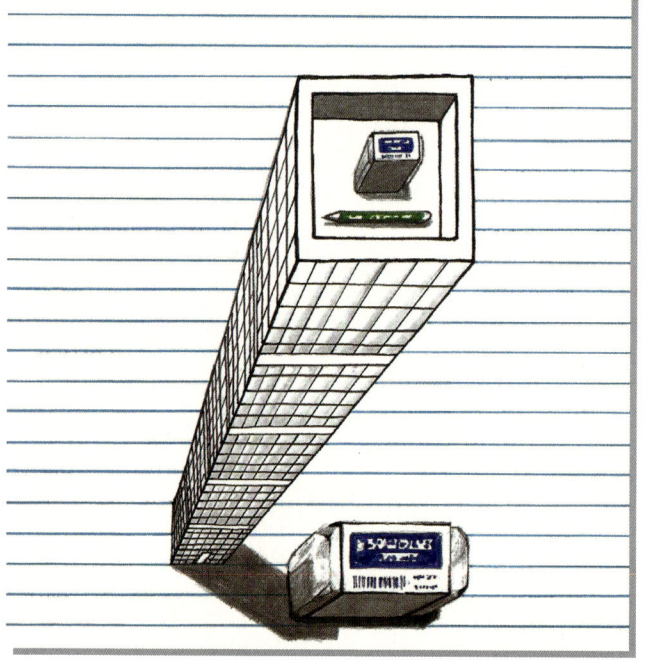

STEP 6

Carefully shade one side of the skyscraper and one side of the top interior edge. Add strong cast shadows to the skyscraper's base, the two erasers, and the pencils.

The clearer the detail, the stronger the image, so spend some time adding the detail you want once you are sure the basic lines are correct. View your drawing from the anamorphic dot you drew to see the full anamorphic effect.

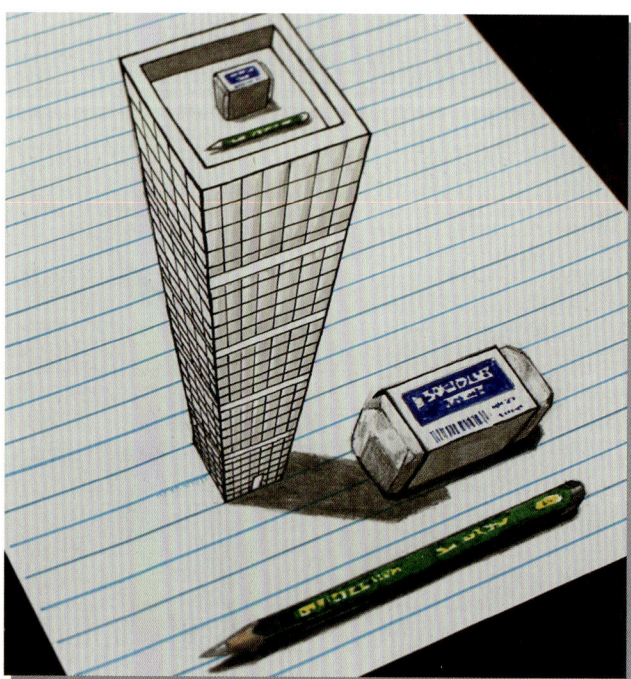

DRAWING WORKSHOP

- Adding color to the trompe l'oeil pencils and erasers will add interest to your drawing.
- You could add lines to the background, so the skyscraper looks like it is rising from a piece of lined paper from an exercise pad.

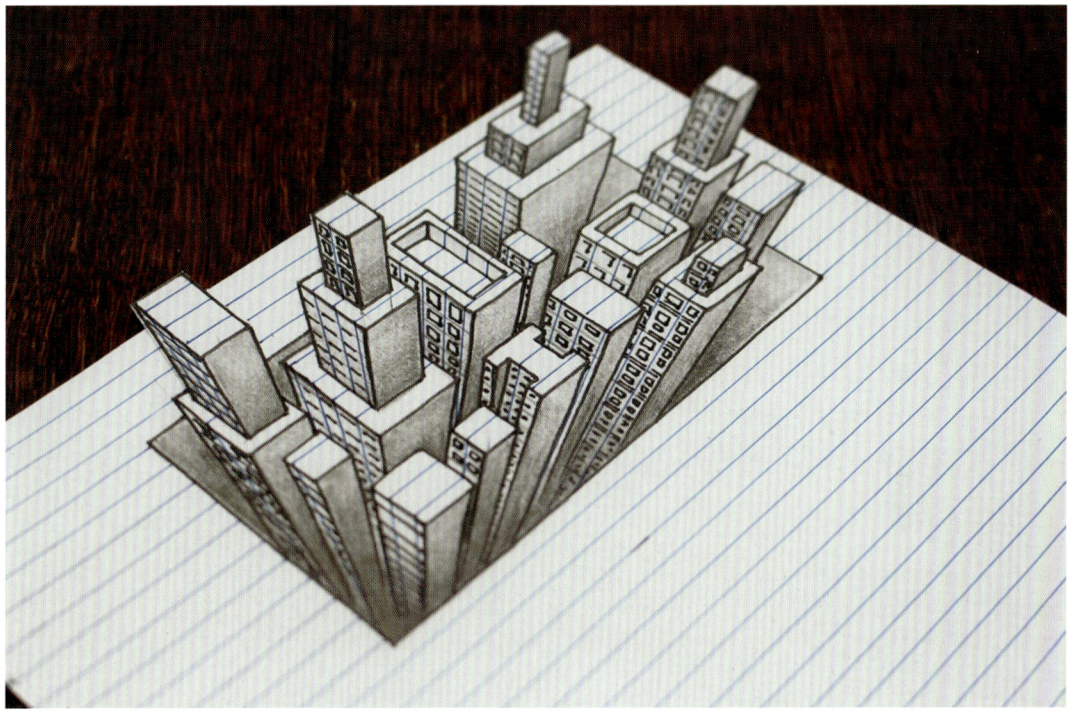

6.4 3D City

A city is a massive subject, so we shall only draw part of a city. In this drawing, we shall draw a group of similarly shaped buildings using anamorphic perspective.

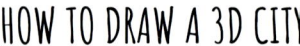

HOW TO DRAW A 3D CITY

Drawing tips: Check that your basic shapes work well at each stage of this drawing.

Consider experimenting with different styles of buildings to create a unique cityscape.

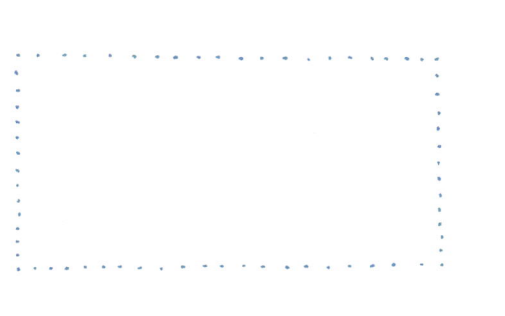

STEP 1

Draw a rectangle that is wider than its height.

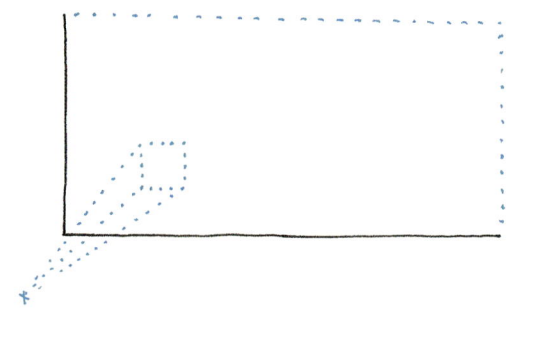

STEP 2

Draw a cross outside your rectangle, to the left and below the bottom-left corner. Next, draw a small square within the rectangle and then draw three lines from the edges of the square toward your cross. The cross represents the anamorphic dot, which shows the view point where the distortion of the image will be revealed as a solid looking 3D illusion.

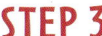

STEP 3

Repeat the process in Step 2 by drawing more small squares and rectangles within the rectangle and some above or to the right of the original rectangle. Then, draw a series of guidelines from the edges of the small squares and rectangles toward your cross.

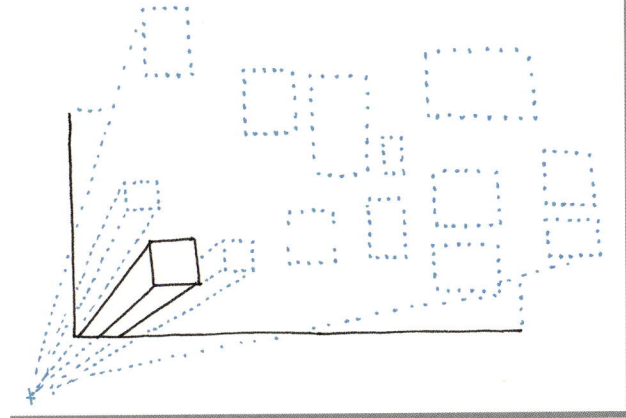

STEP 4

You could add smaller rectangles and squares above some towers and then draw more guidelines toward your cross.

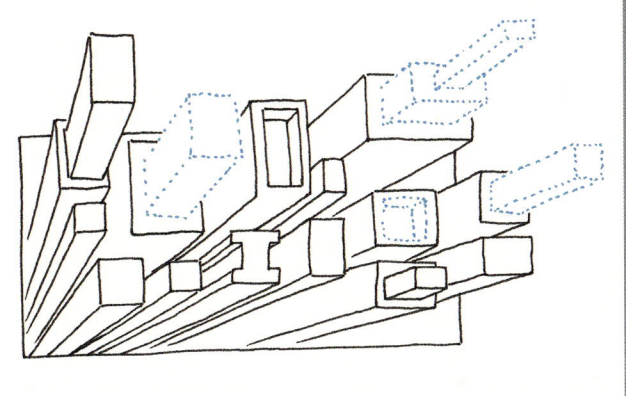

STEP 5

At this stage, you could add details to the skyscrapers and lines to the paper. Use a fine black pen or a sharp dark pencil to draw the small windows and details.

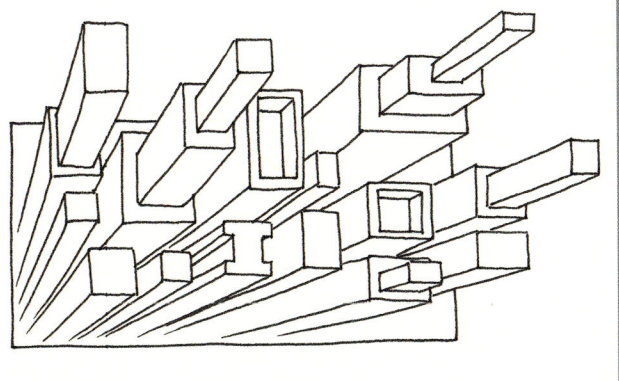

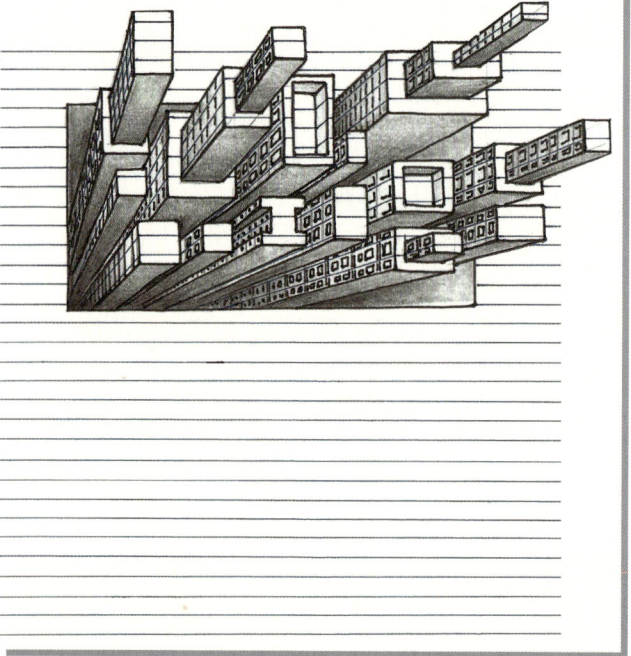

STEP 6

Shade the interior of the original rectangle. Then, shade a graded tonal value on the sides of the buildings, darker on one side than the other. These graded tonal values should get darker as they recede into the rectangular hole.

The smaller the details you add to your drawing the larger the buildings will seem. View your drawing from a low height above the cross to see the full 3D effect of the anamorphic perspective.

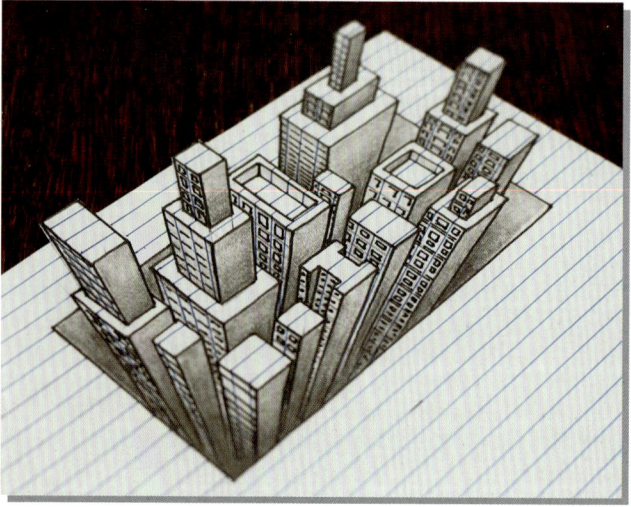

DRAWING WORKSHOP

- Consider adding atmospheric perspective by gradually lightening the tonal values of buildings as they recede into the distance. This mimics the way objects appear less tonally saturated at a distance.
- Experiment by adding roads to connect the buildings and give the cityscape a sense of scale. The smaller the details, the larger the buildings will look. Add details at a distance, such as cars, pedestrians, and streetlights, to bring the scene to life.

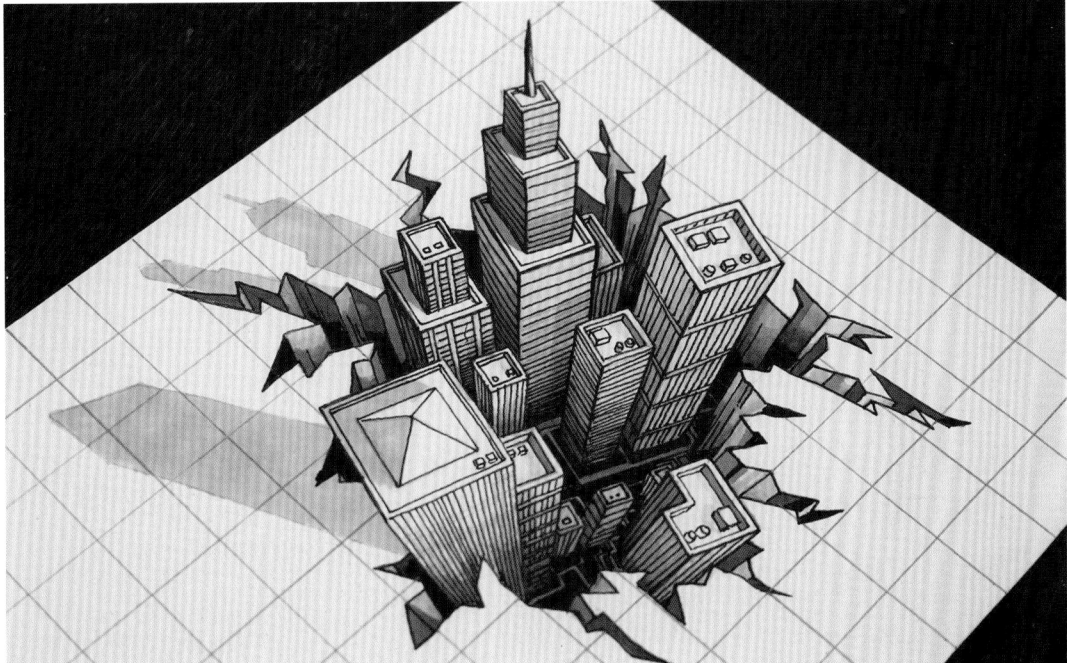

6.5 3D City II

Here is another city challenge. For this drawing, we can be more creative and play-ful in developing the architectural shapes of the building we shall draw.

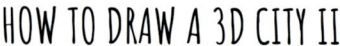

HOW TO DRAW A 3D CITY II

Drawing tips: Consider using reference images of real cityscapes to inspire your drawing. Always start with basic shapes first and check they work well before adding any details to your drawing.

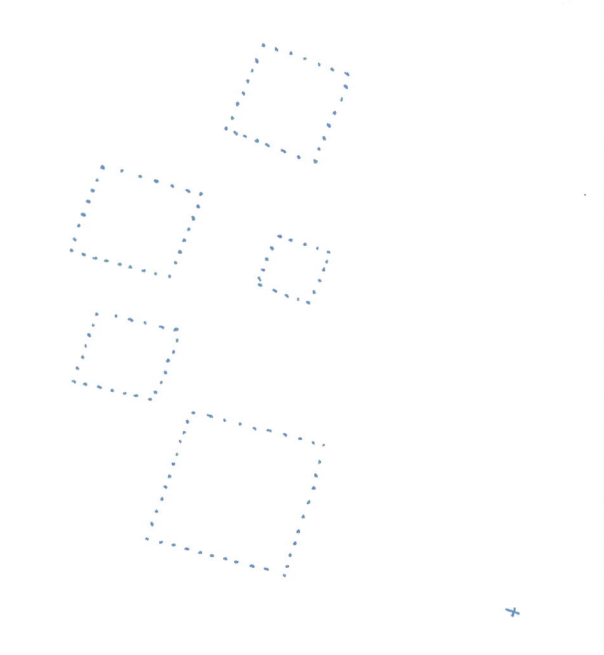

STEP 1

Carefully study all the steps of this drawing before you start. When ready, draw five squares representing the skyscrapers' tops, and draw a cross near the bottom of your paper to mark the anamorphic dot.

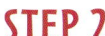

STEP 2

Draw a series of straight guidelines from the corners of the squares toward your cross. Check your drawing from the anamorphic dot to see how the image is looking at this stage.

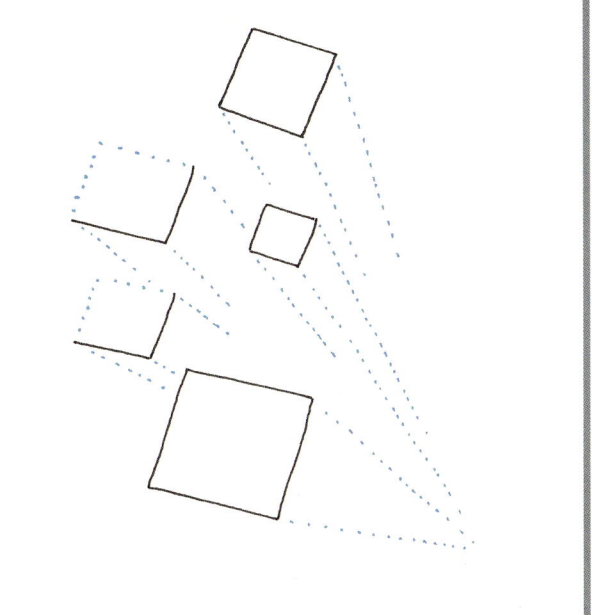

STEP 3

Add some details to the tops of the skyscrapers. Make sure all receding lines go toward your cross. Next, draw a zigzag-shaped hole around your skyscrapers. Ensure the tallest towers are in front of (or overlap) the zigzag-shaped hole.

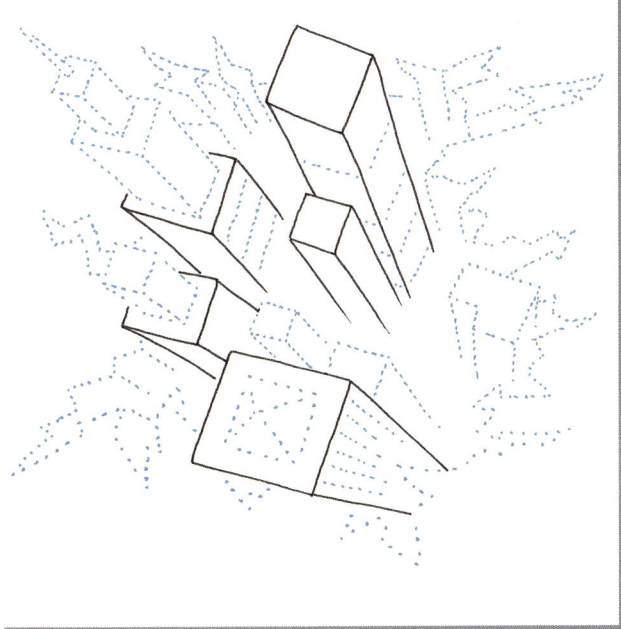

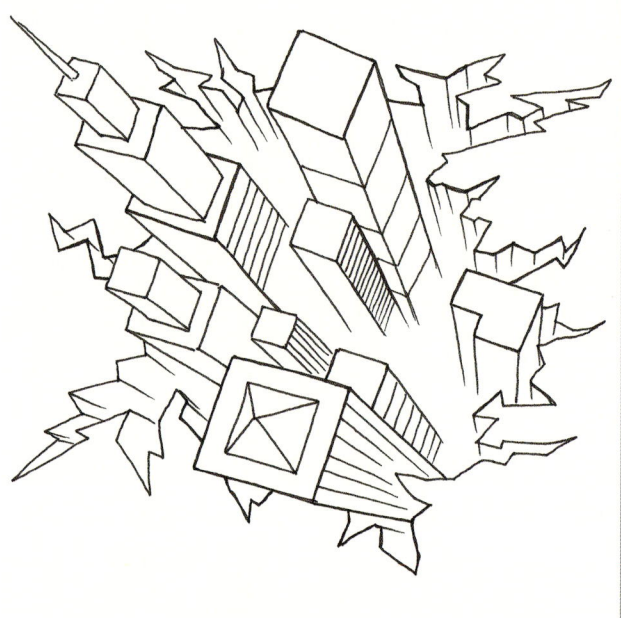

STEP 4

At this stage, add more details to your buildings and clean up your drawing so that it has only the lines and shapes you want.

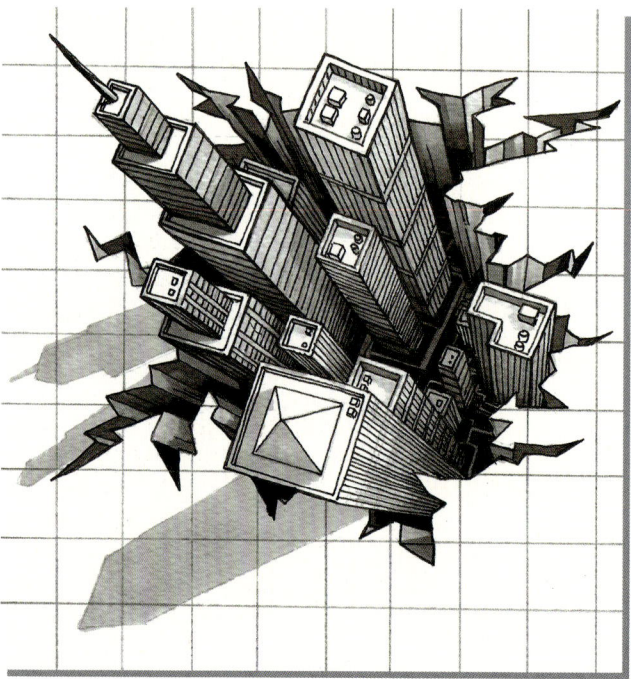

STEP 5

Carefully add some shading to your drawing. Start by shading the sides of the buildings and then add some simple tonal values to the cracks in the hole. Start each tonal value lighter than you might want, then slowly darken the areas by adding layers of tonal shading until you get the shading you want. Add fine detail with a thin black pen or a sharp dark pencil. The last step is to draw a flat cast shadow and add lines or a grid on the paper outside the zigzag hole.

DRAWING WORKSHOP

- Experiment with the contrast between light and shadow to emphasize the three-dimensional nature of the buildings.
- Consider using a set of gray marker pens to add powerful tonal values to your drawing.

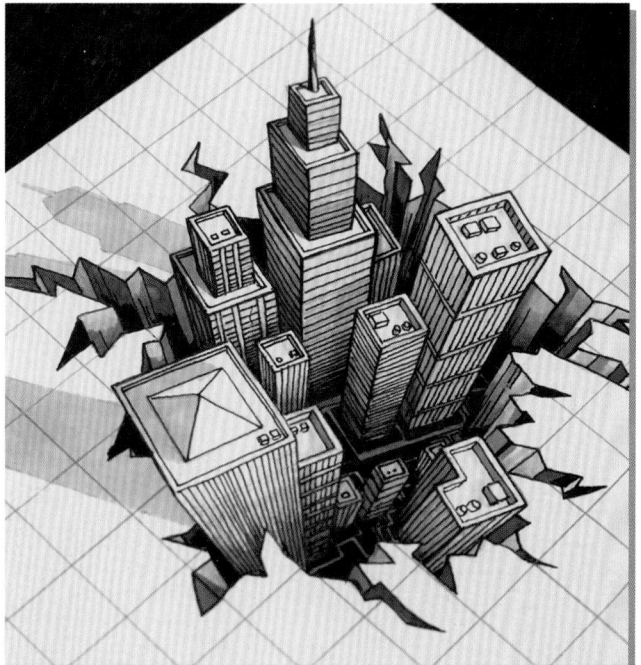

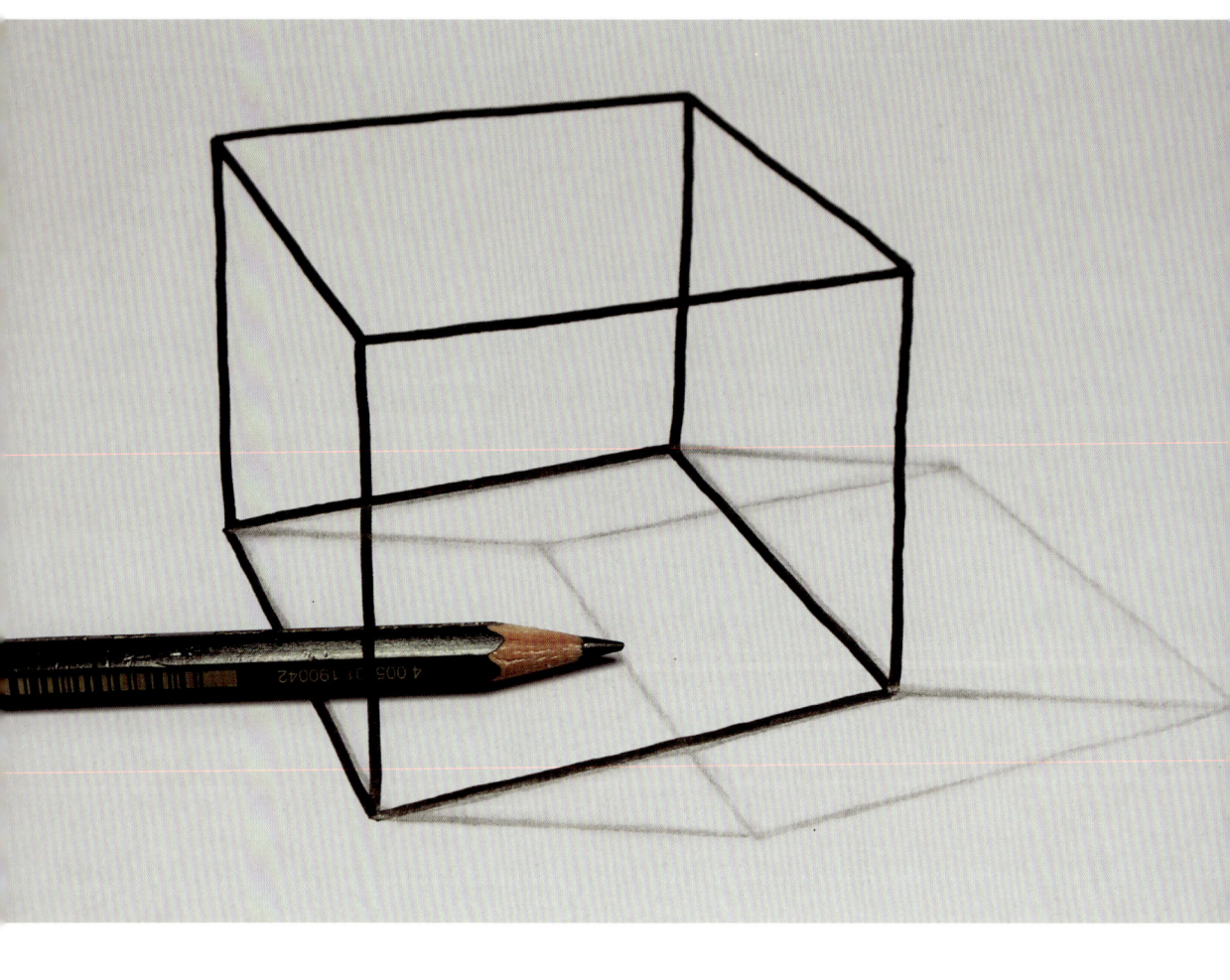

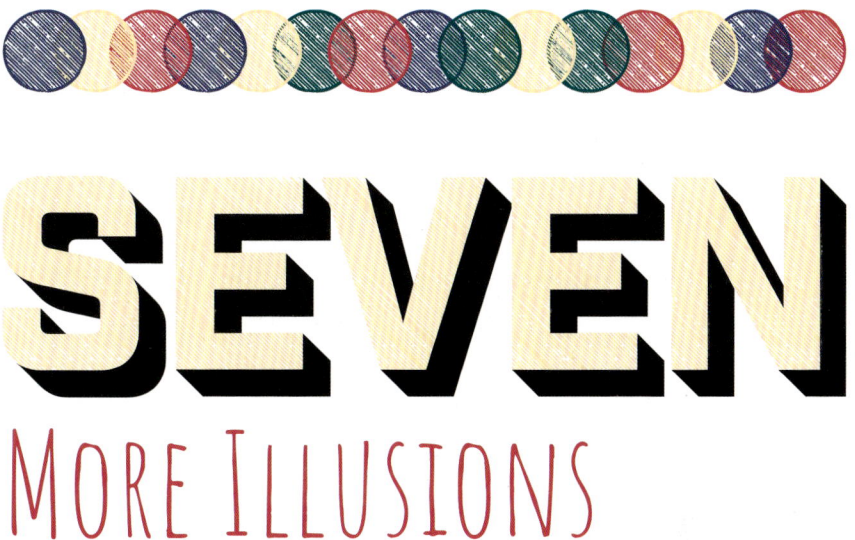

SEVEN
MORE ILLUSIONS

This section provides step-by-step instructions for drawing some of the images from the introduction.

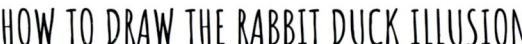

HOW TO DRAW THE RABBIT DUCK ILLUSION

Drawing tips: Make sure the eye you draw is looking directly out towards the viewer.

Make sure the ends of the beak/ears are not quite pointed or round.

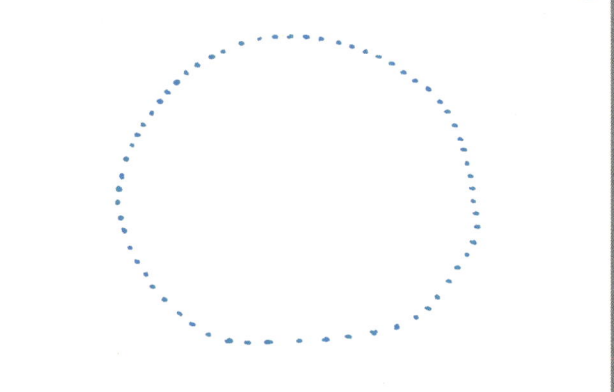

STEP 1
Draw a simple oval for the head shape.

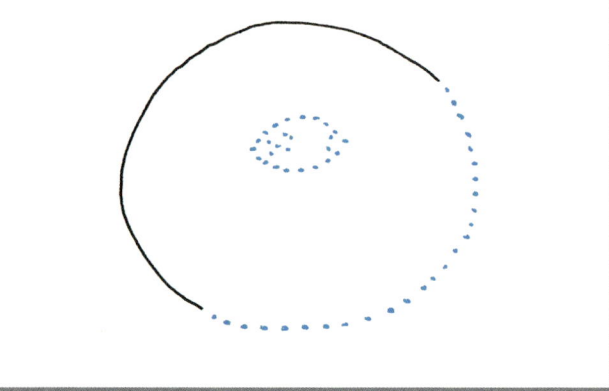

STEP 2
Draw an eye in the center of the oval head.

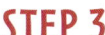

STEP 3

Draw a small button nose on the left side of the head.

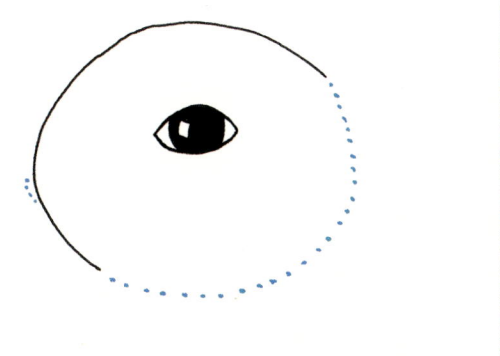

STEP 4

Draw two ears on the right, close together so that they resemble the slightly open beak of a duck.

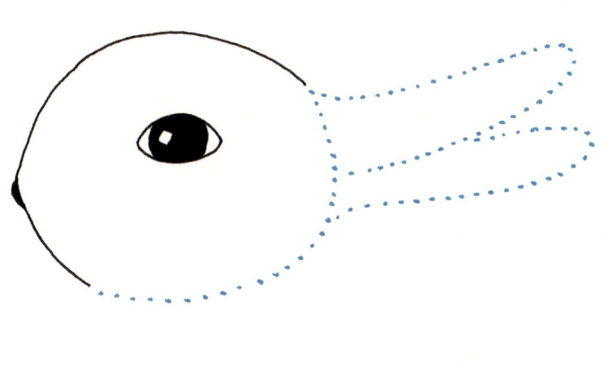

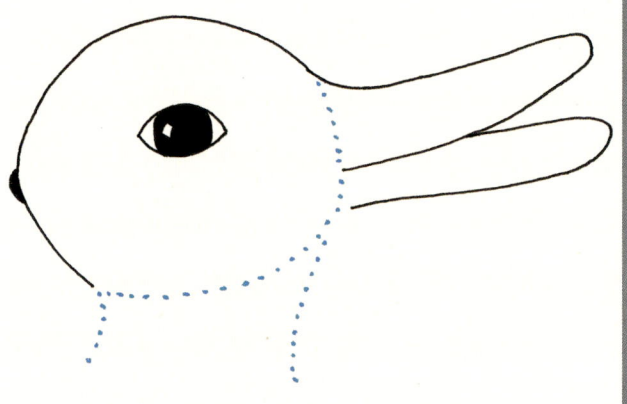

STEP 5

Draw a simple wide neck and erase the oval line between the lines of the neck.

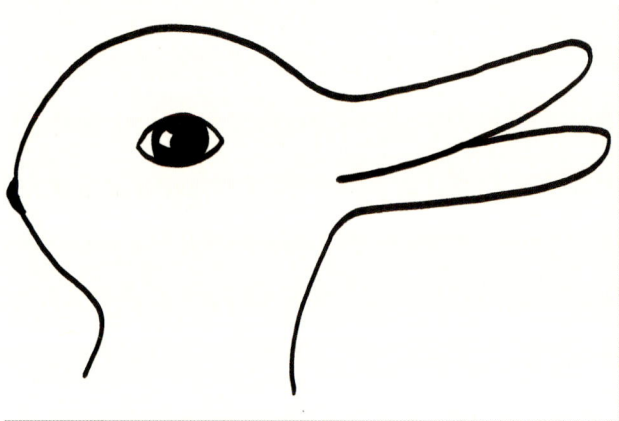

STEP 6

Once you have completed your drawing, check that it looks both like a rabbit and a duck. If your drawing needs improving, look at the ears/beak and see if you can simplify them.

DRAWING WORKSHOP

- You could add some shading to the drawing to add a sense of form.
- You could make makes to represent textures for fur and feathers, following the direction of the image outlines.

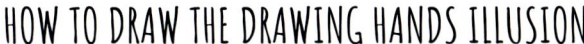

HOW TO DRAW THE DRAWING HANDS ILLUSION

Drawing tips: Study the image before you start your drawing. Notice how the success of this image relies on two realistic-looking pencil points making a line drawing of a sleeve.

You will need two pencils to draw this drawing.

STEP 1

With your dominant hand, the hand you draw with, make a line drawing of your non-dominant hand holding a pencil. Look carefully at the shapes you can see.

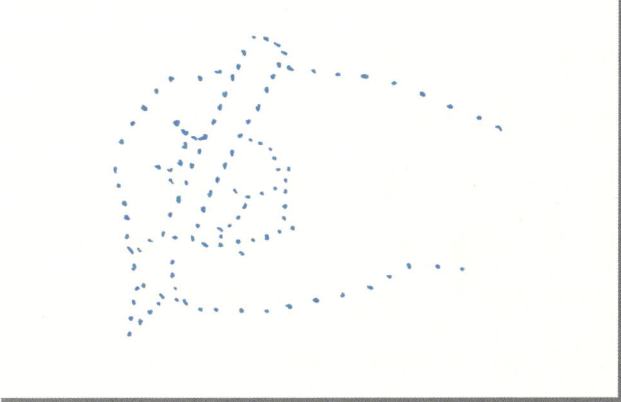

STEP 2

Once you have carefully drawn a hand holding a pencil, draw the wrist and part of the sleeve as a simple line drawing.

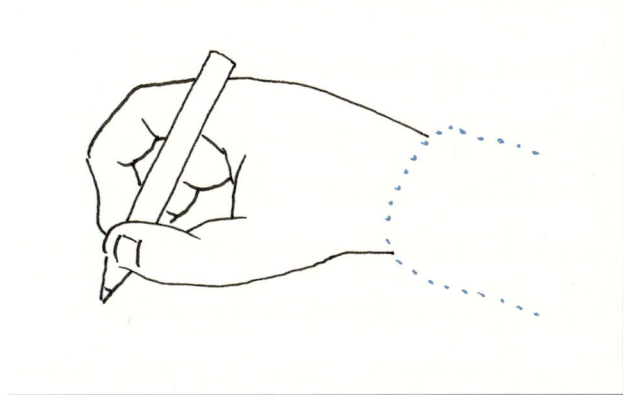

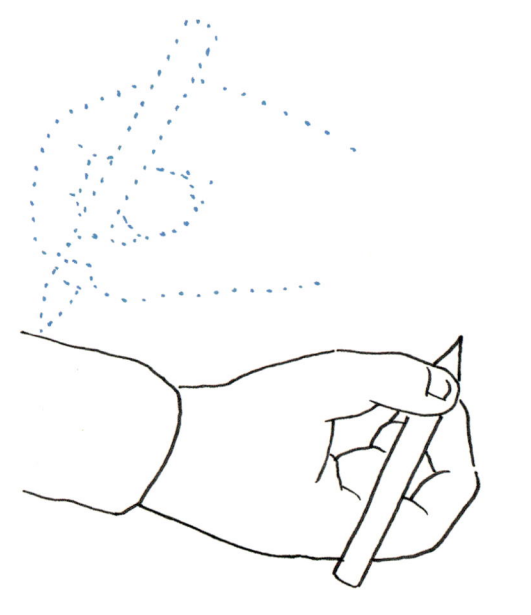

STEP 3

Turn your drawing upside down and repeat Step 2. Make sure you start by drawing the second pencil point on the line of the sleeve from your earlier drawing.

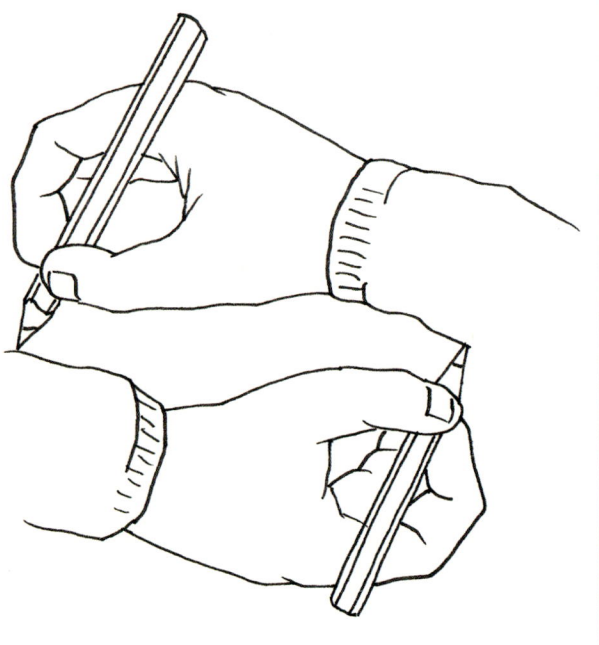

STEP 4

Draw the wrist and part of the sleeve as a simple line drawing so that part of the line drawing of a sleeve touches the pencil point from your first pencil drawing.

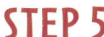

STEP 5

Now, you can add shading to both pencil points, the fingers, and part of each hand. The area of each hand furthest away from the pencil point should remain a line drawing.

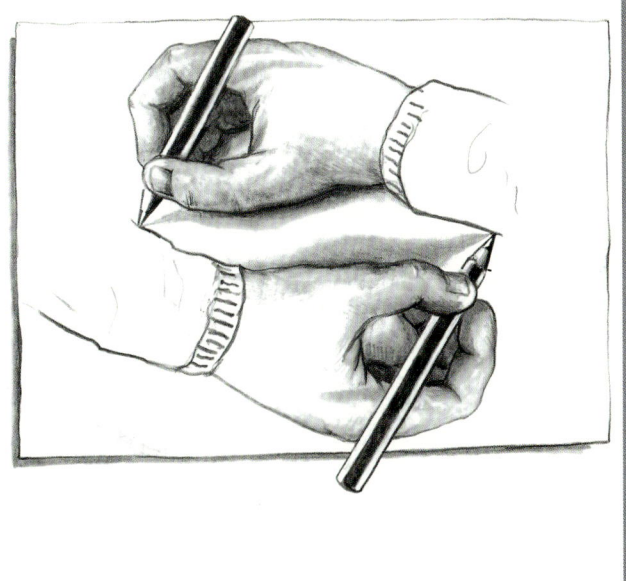

DRAWING WORKSHOP

- Add a cast shadow to each hand. Remember to turn your drawing around so you see each hand the right way up.
- Draw a delicate rectangle around your drawing. Make this rectangle look like a piece of paper by adding a subtle thin cast shadow to some of its edges and a few lines and smudges to represent creases in the paper.
- In each corner, draw the top of a drawing pin and a simple cast shadow, with some careful shading to make it realistic.

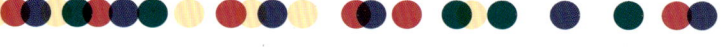

HOW TO DRAW THE TWO-WAY ARROW ILLUSION

Drawing tips: Notice how each diagonal line in this image is at an identical angle that either goes toward the left or the right.

All the other lines that create this illusion are horizontal or vertical.

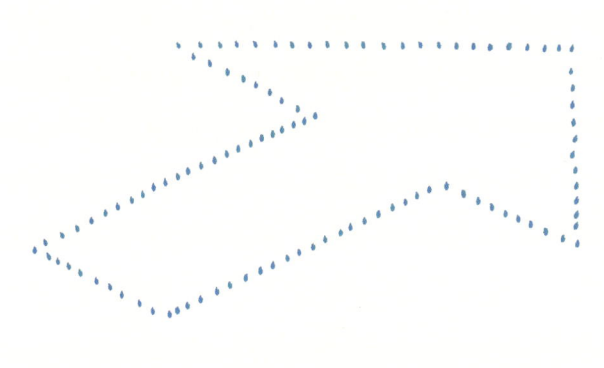

STEP 1

Draw a diagonal arrow towards the right. Ensure the two lines that create the arrow point meet at 90 degrees, a right angle.

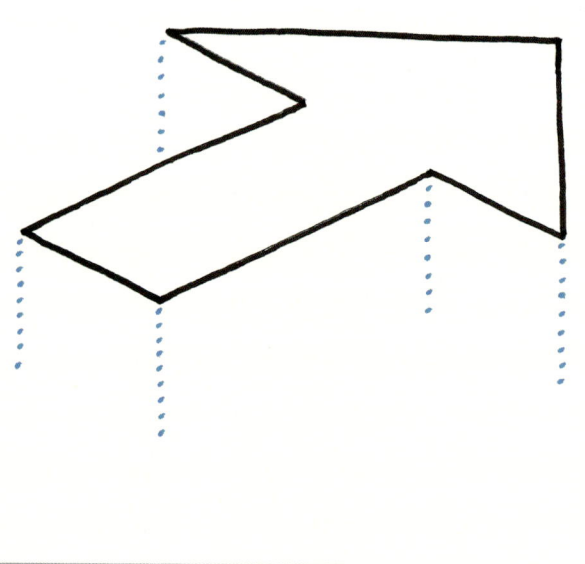

STEP 2

Draw five vertical lines of identical length from the lower edges of your arrow.

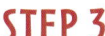
STEP 3

Draw three lines to join the four lowest vertical lines that match the lines they are directly below.

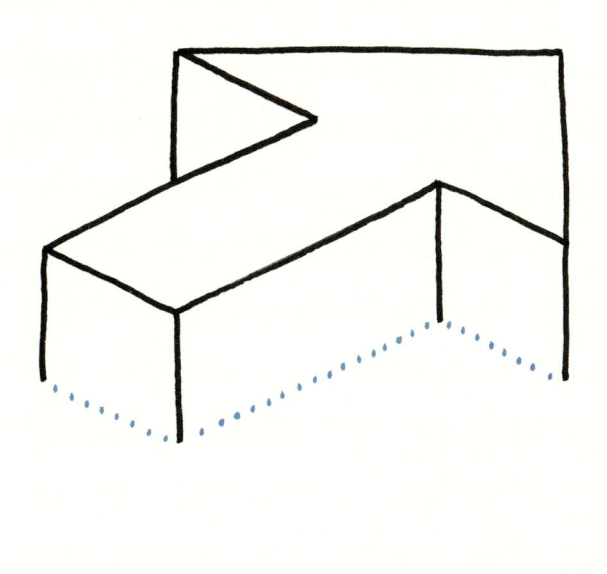

STEP 4

Draw a second arrow identical to the first but pointing in the opposite direction, with its longest edge formed partly by the diagonal back line of your first arrow.

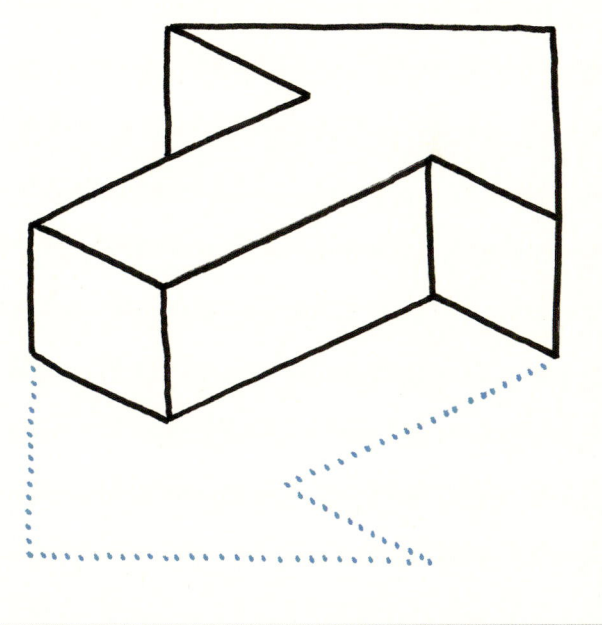

147

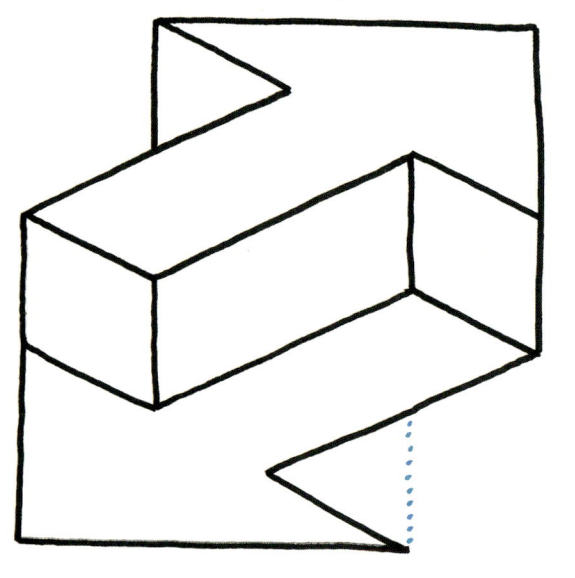

STEP 5

Draw a vertical line from the bottom right of your second arrow, going upwards to the long diagonal line above it.

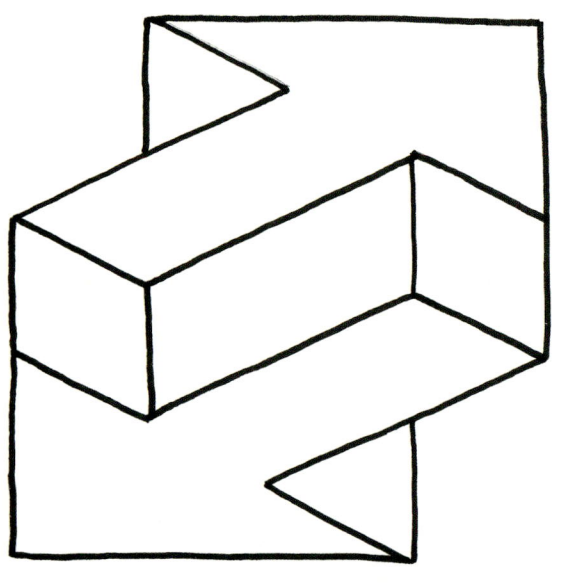

STEP 6

Once you have completed Step 5 it is time to check your drawing for accuracy and see if there are any lines you can improve so that each arrow is an identical shape.

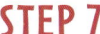

STEP 7

Identify the two shapes that represent the depth of each arrow head and shade them in a dark tonal value. Notice how the three shapes across the middle of this illusion are shared by both arrows.

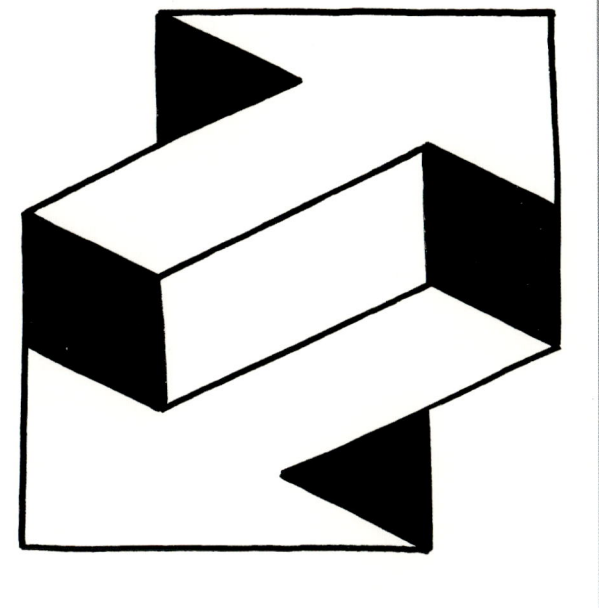

DRAWING WORKSHOP

- You could add your own color combinations to each shape within this drawing to enhance the illusion.
- Rather than shading the surfaces with a flat, even tonal value, you could use graded ones so that each surface changes from light to dark.

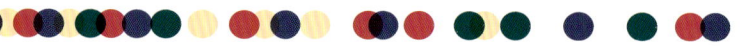

HOW TO DRAW THE SHEPARD TABLE ILLUSION

Drawing tips: You could draw one tabletop shape, cut it out, and then use it as a template to draw the other tabletops in this illusion, ensuring each is the same size.

Check each table leg is the same height.

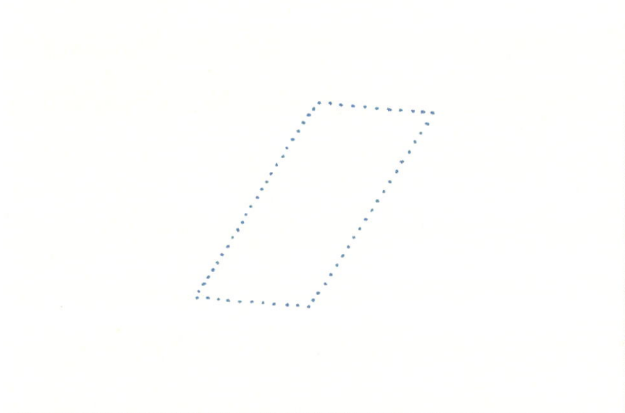

STEP 1

Draw a tall parallelogram, a quadrilateral shape with two parallel sides representing a tabletop.

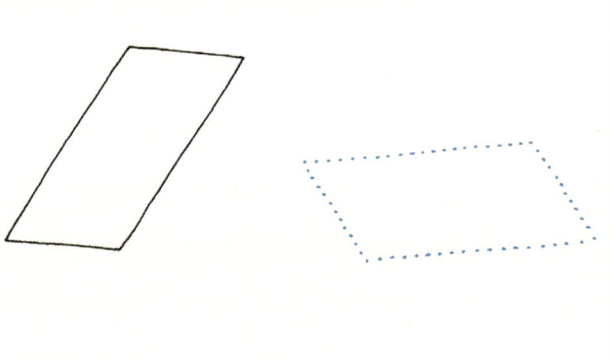

STEP 2

Draw the same shape again, but this time, the long sides of the parallelogram are horizontal.

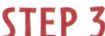

STEP 3

Draw three short and simple table legs of equal length for each tabletop.

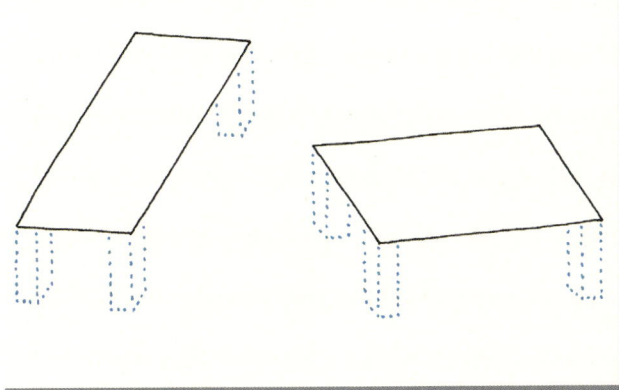

STEP 4

Shade on one side of each table leg.

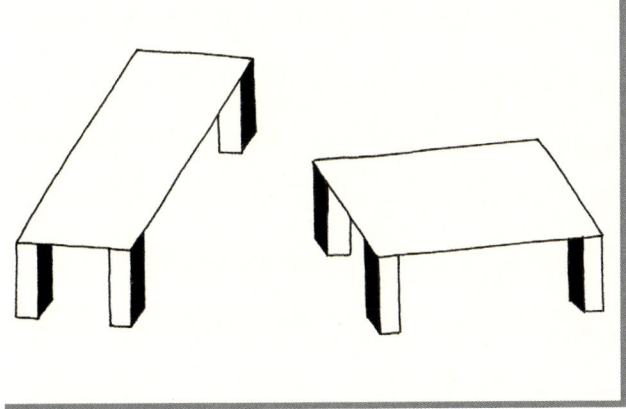

DRAWING WORKSHOP

- You could add colors to this illusion, but it's best to make each table the same color to keep the illusion simple and effective.
- If you want to draw some objects on the tables, make sure they are identically sized on each table so as not to confuse the simplicity of this illusion.

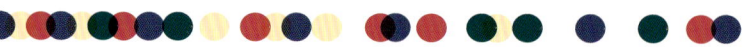

HOW TO DRAW THE SCHRÖDER STAIRS ILLUSION

Drawing tips: Try to draw the front and back walls the same size and shape.

As you develop your drawing, turn your paper upside down and back again to check if it looks the same from both viewpoints.

STEP 1
Draw a rectangle using soft guidelines.

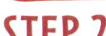

STEP 2

Draw a series of vertical and horizontal lines to create four evenly spaced steps.

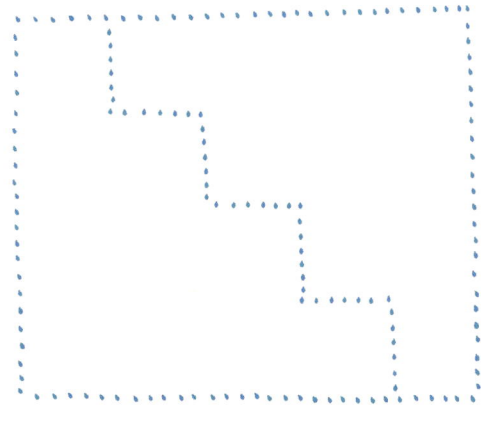

STEP 3

Draw a series of parallel diagonal lines at 45 degrees from the edge points of each step, going towards the right. Make sure each line is the same length.

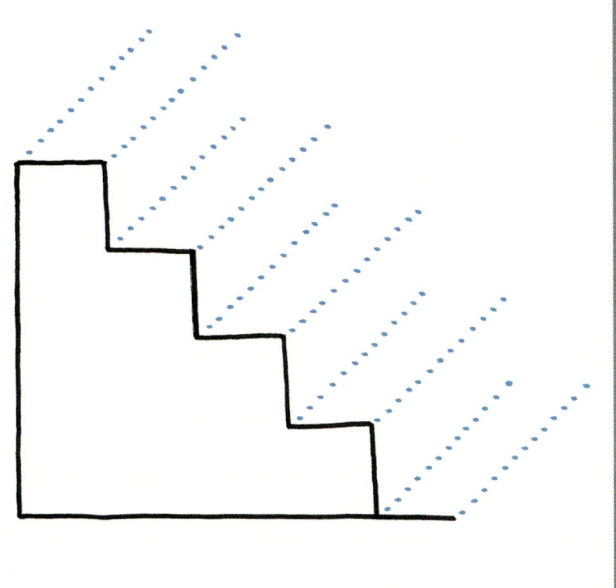

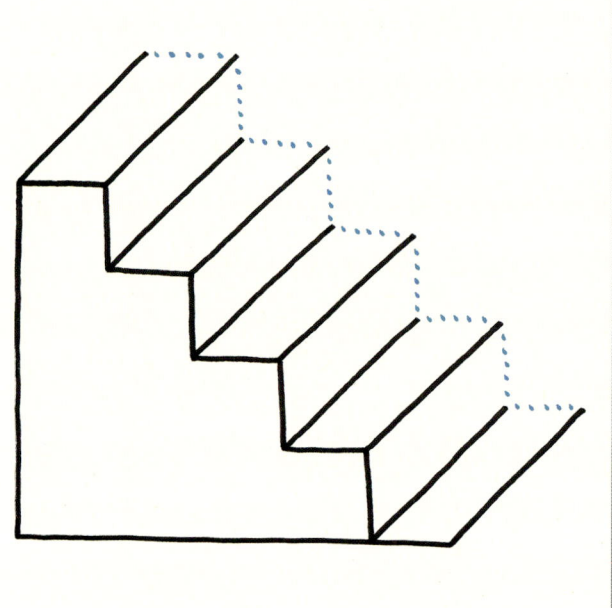

STEP 4

Repeat Step 2 to create the back outline of the steps, joining all the diagonal lines from Step 4 with a series of horizontal and vertical lines.

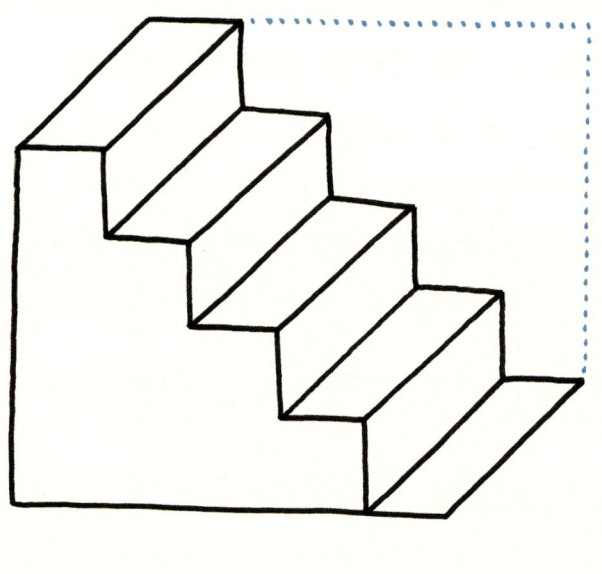

STEP 5

Draw a horizontal line from the top back step and a vertical line from the bottom back step until they meet at a right angle.

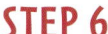

STEP 6

Check your illusion line drawing by turning your image upside down to see the second series of steps.

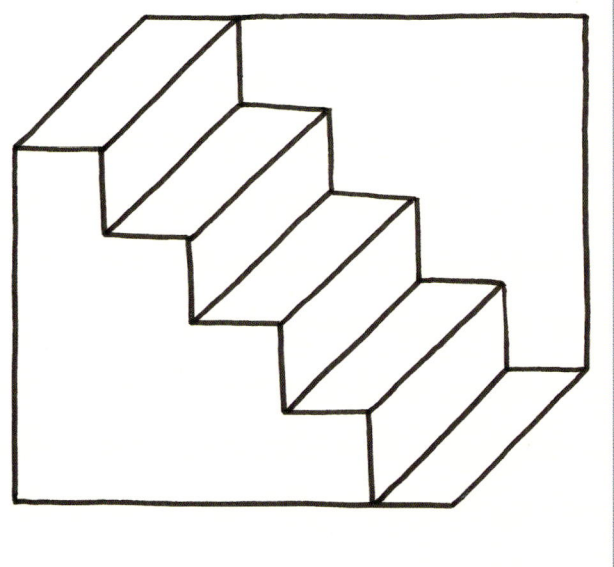

STEP 7

Shade the near and far walls with a different tonal value than the tone on the step risers.

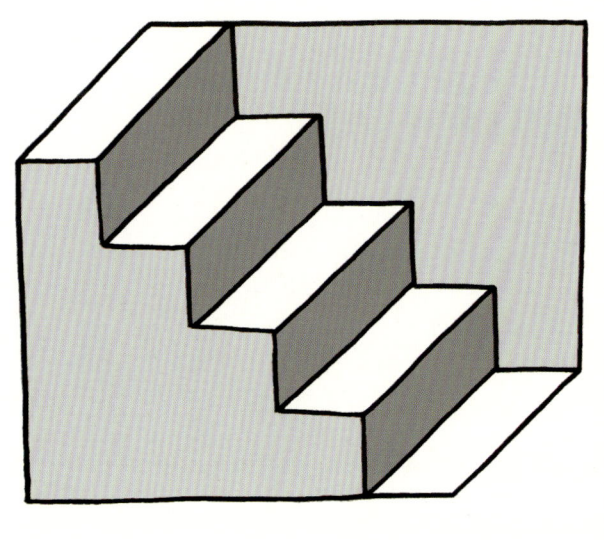

DRAWING WORKSHOP

- Experiment with different colors to emphasize the illusion.
- You could draw a figure walking up the stairs and see how that affects the illusion.

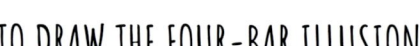

HOW TO DRAW THE FOUR-BAR ILLUSION

Drawing tips: Look at the finished optical illusion before you start this drawing.

Notice that there are just three directions of lines in this illusion: vertical lines, lines to the left, and lines to the right.

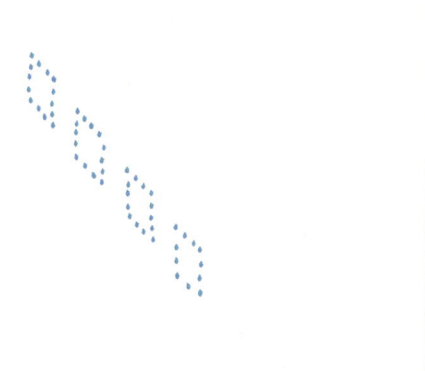

STEP 1

Draw four small parallelograms in a row for the four ends of the bars. Notice how Step 2 works before you start Step 1.

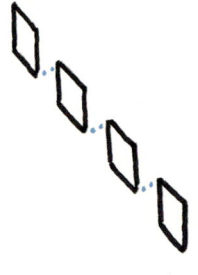

STEP 2

Draw three short diagonal lines to connect the four parallelograms.

STEP 3

Draw three long lines from each of the end parallelograms and then draw two short lines at their ends, the same as the right-hand sides of your original parallelograms, to create two solid-looking bars.

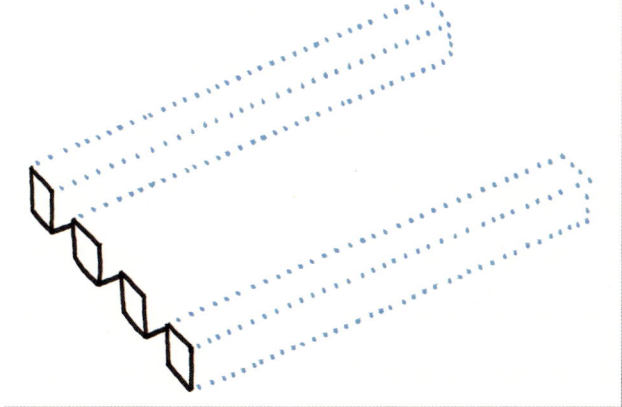

STEP 4

From each of the remaining edges of your original parallelograms, draw three lines to the right and then two short lines to make a third bar end in a row with the first two bars.

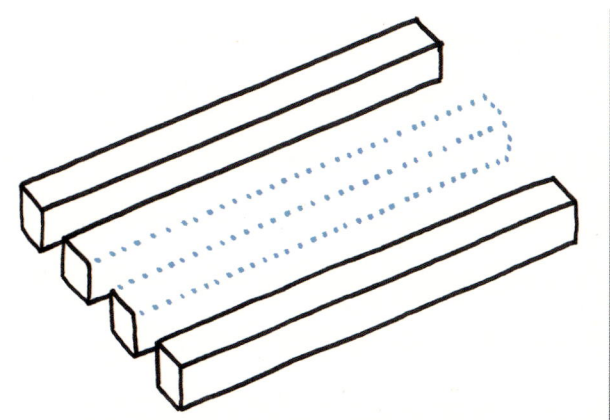

STEP 5

Now that you have created the illusion, look carefully and check the quality of lines you have used and their accuracy and if there is anything you think you could improve, now is the time to improve it.

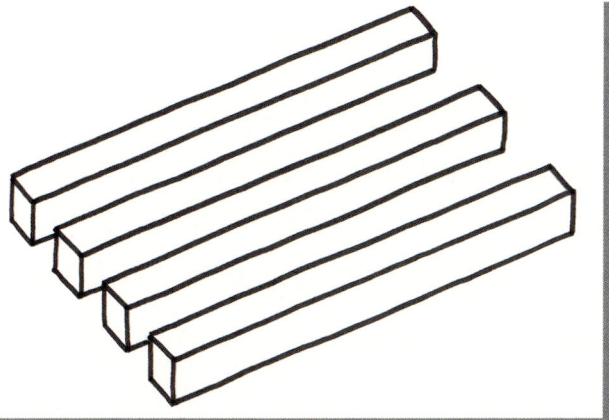

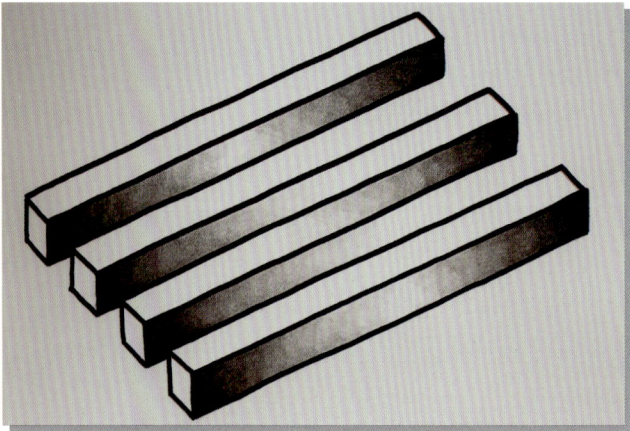

STEP 6

Next, you could shade some of the surfaces of your drawing with graded tonal values, creating dark ends to the four bars on the left and the three bars on the right of your drawing to heighten the optical illusion.

DRAWING WORKSHOP

- Consider using different tonal values to various areas of your drawing.
- Consider using dots and colors to create a unique optical illusion.

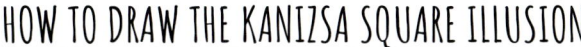

HOW TO DRAW THE KANIZSA SQUARE ILLUSION

Drawing tips: Try to visualize the image on your paper before you start your drawing.

Consider drawing four dots to mark the four corners of a square, rather than actually drawing a square for this illusion.

STEP 1

Draw a square with a soft pencil guideline.

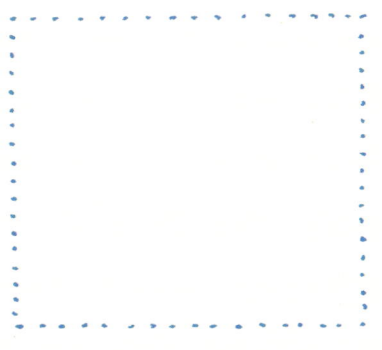

STEP 2

Draw four three-quarter circles of equal size at each of the square's corners.

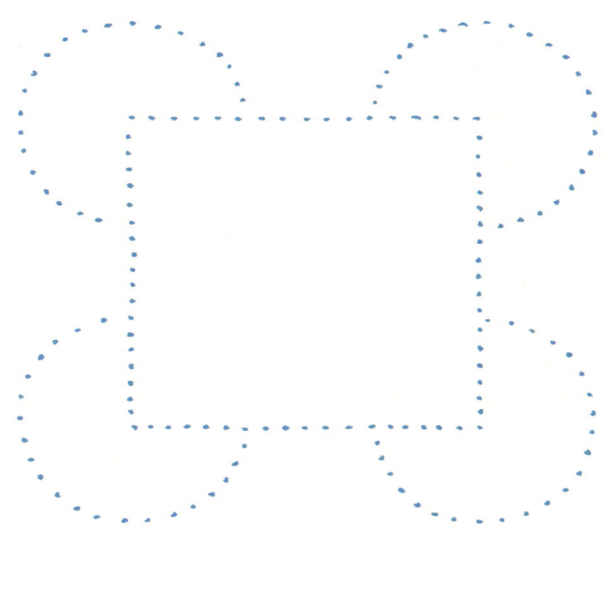

159

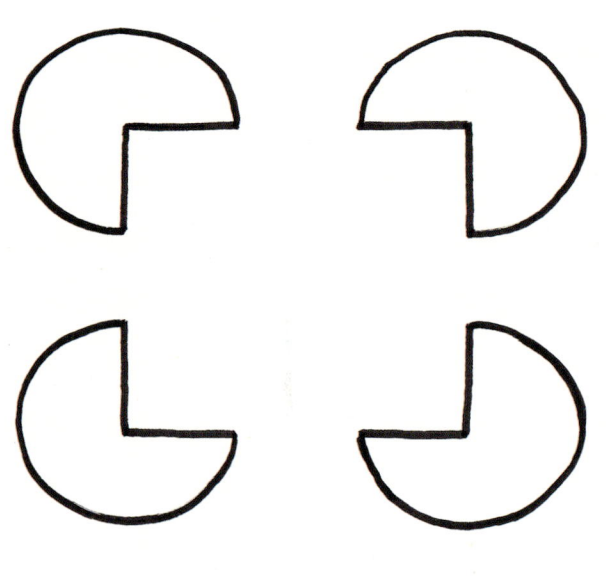

STEP 3

Erase the guideline of the original square you no longer need.

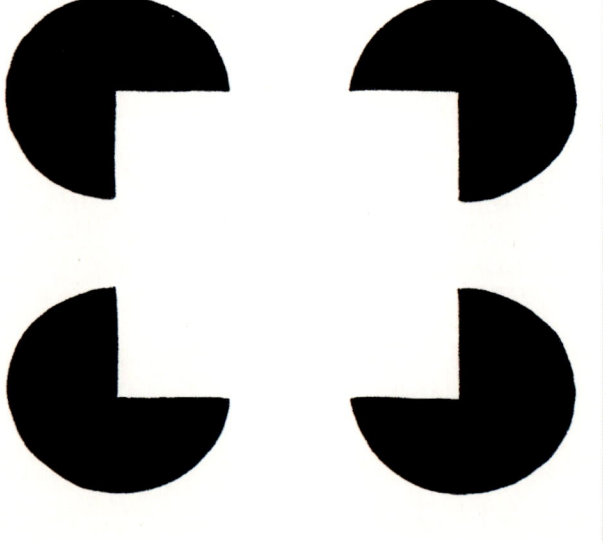

STEP 4

Shade in the three-quarter circles with a dark, flat tonal value.

DRAWING WORKSHOP

- Consider using a color for the three-quarter circles.
- See what other geometric shapes you could create using the techniques in this simple but effective optical illusion.

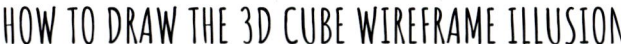
HOW TO DRAW THE 3D CUBE WIREFRAME ILLUSION

Drawing tips: Notice how the tonal values of the lines are vital to making a solid illusion of depth in the wireframe cube, in contrast to the graded subtlety of shading for the linear cast shadow.

Draw lines with a soft tonal value and then darken them later.

STEP 1

Draw a diamond shape for the top of the cube. Make sure the top point of the diamond shape is to the right of the bottom end of your diamond shape.

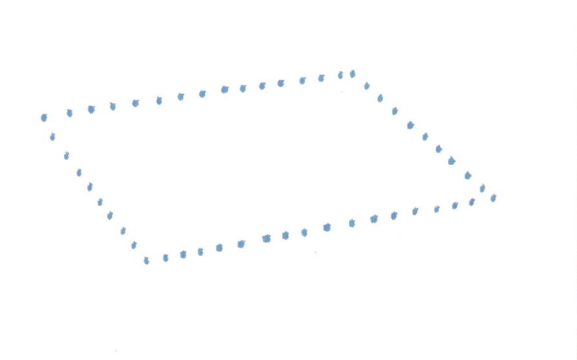

STEP 2

Draw four vertical lines downwards from the four points of the diamond.

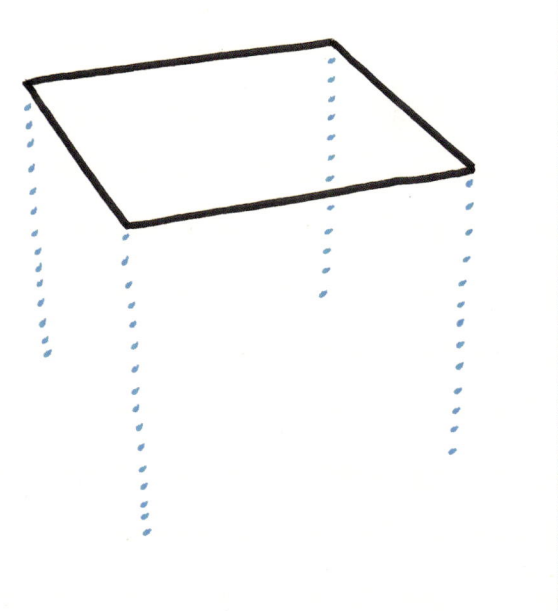

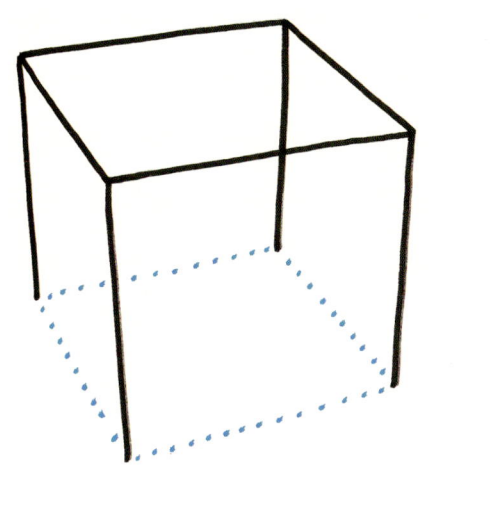

STEP 3

Draw four lines to join your vertical lines from Step 2 and make a new diamond shape to represent the base of your cube.

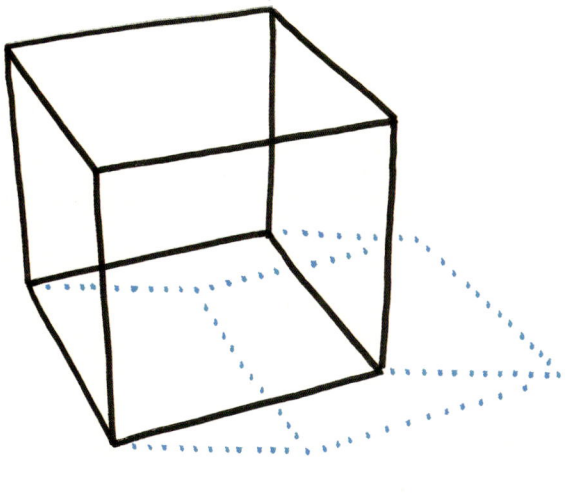

STEP 4

Draw a soft pencil line from each of the points of the base of your cube towards the right, connecting them with four more pencil lines in a diamond similar to the top of your cube.

STEP 5

Darken the lines of your cube with a black pen, but leave the cast shadow as soft pencil lines.

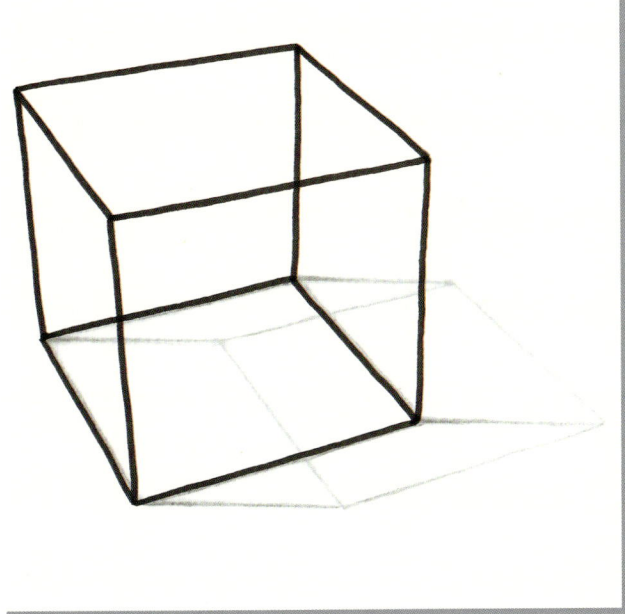

DRAWING WORKSHOP

- Consider drawing a version where the cube is a color and the shadow is a gray tonal value.
- You could use the same technique to draw a range of simple geometric forms, for example a square based pyramid or a cone.

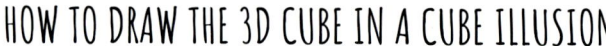

HOW TO DRAW THE 3D CUBE IN A CUBE ILLUSION

Drawing tips: Notice how the outline of each cube is the shape of a hexagon.

There are just two shapes that are each repeated three times within this illusion.

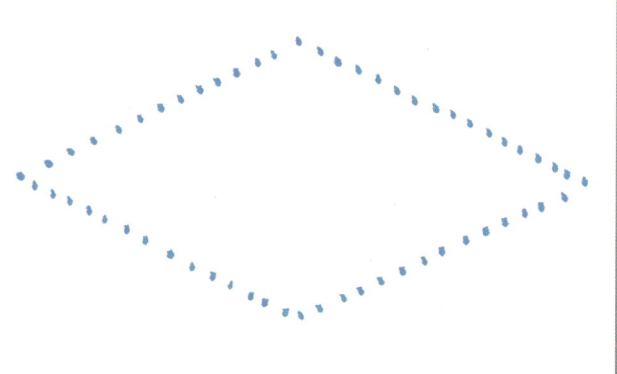

STEP 1

Draw a diamond shape wider than tall for the top of the main cube.

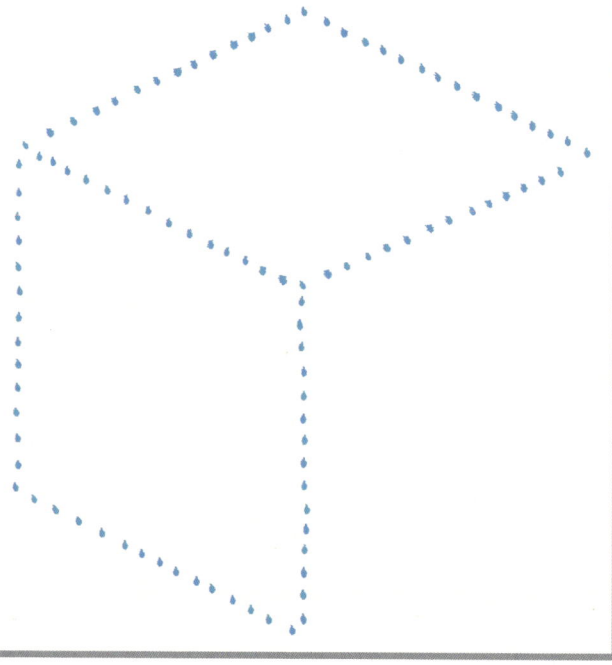

STEP 2

Draw a second diamond shape of the same size below the first and to the left.

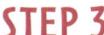

STEP 3

Draw a third diamond shape of the same size to the right, creating three diamonds whose outside shapes create a hexagon.

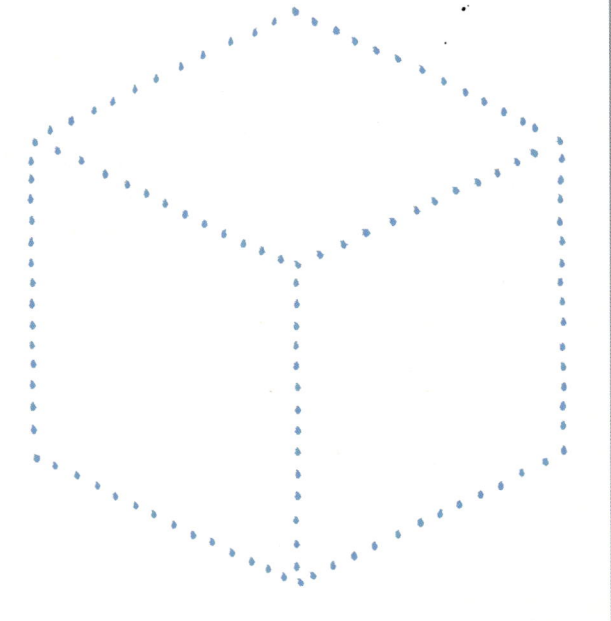

STEP 4

Draw three new diamonds, half the size of the first diamonds, in the center of the hexagon.

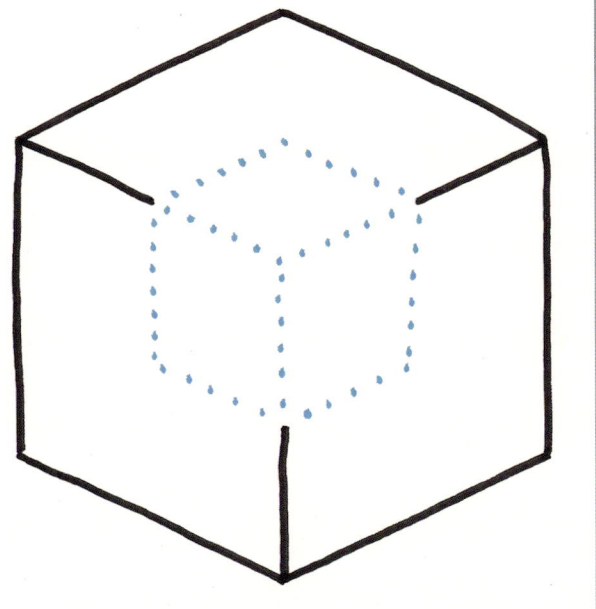

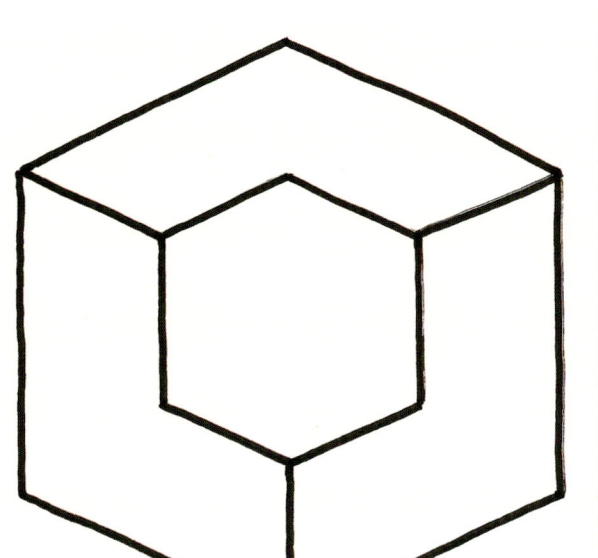

STEP 5

Erase the center three guidelines in your drawing.

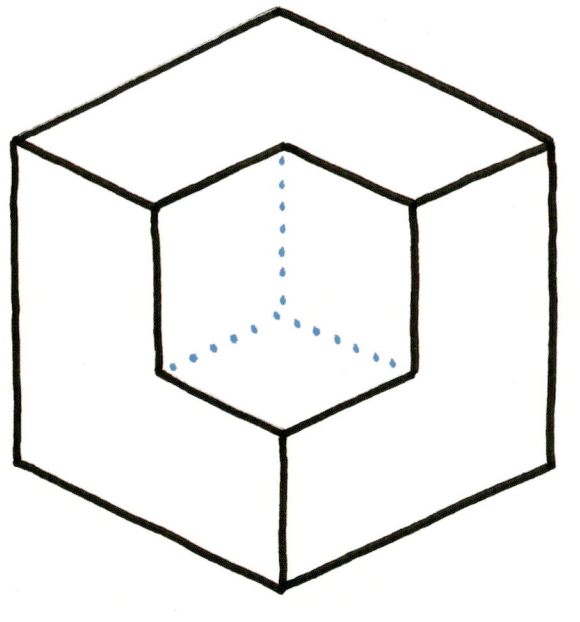

STEP 6

Draw three short lines from three points of the center hexagon parallel to the lines in the same direction until they meet at the center of your drawing.

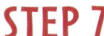
STEP 7

Shade one side of the cube with a dark black and shade another with a gray mid-tonal value. The third side surface of the cube can be left unshaded.

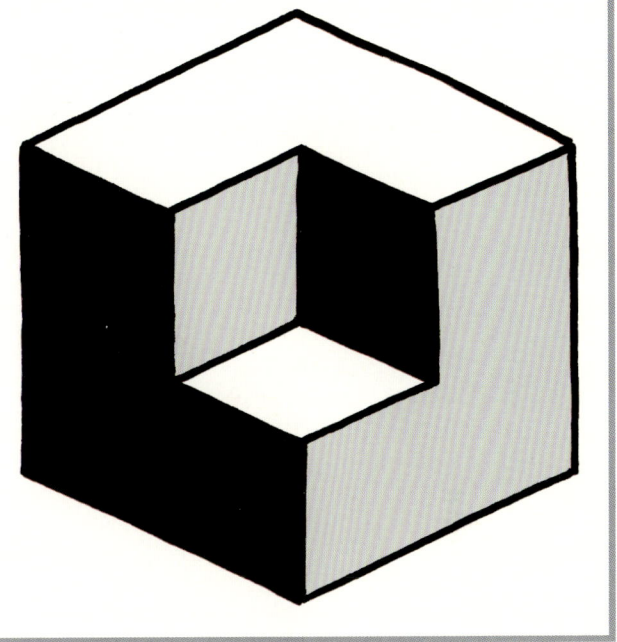

DRAWING WORKSHOP

- Consider using three colors for the three surface planes of the cubes.
- Consider shading your tonal values with textural marks so the image's surface resembles hard stone with a few chips and cracks.

167

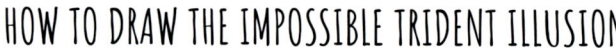

HOW TO DRAW THE IMPOSSIBLE TRIDENT ILLUSION

Drawing tips: Study both ends of the finished image separately by placing your hand over one end at a time before you start your drawing. Make sure you check each step you draw before you move on to the next step.

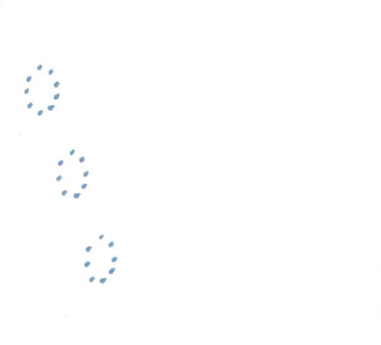

STEP 1

Draw three small circles in a row, seen from the side.

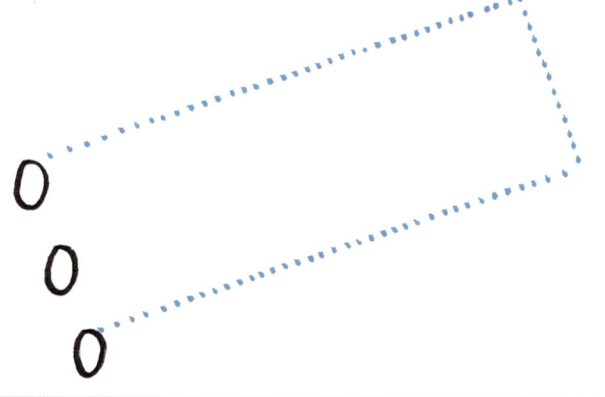

STEP 2

Draw a long line from the top edge of the top circle towards the right, draw another long line parallel to the first long line from the top edge of the bottom circle to the right, and then join these two long lines together by drawing a shorter right-angled line.

STEP 3

Draw another long line parallel to the long lines in Step 2 from the bottom of the bottom circle to the right, then a very short vertical line from the base of the right angle on the right down to the new long line.

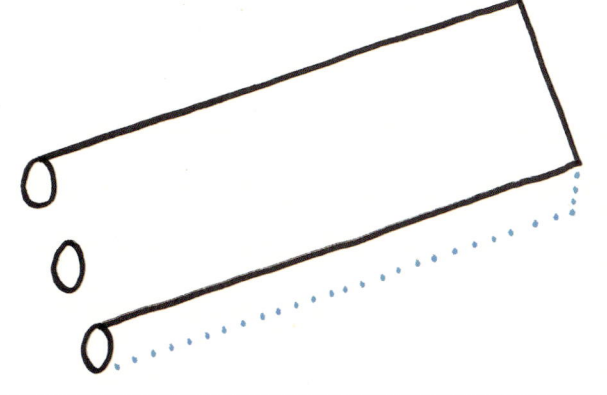

STEP 4

Draw two more long lines parallel to the three other long lines in your drawing, one from the base of the top circle and one from the base of the middle circle to the right. Then, join these two lines with a shorter line at right angles.

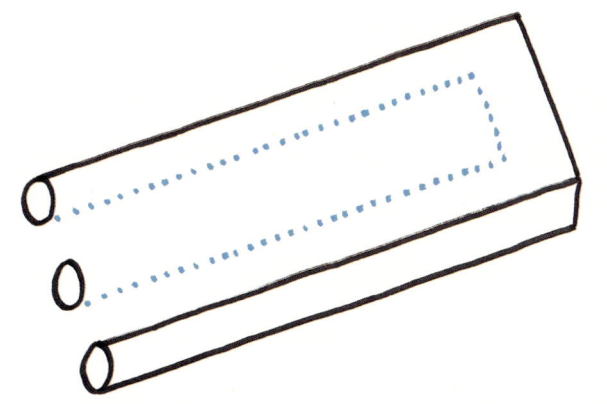

STEP 5

Draw one more long line, parallel to your other long lines, from the top of the middle circle towards the right. Then draw a short downward vertical line from the top of the inner right angle and, lastly, a short line from when the long line and vertical line meet, which is parallel to the right-hand edge of your image.

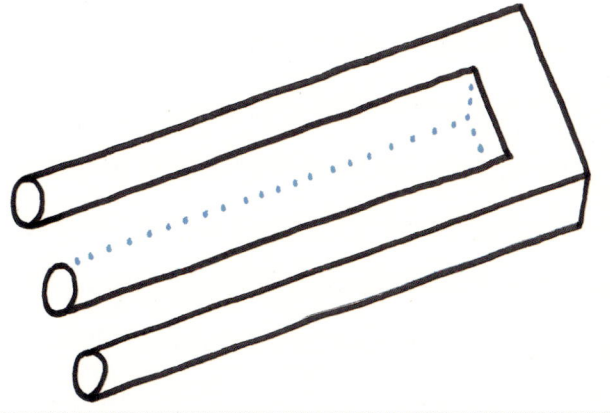

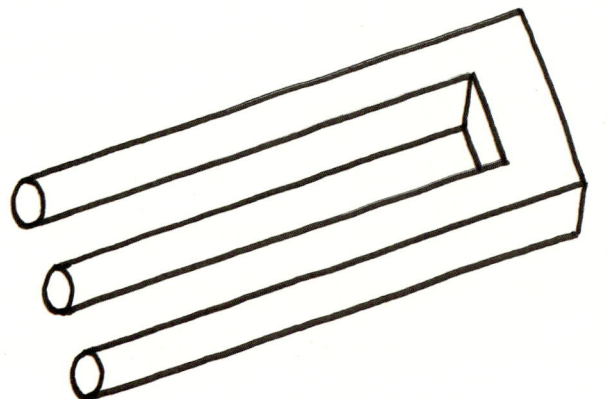

STEP 6

You could go over your pencil lines with a thin, dark black pen.

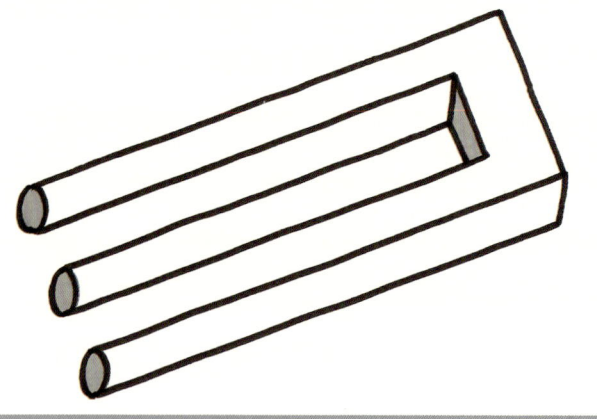

STEP 7

You could add some shading to your drawing to emphasize the optical illusion.

DRAWING WORKSHOP

- Consider using graded tonal values to shade the surfaces of your drawing.
- Consider using colors to make your own unique illusion.

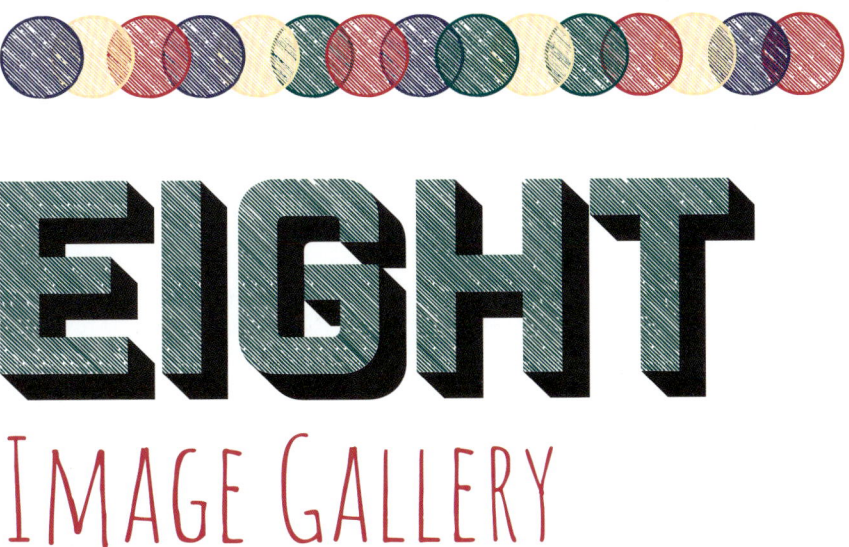

EIGHT

Image Gallery

In this section, you will find a gallery of optical illusions to inspire creativity.

Anamorphic Impossible Triangle

An example of an impossible triangle in an anamorphic perspective. For this drawing, I first drew a basic impossible triangle, then looked at my drawing from a low-down angle and drew a new drawing of what I could see. Then, I drew a notepad, added some shading and a reflection of the triangle on the notepad, cut the drawing out, and viewed it from a low position above the anamorphic dot to make the illusion of a solid impossible triangle on a notepad visible.

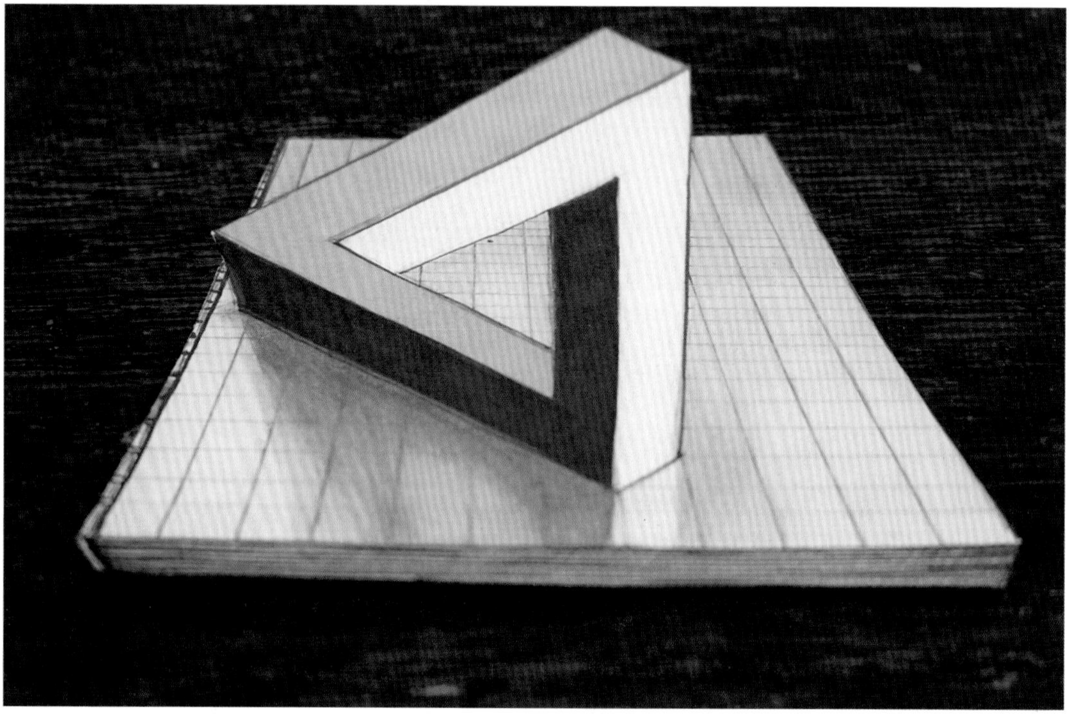

Falling Cubes

For this drawing, I drew a grid on paper with a pencil, then the shape of a hole in the squares. Next, I drew a depth to the hole using vertical lines. Then, I drew some cubes on the surface and some smaller cubes in the hole. The last stage was to go over the grid with a black pen, darken the hole, and use a grey marker pen to shade the sides of the cubes.

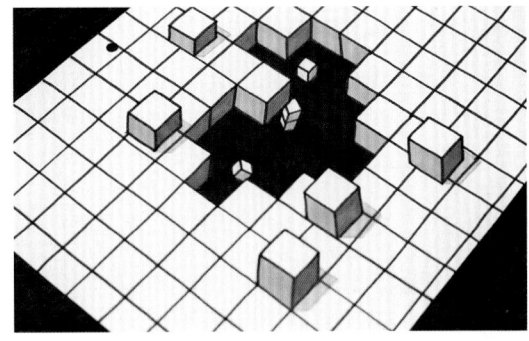

Endless Waterfall

I simplified the image based on M.C. Escher's famous 1961 lithographic print of a waterfall. When drawing the image, I found the key was to keep the two towers straight and then try to understand how the waterfall's zigzag interacts with the towers' columns. Once that relationship is understood, the illusion of an endless waterfall will work.

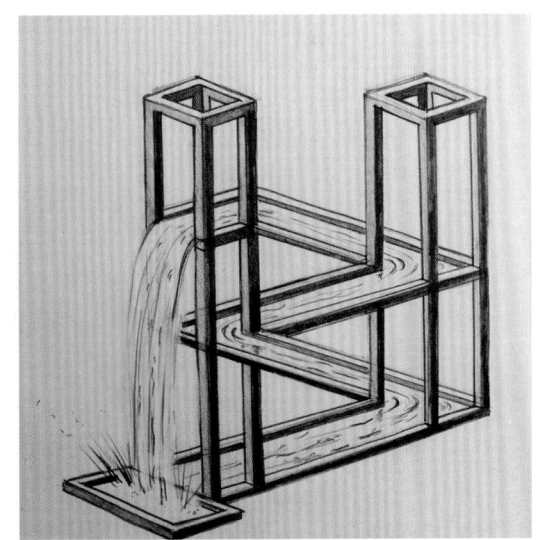

Cube Doodle

I was playing with the idea of intersecting elements in a wireframe cube for this drawing. I kept the image symmetrical, as I found it easier that way.

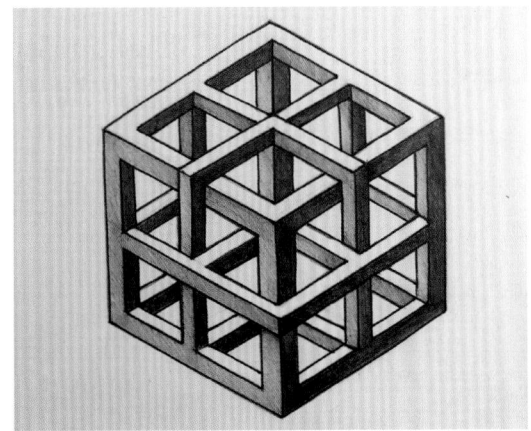

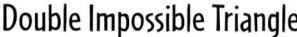

Double Impossible Triangle

To draw an impossible triangle within a larger impossible triangle, I started by drawing the larger triangle. Then, I added three short central bars from the middle lengths of the larger triangle to the corners of a smaller impossible triangle. This drawing looks complex, but just three line angles are needed to make the image.

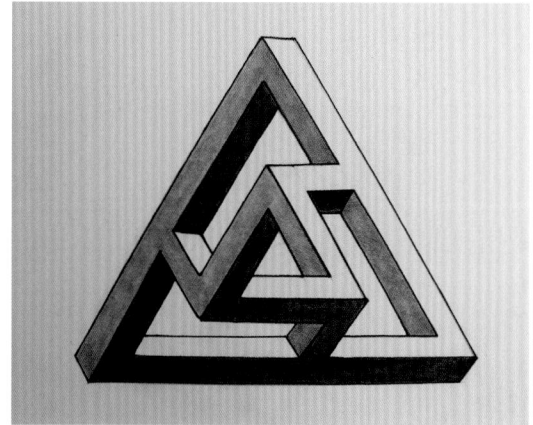

Falling Cubes in a Paper Hole

One way to create a new optical illusion is to combine two different illusions in one new drawing. For this image, I used graph paper, choosing a style with pale grid lines. Then, I drew a stylized trompe-l'oeil paper hole and a series of receding 3D Cubes falling backward into a dark void.

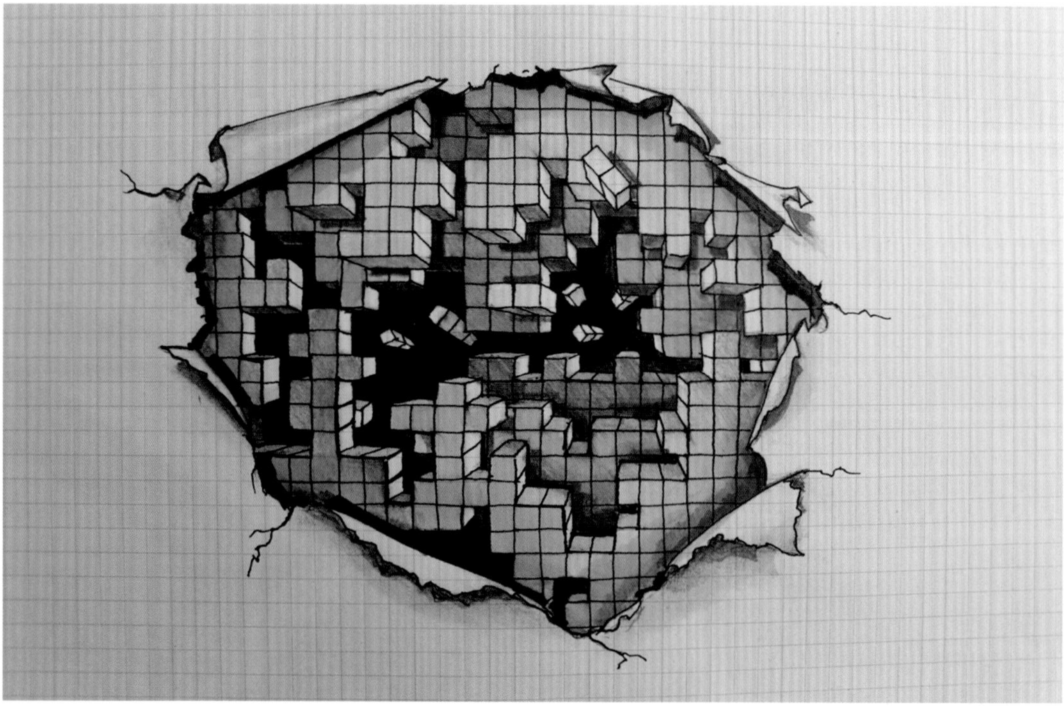

Impossible 3D Star

For this drawing, I started with a small pentagon as the hole in the middle of the star. Next, I drew a series of extension lines from the pentagon edges. Then, I worked out a series of lines radiating from the center. The next stage was to create the five-pointed star and work out how the negative and positive shapes create a solid-looking triangle, where we can see two sides of each of the five points. The last stage was to notice how the inner structure of the stars impossibly crossed over each other.

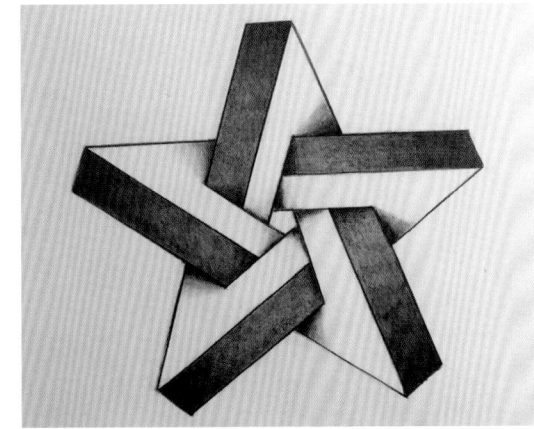

Anamorphic Steps in a Cube

Starting with grid paper, I drew a square and then chose an anamorphic dot below the square, far off the edge of the paper. The vertical edges of the cube go towards this anamorphic dot, and the receding lines follow the lines of the grid paper. Remember that all anamorphic drawings only reveal their 3D structure when viewed from the anamorphic dot.

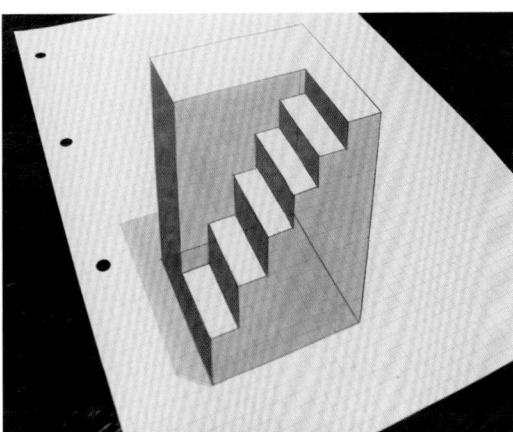

Endless Stairs with People

For this drawing, I added a few people and some extra buildings to the impossible steps. I tried to have the extra buildings overlap each other to add a sense of depth to the image.

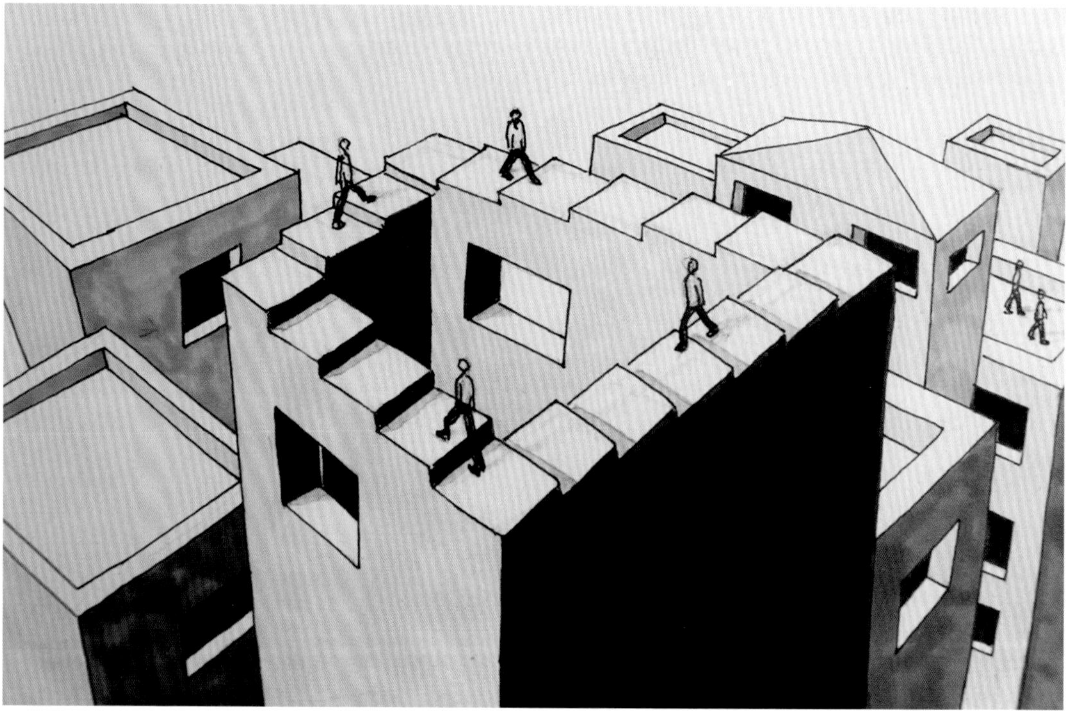

The Impossible Cube

I used very thin lines for this version of the impossible cube and then added some color at the end.

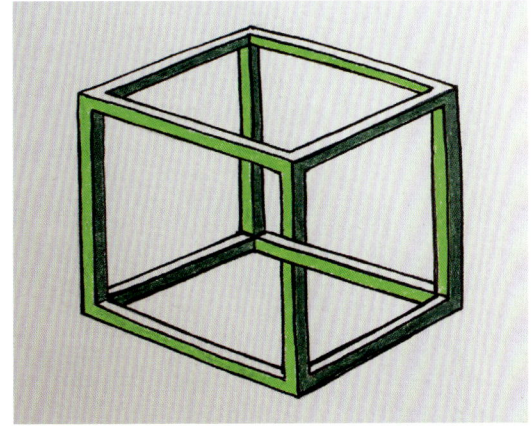

2022 3D

I drew a year using an anamorphic perspective. The focus was to develop a range of tonal values within the depth of the numbers using a 4B pencil and some time. I wanted to contrast the darkness of the numbers with the trompe l'oeil paper they are resting on. Getting a cast shadow that worked with the numbers took a while.

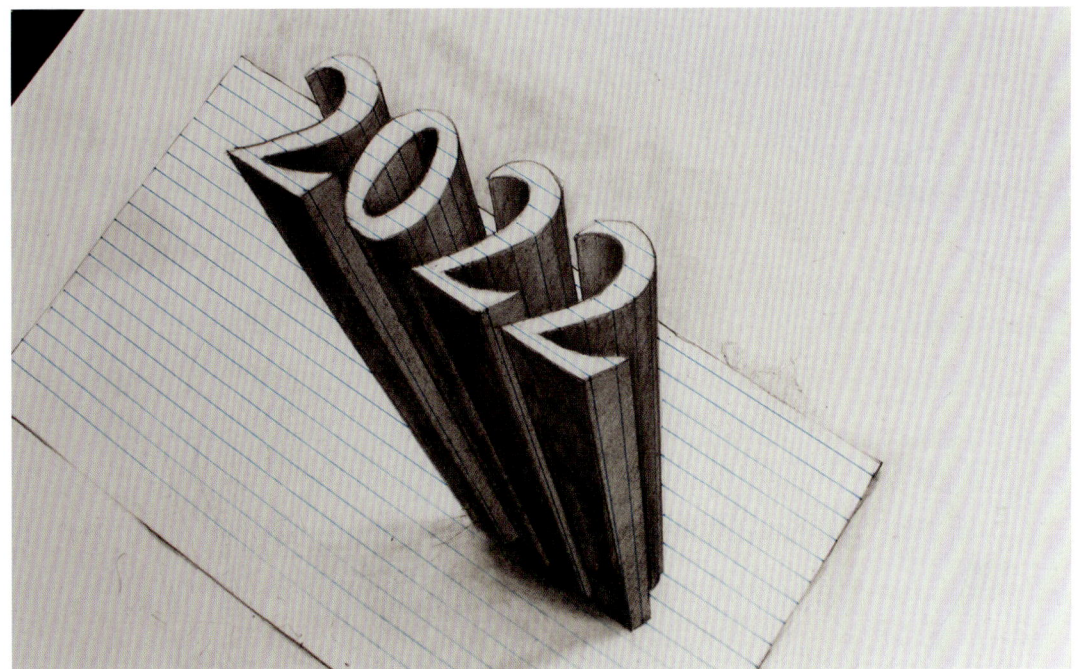

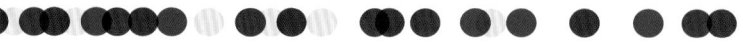

3D Arrows Optical Illusion

When I'm trying to draw an optical illusion, I always start by looking at the basic shapes and trying to figure out how the positive and negative shapes work together. For this illusion, I began by drawing three cubes in the center. Can you work out the next step?

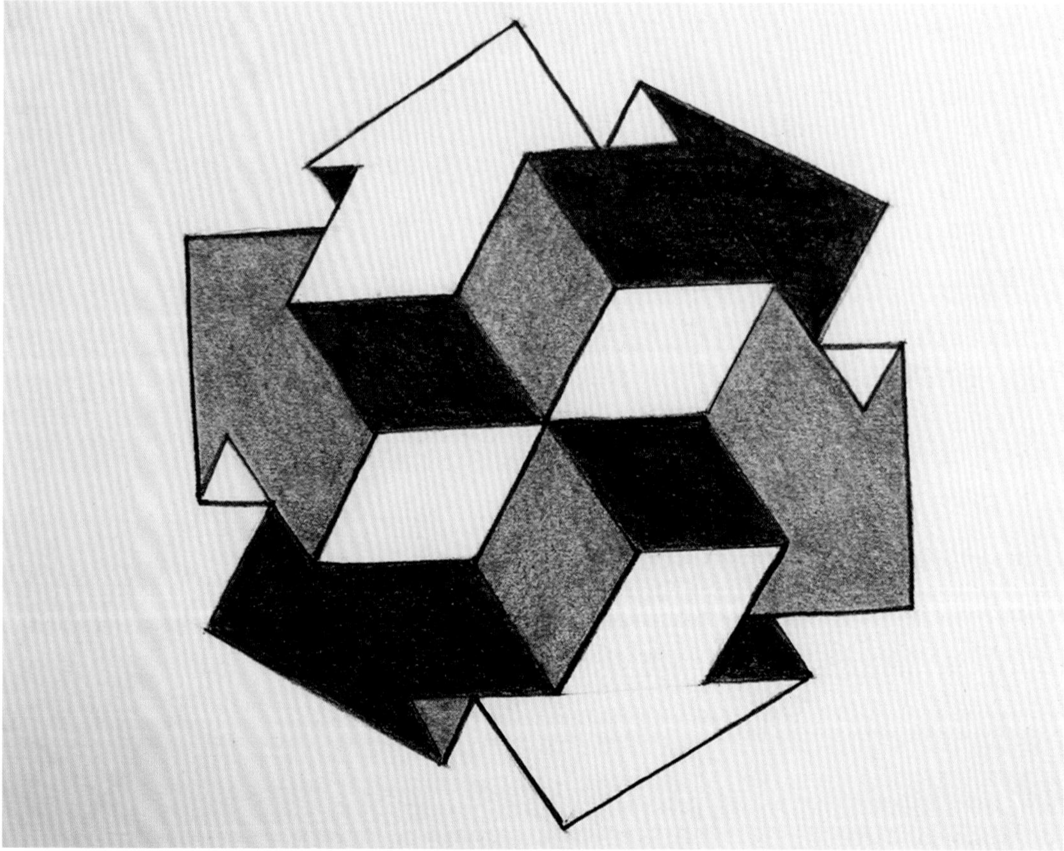

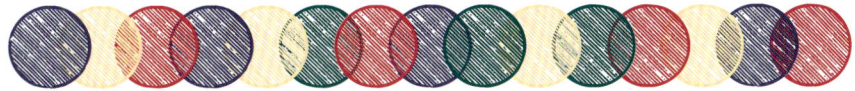

Glossary

In this section, you will find a glossary of drawing terms from the book.

Ambiguous: Something open to multiple interpretations.

Ambiguous Illusion: An optical illusion that presents an image or situation that can be perceived in multiple ways.

Anchor Shadow: The thin, dark cast shadow on the surface directly adjacent to an object.

Angle: The space between two intersecting lines or surfaces measured in degrees.

Anamorphic Dot: A point used in anamorphic perspective to establish the viewpoint from which the illusion can be viewed without distortion.

Anamorphic Perspective: A distorted perspective that requires a specific viewing angle or device to perceive the image correctly.

Ascending: Moving or rising upward.

Atmospheric Perspective: A technique used in art to create the illusion of depth by making distant objects appear lighter and less detailed.

Camera Obscura: A device used in art and photography to project images of external scenes onto a flat surface.

Cast Shadow: A shadow created by an object blocking light from falling onto a surface.

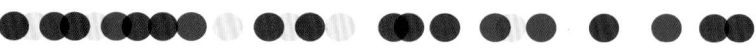

Cognitive: Relating to mental processes such as perception and memory.

Composite Perspective: In art, an image that combines two or more different viewpoints to form a single representation.

Converge: To get closer together.

Cube: A three-dimensional shape with six square faces, each meeting at right angles.

Depth: The distance from the front to the back of an object or space, often associated with the perception of distance.

Descending: Moving or falling downward.

Diagonal: A straight line connecting two nonadjacent corners of a rectangle or another polygon.

Digital Age: A period characterized by the widespread use of digital technology.

Distorting Illusion: An optical illusion that distorts the perception of size, shape, or depth.

Drop Shadow: A drawing technique that creates depth by adding a shadow behind an object.

Equilateral Triangle: A triangle with three sides of equal length and all interior angles measuring 60 degrees.

Euclidean Geometry: A branch of mathematics concerned with the study of flat surfaces and shapes based on the ideas of Euclid.

Eye-Brain Partnership: The collaborative function of the eye and brain in processing visual information.

Eye Level: The height at which the viewer's eyes are positioned when looking straight ahead, represented in linear perspective as the Horizon Line.

Field of View: The extent of observable surroundings seen from a fixed viewpoint.

Form: The shape and structure of an object or entity, including its outline and internal composition.

Form Shadow: The area of an object not directly illuminated by light, resulting in a shadow.

Foreshortening: A distorting perspective used to depict objects receding or extending dramatically.

Freehand: In art, drawing without the use of guiding tools, such as rulers or grids.

Geometric Shape: Shapes such as circles, squares, triangles, and rectangles defined by their mathematical properties.

Geometry: The branch of mathematics concerned with studying shapes, sizes, and properties of space.

Geographic Horizon Line: The line where the earth's surface and the sky appear to meet, as seen from a particular point.

Graded Shading: A shading technique that smoothly transitions from light to dark tonal values.

Grayscale: An image or display that uses varying shades of gray to represent different levels of brightness or intensity.

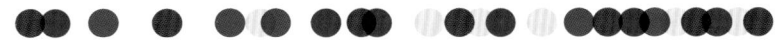

Growth Mindset: A concept referring to the belief that our abilities and intelligence can be developed and improved over time through dedication and effort.

Guideline: A line used as a guide for drawing or positioning elements in a composition.

Highlight: The brightest part of an object or surface, often indicating where the light source most directly hits the object.

Horizon Line: In linear perspective, an imaginary line that represents the viewer's eye level when looking straight ahead.

Impossible Shape: A geometric shape that creates the illusion of a three-dimensional form but cannot exist in reality.

Interlocking: Shapes or forms fitting together like puzzle pieces, often with interconnecting parts.

Intersecting: Shapes or forms crossing or meeting at a common point or line.

Light Source: The original light source in a scene, such as the sun, a lamp, or a flashlight.

Light Tone: A shade or tonal value that is pale or bright.

Line: In art, a continuous mark made on a surface, often used to depict shapes, forms, textures, and patterns.

Line Drawing: A drawing technique consisting mainly of lines used to represent shapes, forms, textures, and patterns.

Lithographic Print: A printmaking process in which an image is drawn on a flat stone or metal plate, inked up, and transferred to paper.

Linear Perspective: A technique used in art to create the illusion of depth and distance by representing parallel lines as converging towards a vanishing point.

Mid-Tone: A shade of tonal value found between the light and dark tones.

Muscle Memory: The ability of muscles to remember and repeat specific movements or actions through repeated practice.

Negative Shape: The shape of the background space that surrounds an object.

Observation: The act of closely watching or monitoring something, often to gather information or study.

Optical Illusion: An image or visual phenomenon that tricks the brain into perceiving something that is not actually present or is different from reality.

Organic Shape: Shapes that resemble those often found in nature, usually characterized by irregular, flowing contours.

Parallel Lines: Lines that are equidistant from each other and never intersect.

Paradox: A statement or situation that seems contradictory or absurd but may be true.

Pareidolia: The tendency to perceive meaningful shapes, such as faces and animals, in random or ambiguous shapes like clouds or trees.

Parallelogram: A four-sided figure with opposite sides that are parallel and equal in length.

Perception: The process of interpreting sensory information, often influenced by personal experiences, expectations, and biases.

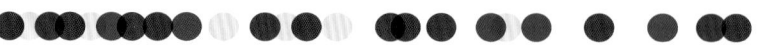

Perpendicular: Intersecting lines or planes at right angles, forming a 90-degree angle.

Persistence of Vision: The phenomenon by which the human eye retains an image for a fraction of a second after it disappears, allowing for the perception of continuous motion in film and flip-books.

Perspective: A drawing technique used to create the illusion of depth and spatial relationships in two-dimensional art.

Polygon: A closed shape with straight sides, typically more than three.

Positive Shape: The shape of an object, in contrast to the negative shape of its surrounding background.

Proportion: The relationship between the sizes of different parts of an object or scene, often expressed as ratios or percentages.

Psychologist: A professional trained in studying behavior and mental processes, including perception and cognition.

Quadrilateral: A polygon with four sides and four angles.

Reality: The state of things as they exist, as opposed to how they are perceived or imagined.

Rectangle: A four-sided shape with four right angles.

Renaissance: A period in European history spanning roughly from the 14th to the 17th century characterized by a renewed interest in art, science, and culture.

Right Angle: An angle that measures exactly 90 degrees.

Scale: The ratio between the size of an object in a drawing or model and its actual size in the real world.

Shadow: A dark area or shape produced by an object blocking light.

Shading: The use of light and dark tonal values to create the illusion of form, volume, and depth in a drawing or painting.

Size: The physical dimensions of an object or area, measured by height, width, and depth.

Space: The continuous area or expanse around or within objects.

Square: A four-sided figure with all sides of equal length and all interior angles measuring 90 degrees.

Template: In drawing, a pre-designed shape used to guide drawing more of the same shapes.

Three-dimensional: A 3D space has height, width, and depth.

Triangle: A polygon with three sides and three angles of a sum of 180 degrees.

Trompe L'oeil: A painting or artwork intended to deceive the viewer into believing that the objects depicted are real and three-dimensional.

Two-dimensional: A 2D space has height and width with no depth.

Typography: The design and arrangement of letters and numbers to make written language legible and visually appealing.

Vanishing Point: In linear perspective, an imaginary point, often on the horizon line, where parallel lines appear to converge.

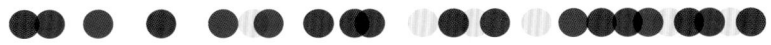

Vertical Line: A straight line that goes up and down.

Vision: The ability to see or perceive visual information.

Visual Cortex: The part of the brain responsible for processing visual information from the eyes.

Wireframe: A skeletal representation of a three-dimensional object consisting of lines and points that define its shape and structure.

Zoetrope: A device used to create the illusion of motion by rapidly displaying a series of still images in sequence.

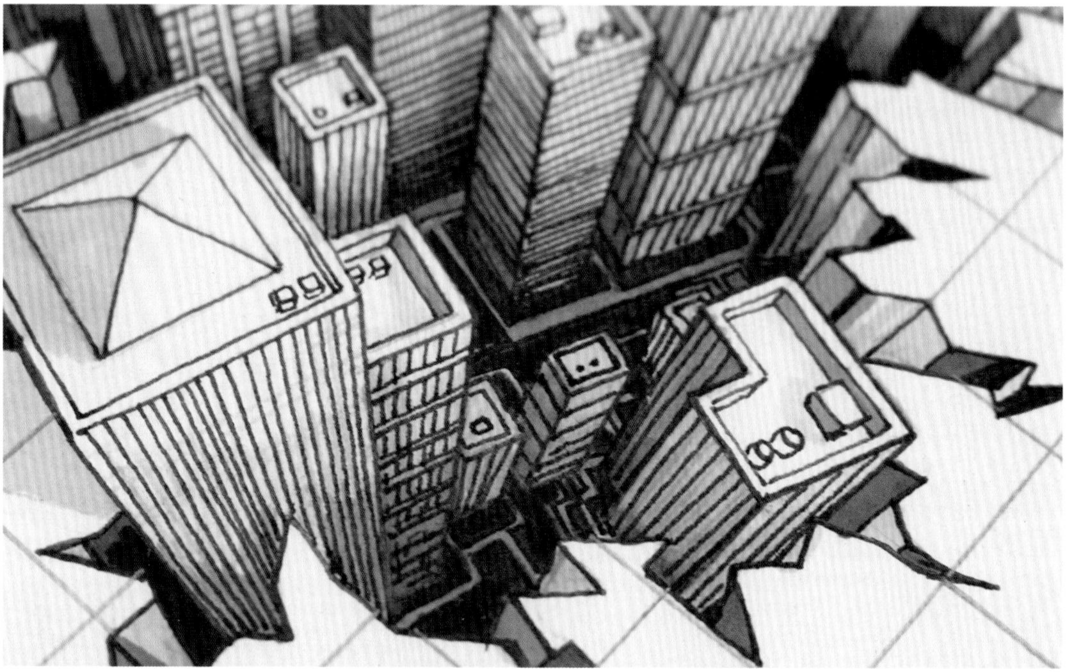

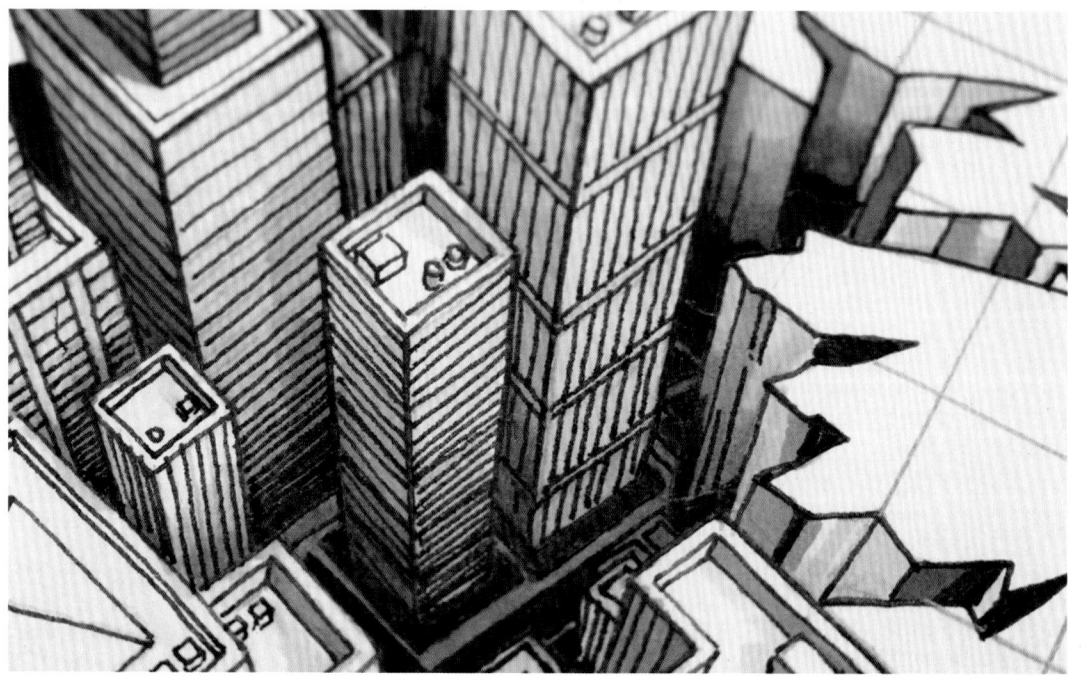

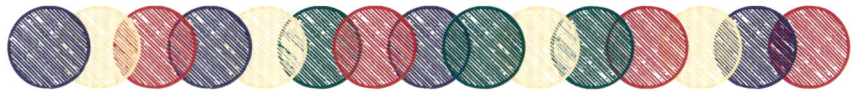

Conclusion

The Art of Deception

Optical illusions rely on fooling our brains into seeing things that aren't there. So, make sure you draw your illusions as neatly and realistically as possible so that they can trick and engage the viewer.

To continue your drawing journey, you will need a positive outlook and a growth mindset. Drawing is a journey of discovery; it is not a fixed destination. There is always more to explore. Aim to notice what works well and do more of that, and over time, you will do less of what does not work so well.

Simplifying seemingly complex forms into their fundamental shapes and tonal values is critical. Enhance your ability to observe the visual world with deep focused attention.

Try to perceive lines and their angles. Look for shapes and patterns. Be more observant. Look closer.

I hope you are inspired to continue pushing the boundaries of perception by creating amazing optical illusions.

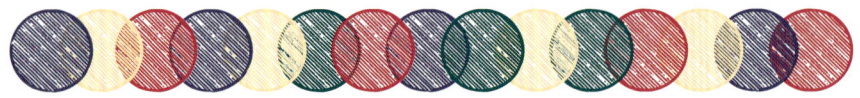

ABOUT THE AUTHOR

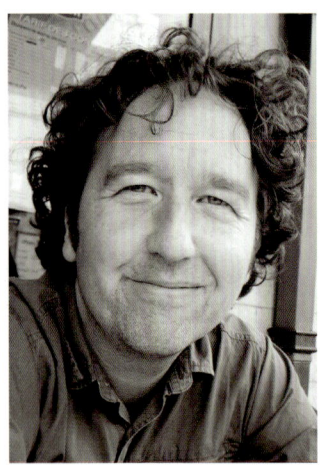

Tom McPherson is the creative force behind Circle Line Art School, a platform that provides online engaging and insightful drawing tutorials. He holds a Fine Arts degree from Central St. Martins School of Art in London.

Based in England, Tom is an experienced artist and freelance art teacher. His tutorials reflect his expertise in drawing fundamentals, offering accessible lessons for artists of all levels. Driven to inspire and empower others, Tom founded Circle Line Art School to share his knowledge globally. His clear instructions have been viewed by millions of students keen to develop their drawing skills. Circle Line Art School remains a trusted resource for artists seeking to expand their horizons, offering valuable insights and guidance, focusing on drawing architecture in perspective.

The Resource Package

Would you like to continue your creative journey?

A unique resource package has been created for this book, which includes a comprehensive workbook, drawing exercises, and instructional videos. You can find the resource package at www.circlelineartschool.com/resources